Anonymous

The Old College

Being the Glasgow University album for MDCCCLXIX

Anonymous

The Old College
Being the Glasgow University album for MDCCCLXIX

ISBN/EAN: 9783337036218

Printed in Europe, USA, Canada, Australia, Japan

Cover: Foto ©ninafisch / pixelio.de

More available books at **www.hansebooks.com**

BEING

The Glasgow University Album

FOR *MDCCCLXIX.*

EDITED BY STUDENTS

GLASGOW
JAMES MACLEHOSE, BOOKSELLER TO THE UNIVERSITY
61 ST. VINCENT STREET
1869

CONTENTS.

	PAGE
OUR OLD UNIVERSITY,	1
OLD ALICE,	34
GREEK ETHICS,	35
TO ELIZA,	76
CUI BONO,	77
HEINE,	78
FROM HORACE,	95
LAW AND HISTORY,	98
THE RIVER,	114
AFTER MANY YEARS,	116
THE NATIONALITIES OF SHAKESPEARE,	118
GLAUCUS,	130
A LECTURE ON DRAMATIC POETRY,	139
IMITATION OF THE OLD BALLAD,	160
FUGA TEMPORUM,	161
GREEK VERSES,	162

CONTENTS.

OUR ENGLISH PROMETHEUS,	164
LET'S LOVE WHILE LOVE WE MAY,	191
AUTUMN,	192
SPINOZA—THE MAN AND HIS SYSTEM,	193
THE APPLE-TREE,	233
ON SOME CHARACTERISTICS OF SCOTT'S POETRY,	234
FROM HEINE,	242
WILLIAM WORDSWORTH,	243
SPRING SONGS,	260
THE CENTAUR,	263
AMOR VINCIT,	273
ÆSTHETICS,	275
LOVE,	289
NOTES OF A LECTURE BY GEORGE MACDONALD,	290
PROOEMION,	305
PANTHEISM,	306
FROM THE BELLEROPHON OF EURIPIDES,	326
DRAMATIC REPRESENTATIONS IN THE UNIVERSITY,	327
ANSWER,	354
THE TRADITION OF THE ELDERS,	354

THE OLD COLLEGE.

OUR OLD UNIVERSITY.

" Dura sed emovere loco me tempora grato."—Hor.

THE History of Glasgow University has yet to be written. Why this should be so, it is hard to say, considering the importance of the subject, and the abundance of materials from which such a work might be compiled. We are not ambitious on this occasion of attempting the task, being content to discourse briefly, and after an easy and rambling fashion, befitting not the sterner and more decorous style of the historian, concerning a few of the leading events in the history of the College.

It is difficult for us who live in an age of telegraphs, steam-engines and the penny press, to realise the ignorance and barbarity in which our ancestors of the middle ages were sunk. Italy, Germany and France were first to throw off the lethargy in which for centuries they in common with the western world had slumbered, and during the fifteenth century, thanks to the exertions of Pope Nicholas and other illustrious pioneers of thought, opportunely aided by the invention of the art of printing, knowledge had begun to permeate even the humbler grades of society, and a study of the classics, by revealing the greatness and culture of Greece and Rome, had already to a certain extent humanised and cultivated the modern world. Scotland, although remote from the centres of learning, was not slow to catch the spirit of the Renaissance, and even during the preceding century had made great and marked progress in material prosperity and increased civilization. In addition to the schools attached to the monasteries and cathedral churches, there were many public grammar schools, though schools of a higher kind were of a much later date. Prior to the fifteenth century, a Scotchman desirous of education had to betake himself to one of the foreign universities, of which Oxford and Paris, and after them Cambridge and Cologne, were most patronised by our countrymen; though just as Scotch generals and Scotch cohorts were at that time to be found in the service of every foreign prince, so Scotch students and Scotch professors studied and taught in every university in Europe. Towards the end of the fourteenth century, crowds of young Scotchmen flocked to Oxford, although they were never popular there, and just then the papal schism embittered the ill-feeling. In 1382 Richard II. of England addressed a writ to the Oxford authorities forbidding them to molest the Scotch students notwithstanding their "damnable adherence to Robert the Antipope" (Clement VIII.).

These inconveniences hastened by a few years the establishment of Scotch Universities, an event which the increased requirements and civilization of the country had rendered inevitable. In 1410 the University of St. Andrews was founded, and forty years later, on the 7th day of January, 1450-1,* Pope Nicholas V. granted the charter of Glasgow University. The honour of the idea belongs to James II., who requested William Turnbull, Bishop of the Diocese of Glasgow, to apply to the Pope for the required Bull; and the neighbourhood of that city, as being "a noteable place and fitted for the purpose by the temperature of the air and the plenty of all provisions for human life," was chosen as the site of the proposed *studium generale* for the teaching of Theology, Law and Arts, "and every other lawful faculty." Bologna—at that time, with the exception of Paris, the most celebrated, as well as the oldest of European universities—was expressly mentioned as the model of the new foundation; but it is probable that their actual resemblance consisted in little more than the possession of the privilege of conferring degrees, the right of granting which privilege belonged exclusively to the Holy See. Mr. Cosmo Innes considers the real analogue of the new University to have been rather Louvain in Belgium, the customs of which were much imitated at the time by the universities of the Northern countries. This, however, seems doubtful, since Louvain was only erected in 1425, and a very short time had elapsed for testing its constitution; more-

* "1450-1," 7th Jany. 1450, is equivalent to 7th Jany. 1451, of the historical year. Pope Nicholas used the same style, then common in Scotland, beginning the year on the 25th of March, which continued to be the custom of this country till the year 1600.

over Bologna had been also chosen for the pattern of the University of St. Andrews. One curious remnant of Continental influence still survives in our division of students into four "nations," indicating in a rough way the quarters of the globe from which they have come. In old times the "nations" (then including all members of the University) elected four Procurators, who in turn elected the Rector and other officials. In the latter part of the seventeenth century, when the relative proportions and influence of the members of the University had greatly altered, a keen controversy arose as to whether the electoral constituency (in the case of the election of Rector) was properly confined to the permanent members of the University, or should be extended to all matriculated students. The dispute was settled by a Royal Commission in 1727, who declared that the right lay with the matriculated members, masters, and students of the University. Thereafter, accordingly, the Comitia, consisting of the Rector, Dean of Faculty, Principal, Professors, and Matriculated Students, elected the Rector, and continued to do so until, on the abolition of the Comitia, the right of election was vested, as it is at present, in the students alone.

By the exertions of Bishop Turnbull and his Chapter, a body of Statutes was prepared, and the University opened in 1451. It consisted of a Chancellor (the Bishop himself), a Rector,* of Masters and Doctors in

---

* Master David Cadzow, Precentor of the Church of Glasgow, was our first Lord Rector, and read in the Chapter House of the Dominicans on 29th July, 1460, at nine o'clock a.m., in presence of the clergy

the four faculties, and lastly of incorporated students of these Faculties, who might be promoted to degrees after the usual course of study. The Chancellor conferred all academical honours, and the Rector, with the advice of the four Deputati, exercised supreme judicial and executive power over all members of the University. By Royal Charter, dated 20th April, 1450, James II. had granted to William Turnbull, Bishop of Glasgow, and his successors, the City and Barony of Glasgow and lands called Bishop Forest, to be holden in free, pure and mere regality in fee and heritage for ever. By this grant the Bishop was enabled to confer extensive privileges on the University. Accordingly, on 1st December, 1453, he gave to the University full power to buy and sell in the city and regality all goods and necessaries of life brought thither not for trading purposes but private consumption, and without exaction of custom or asking leave. All members were further exempted from taxation,—a privilege often afterwards renewed by successive governments. In 1456 the University obtained from the Bishop the further right of "plenary jurisdiction" over its own members, in all matters, civil and criminal. Every member could claim to be tried before his peers. There is a case on record so late as 1670, in which a student, accused of the crime of murder, was tried before the Rector and acquitted. Even to this day there would appear to be a sort of nominal sanctuary afforded to students by the college walls, and it has very recently

and masters, the Rubric of the 3rd book of Gregory's Decretals, viz., De vita et honestate clericorum.

been questioned whether a civil officer can legitimately insist upon invading the sacred precincts for the purpose of executing the warrant of a judge, without permission from the head of the University.

In the earliest ordinances all general meetings were directed to be held in such place as the Rector might appoint. The Chancellor and Rector being generally the Bishop and one of his canons, these meetings were usually held in the Cathedral. The first place actually used for this purpose was the Chapter House of the Dominicans (Friars' Preachers, as they were called), which occupied the site of the present College Kirk. Here the University held its first general chapter on the 14th of October, 1452, but ever after, down to the time of the Reformation, its general meetings were held, as we have said, within the Chapter House of the Cathedral. The University was necessarily very poor during its infancy, its income being derived solely from some small perquisites connected with the granting of degrees, and the patronage of two or three small chaplainries. Such was its native vigour, however, and the efficiency with which it discharged its functions, that within two years after its establishment, more than 200 students had been enrolled, and two years later the number matriculating in the Faculty* of Arts had increased so much that it was thought necessary to provide

---

* A 'Faculty' was the body of teachers or graduates, who not only had the privilege of lecturing, and examining, and admitting candidates for degrees into their body, but also of making statutes, choosing officers, using a seal, and doing all that pertains to a privileged corporation to raise money.

them with a regular set of teachers, and a place of residence. For the former purpose the Crypt of the Cathedral was allowed them by the Bishop, in which to attend the lectures in the Faculties of Theology and Canon Law. The house provided for their accommodation was the Pædagogium (the first actual collegiate building), which belonged to the Faculty of Arts, and was situated on the south side of the Rotten Row.

The College of Arts appears to have been the most useful and flourishing branch of the University, for so early as 1458 the Faculty rented a piece of ground on the east side of the High Street, whereon they began to erect a new Pædagogium. Their circumstances were, however, so straitened, that with all their efforts to raise money, they might have found themselves unable to compass their object, had it not been for the liberality of Lord Hamilton, who in 1459-60 made them a present of the ground. The seisin is made out in name of Duncan Bunch, the first Regent of the Faculty, and his successors in office. The ground is described as a tenement on the east side of the High Street, lying between the house of the Friars' Preachers on the south, and the lands of Sir Thomas Arthurlie on the north, with four acres of the Dowhill beside the Molendinar Burn, to which possession the name of the "Land of the Pædagogue" was for a long time afterwards applied.* A century later we find the same four acres described as a "greit orchart," and the remainder of the Dowhill tastefully laid out in gardens, rich in summer time with flowers and fruits, and surrounded by well-

* For detailed history of ground see Note, p. 31.

trimmed hawthorn hedges. To this place, then, about the year 1465,* the teaching and residence of the members of the University were transferred, in whole or in part, and the name of Pædagogium or College was given to the new buildings.

Lord Hamilton's gift soon received many additions, and in 1466 the adjacent house and lands were bequeathed to the College by Sir Thomas Arthurlie, chaplain. This land, amounting to about two acres, adjoined the College on

---

* This action on the part of the College was of great importance, deciding as it did one of the most practical and vexed questions in the early history of universities, that, namely, of the residence of students. At first the custom of outside residence, which obtains with us at present, was followed. But the increase of students causing a corresponding increase in rents, the price of lodging soon became so exorbitant as to render immediate action on the part of the College necessary. Bishop Turnbull accordingly enacted that all houses and lodgings for the members of the University within the city were to be let by the arbitration of an equal number of members and citizens sworn as umpires, and no one was to be disturbed in his possession so long as he paid his rent and conducted himself properly. As a further remedy for the evil the religious orders began to establish in University towns hospitia or hostels for such of their members as resorted thither. In imitation of these, houses were provided by charitable persons, in which free lodgings, and ultimately free board, were provided for the poorer students. Such establishments were called inns, halls, or colleges, the last name being generally restricted to foundations *endowed* for the support of graduates. The term *collegium* was also sometimes applied to the place in which the students were taught, although the more general name was Pædagogium. On the disuse of the common table at the end of the last century the practice of residing within college was discontinued, or at least confined to a very few students of standing and repute.

the north side, and stretched along the Vicar's Alley (the New Vennel) back to the Molendinar. It was annexed to the Pædagogy in 1475, and the front portion of it became in later times the site of some of the Professors' houses.

In all probability the Faculty of Arts alone received a definite constitution, and afforded a regular course of instruction. It had its own proper dean, and peculiar statutes, and as it possessed the greater part of the funds, it ultimately assumed the entire control of the University. By one of the statutes it was ordained that every student of sufficient means should live at table with the regents, and should on no other condition be admitted to the study of Arts. It was impossible to get a dispension. Students who were unable, from poverty or otherwise, to live at table were ordained to pay a noble each to the regents, and as many should be allowed to sleep in the College chambers as could be accommodated. By another statute the gates were ordered to be closed in winter at nine, and in summer at ten o'clock, the chambers of the students having first been visited by one of the regents.

In this way the College went on gradually developing and increasing in usefulness till the time of the Reformation, when along with other constitutions of Roman Catholic origin, it was thrown into confusion by the loss of the support, which it had previously derived from the church. When the Crown absorbed the benefices by which the regents, who were all churchmen, were supported, men could with difficulty be found to accept the office of regent without the salary. The Chancellor, James Beaton, fled to the continent, carrying with him the cathedral plate, as well as the charter, and titles both of the See and of the University. The buildings at this time are described as ruinous, and the teaching as almost extinguished. The College of Arts, however (owing to its principal, John Davidson, having embraced the Reformed doctrines, and continued in office), survived the storm, but in so shattered a condition that in a charter by Queen Mary, dated 13th July, 1683, it is stated that "ane parte of the sculis and chalmeris being biggit, the rest thairof alsweill dwellingis, as provisioune for the pouir bursouris and maisteris to teche ceissit, sua that the samyn apperit rather to be the decay of ane Universitie, nor ony wyse to be reknit ane establisst fundatioun." For which reasons the Queen founded five bursaries for poor youths, for the endowment of which she granted to the University the manse and church of the Friars' Predicators, thirteen acres of ground adjoining, and certain other rents and property, confiscated from the Roman Catholic Church. In 1572 the Magistrates and Council of the town, sensible of the loss which the community sustained from the decay of the University, conveyed to the College certain church property which had been granted to them by the Queen. The Act of Parliament confirming this charter shows at what a low ebb the affairs of the University were at this time, the whole of the resident members, regents and students, only numbering some fifteen persons, and the entire annual income of the College not exceeding £300 Scots (£25 sterling).

In 1574 a fresh stimulus was given to the whole University system by the advent of the celebrated Andrew Melville, whose nephew, alluding to this period in its history, writes, "There was na place in Europe comparable to Glasgow for guid letters during these yeirs for a plentifull and guid chepe mercat of all kynd of langages, artes, and sciences." These words must, however, be accepted with a reservation, as it is difficult to reconcile them altogether with the facts stated immediately below. Melville, on finishing his course of study at St. Andrews, left that University with the character of being "the best philosopher, poet, and Grecian, of any young master in the land." He afterwards studied at Paris, and on returning to Scotland was appointed Principal of Glasgow University, which office he held till 1580, when he was translated to St. Andrews to fill a similar situation. During his connexion with these universities he introduced many improvements into their system of teaching and internal discipline, and eminently contributed to extend their usefulness and increase their reputation. In 1577 James VI., then in his minority, was advised by Regent Morton to remodel the constitution of the University, and grant a charter, making over to it the Rectory and Vicarage of the Parish of Govan. This deed is commonly called the *Nova Erectio*, and forms the basis of the present constitution—the Magna Charta, as it were,—of our College. The preamble contains a doleful account of the state into which the University had fallen. "Seeing that among other losses and inconveniencies of our kingdom we observe our schools and gymnasia to have almost perished, and that our youth, who formerly were distinguished by uprightness of life and purity of moral character, are languishing in idleness and vice, we desire to renew, restore, and endow on a new foundation our Pedagogy in Glasgow, which for want of funds has almost perished, and in which, through poverty, study and discipline are in abeyance." By this charter twelve officers were appointed, including a Principal, who was to teach Theology, Hebrew, and Syriac, and three Regents or Professors, one for Greek and Rhetoric, another for Dialectics, Morals, and Politics, with Arithmetic and Geometry, and the third for Physiology, Geography, Chronology, and Astrology. Besides these there were also four Bursars (poor students), a House Steward, a Servant to the Principal, a Cook and a Janitor. These were all to live within the College, and the provision for their support was purposely limited, in order that by frugality in their meals they might be incited to greater zeal in their studies. They might with propriety have adopted for their motto the line suggested by the witty Canon for the *Edinburgh Review*, "Tenui musam meditamur avena." The provisions regulating the domestic lives of the students are very minute. The effeminate youths of modern days who grumble at having to attend classes at eight o'clock a.m., may be glad that they were not members of the College during the fifteenth and sixteenth centuries, when every one at a given signal had to turn out at five o'clock in the morning, at which hour one of the Regents (styled the Hebdomadar) went round their bed chambers to rouse them from their slumbers. The duties of the toilette over, lessons followed from six to eight, when they all assembled to morning prayers, which occupied only half an hour. After prayers they retired to their different rooms to study till breakfast time (nine o'clock). At ten studies were resumed, and at a quarter past eleven the cook received warning to have all things ready for dinner at twelve. After dinner thanks were returned and a psalm sung, during which all stood. The rest of the day was spent in the schools until late in the evening. At nine p.m. the Hebdomadar went his rounds again to see if everybody was in, and take a note of the absentees. On certain days, after dinner and supper, disputations were held, of which, we are told, Principal Melville was exceedingly fond. From dinner till four p.m. every second, fourth, and sixth day in each week was set apart for 'play,' one of the many duties of the unfortunate hebdomadar being to accompany the students to the fields where they went to "disporte themselves." By an order in the reign of Charles I. the 'Scholars at Glasgow' were to be exercised in lawful sports, such as "gouffe, archerie, and the lyk," and were prohibited from indulging in unlawful games as carding, dicing, and for some strange reason *bathing or swimming*—we presume in the Molendinar—indulgence in which was strictly prohibited under a pain of "many stripes and ejection." It must not be supposed that their amusements were limited to such as are only exercised in "green fields"—they even included dramatic representation. It was ordained in 1462 that ever after on 9th May (the day of Saint Nicholas) at a general congregation to be held at the doors of the Cathedral, "two discreet masters should be elected to provide the necessaries and utensils for a grand banquet of the College of the Faculty of Arts, on the Sabbath day (*i.e.*, Saturday) or Feast following said day of St. Nicholas, as the Faculty should judge proper, and weather permit," to which every master holding a benefice should give 3s., and all non-beneficed masters, bachelors and students, 1s. 6d. each. On the day fixed all should assemble, under a penalty of 2s., at eight a.m., in the Chapel of Saint Thomas, and there hear Mass, after which they should, in a becoming and solemn manner, receive flowers and branches of trees, and all should proceed on horseback in a grave and stately procession through the public street, from the higher part of the city to the Cross, and return the same way to the College of Arts, where, amid the joy of the Feast, the masters should take council concerning what might promote the interests of the Faculty and its members. The feast over, the banquetters were to repair to a place more fitted for amusement, where some of the masters and students should perform an interlude or other show whereby to delight the people; the actors being granted special powers and prerogatives for their trouble. Even in 1574, three years after the death of Knox, the performance of comedies on Sunday was not altogether discontinued, though one year later an Act was passed by the General Assembly prohibiting them.

The discipline maintained in College was very strict.

No resident student who was not cunning in the Latin tongue was allowed to have a servant, and so late as 1705 the Principal ordered every Regent to appoint a secret censor to spy among the students, and report on such as were guilty of the heinous crime of speaking their mother tongue. The wearing of arms was (and is) strictly prohibited, as also was intrusion by scholars into the sacred region of the kitchen. All students convicted of robbing the orchards were severely punished, and Masters of Arts were enjoined not to be familiar with non-graduates. Corporal punishment was a thing of daily occurence. Originally the Principal *propria manu* inflicted the chastisement on the delinquent's bare shoulders, in the common hall, in the presence of the masters and students therein assembled. Andrew Melville was the first to disregard the custom, and devolved the task upon his regents. Squibs—which we dare say many of our readers imagine to be a recent importation within our College—were very common with students in the seventeenth century, as we read of Principal Gillespie being bitterly wroth at certain lampoons against himself and colleagues which were affixed "diverse tymes on the Colledge gate, and scattered in the Colledge close, and put in the mouth of all the schollars." These squibs are described by the enraged principal as "most base and scandalous Latine verses, abusing myself and Mr. John Young (Professor of Theology) very vylelie, and scoffing at all the Regents." The learned and irate authorities were unable to discover the author, although "sundrie boys were scourged publiclie," which "remedie," we are naively told, "appeared not to have too much effect, for every other day new papers of many base villanies were spread and sent out all over the countrie." In 1725 a censor was appointed, for the "better preservation of order without the College," to visit the streets and "billiard rooms and other gaming places," and "observe what gentlemen of the College they might find there at unlawful hours." This and a curious letter, dated 3rd April, 1716, from Gerschom Carmichael to Principal Stirling of Aberdeen, proves the truth of the adage that "youth will be youth," or rather has always been youth. "There were some," writes Carmichael of his fellow-students, "that kept ill hours, coming late into the College by backways, and by your house among the rest, &c."

The Nova Erectio ordained, among other things, that the professors were not, as had hitherto been the custom, to carry on their students through the three years course, but had each to confine himself to his own department, so that the student had a new professor every year, a system which was altered in 1642, but reintroduced after the Revolution. Professors were enjoined to observe celibacy, and in the event of their marrying were strictly prohibited from bringing their wives within the walls.

In 1581 the Archbishop of Glasgow, then Chancellor of the University, in order to augment the yearly duty paid to it by the town, mortified the whole customs of the Trons, great and small, and those of fair and market, measure and weight, within the burgh, by which donation the College was enabled to institute a separate Greek Chair. Again in 1615 the Bishop of St. Andrews presented the College with the land lying between it and its garden, of which mention has been made above. Notwithstanding all these acquisitions, however, the buildings in 1617 had advanced very little, and were still in a disgraceful state of decay. Concerning the original buildings we know little or nothing. No remains of them are now extant, except perhaps a part of the building between the two oldest quadrangles. It was not until 1632, when its appeal to the public for aid was liberally met, that the College was enabled fairly to begin the work of restoration. Attention was first directed to the inner of the two courts, the greater portion of which was rebuilt within the next seven years. An interval of about fifteen years then elapsed, during which time the College received the magnificent donations of Zachary Boyd, which were applied chiefly for the erection of the steeple. The impression is pretty general that Zachary was rather badly treated by his disponees, having left his property to them under the condition that a small portion of the funds should be devoted to the publication of a portion of his MSS. works, a condition which was never fulfilled. We are inclined to think that, apart from the strictly legal or moral aspect of the question, the College exercised a wise discretion in not fulfilling Zachary's instructions to the letter. It is not to be supposed that his two most intimate friends, Dr. Strang and Mr. Robert Baillie, to whom he had primarily committed the revisal of his MSS. for the press, should have neglected to insist on the publication without good cause. The probability is that they were overruled or persuaded by a more powerful party, headed by Principal Gillespie (of whom hereafter), who were desirous of completing the buildings, and that the preparations for publication being deferred to a more convenient season, which never came, the matter dropped altogether out of sight. Indeed, when we consider the nature of the task imposed by Zachary upon his two reverend literary friends, we are not surprised that they were persuaded to defer its execution. The prospect of having to wade through a mass of MSS., consisting of nearly 2000 pages, closely written, and of no preeminent literary merit, might have appalled bolder men. However this may have been, thanks mainly to Zachary's donations and Principal Gillespie's zeal, the work of building was pushed on with great vigour. About the year 1654, and during the four following years, the steeple and the remainder of the inner court, particularly on the south side (but excluding the portions of the original building allowed to remain), were finished, and the work began to proceed in the first court. It is probable that up to this time (1659) the front court was merely an open space off the High Street, and that the only approach to a quadrangle was an imaginary square formed by the continuation of a projecting portion at each end of the building, and a line drawn at right angles to the lines so formed along the border of the street. The whole front therefore, nearly as it now stands, containing the fore hall, staircase, the Principal's house, and the arched entrance, is just about 210 years old. Six of the Professors' houses had been built by this time, and in 1698 the stone ballusters of the great staircase, and the lion and unicorn on the pedestals at its foot, were erected. Writing of·the Professors' houses, Mercuri says—" Of late there is a third court erected, two parts whereof are already built for the use of the masters of the University to lodge in, and when this court is finished (as is projected) it will be the largest court, looking rather like a king's palace than any other lodging. . . . The primar or principal has a most stately and convenient lodging in the south side, and adjacent to the University, so that it is an universal saying, that the primar of the College of Glasgow (even when episcopacy took place) was the best lodged clergyman in the Kingdom."

The history of the rest of the building is well known. The library was added about 1730, the Hunterian Museum in the earliest years of the present century, and the east side of the inner quadrangle, containing the common hall and several large class rooms, with an archway admitting to the back, was erected in 1812. To Principal Gillespie's enterprise and perseverance we are greatly indebted for our present pile of buildings, which is not without architectural beauties, and whose walls blackened by the smoke of ages, have so well withstood the tear and wear of the elements. The name of its architect—if it ever had one—is unknown. In these later days each builder of a petty dwelling house, must needs carve his name and the date of foundation on its front, while on our magnificent old College only the Royal arms, with C(harles) R(ex) are engraved above the arched gateway, fronting the High Street.

In the beginning of the seventeenth century, greatly owing, as we have seen, to the patronage of James VI. and the presidency of Andrew Melville, the College had greatly increased in influence and prosperity, so much so indeed as to attract to its halls large and ever increasing crowds of students—among others one who was destined in after years to do it notable service, the well known and much misrepresented Zachary Boyd. It would be unfair, and disrespectful to the memory of one whose fortunes will ever be identified with those of the College which he loved so much and served so well, were we to pass over without some brief notice the name of Mr. Boyd. To the general public and even, we suspect, to the majority of our students, the venerable Zachary is little more than a myth,—associated in their minds with one of Grant's novels,—certain ludicrous misrenderings of holy writ erroneously attributed to his pen, and a smoke-begrimed monument of a rather austere cast of countenance, that has looked down on the inner quadrangle of the College from time immemorial. That he was a clergyman of more than ordinary attainments and exact scholarship, possessed of great courage and unblemished character, one moreover who literally gave his *all* to the institution with which he was so long and so honourably connected—not many, we dare say, even of our academical readers are aware. We shall not therefore apologise for this digression, necessary as it is, moreover, to the satisfactory elucidation of our subject. Zachary, then only sixteen years of age, matriculated in Glasgow University in 1601, from which two years later he removed to Saint Andrews, where he took his degree of M.A. in 1607. After passing sixteen years in France, studying part of the time in the College of Saumur, he returned to Scotland in 1623, and shortly after his arrival was installed as minister of the Barony Parish of Glasgow. At the time of his ordination the population of the whole City did not exceed 7,000, and the houses generally were of a mean appearance, covered with turf, heather, or straw thatch. Mr. Boyd was three times elected Dean of Faculty, twice Vice-Chancellor, three times Rector, and while he held these offices the Records of the University bear evidence to his having been a faithful and hard working friend to its internal prosperity. From 1629 until the close of his life he was continually subscribing large sums to the College, and in 1652 he granted a Deed of Mortification in its favour, in which, reserving the life rent to his spouse, in the event of her surviving him, he conveyed to the College almost all his property. Although, as we have seen, his disponees failed to fulfil all the conditions of his will, they showed themselves not insensible to his liberality, by causing a marble statue* to be erected to his memory,

* The inscription on the statue is as follows :—

MR ZACHARIAS BODIVS FIDELIS ECCLESIÆ
SVBVRBANÆ PASTOR 20000 LIB. QVA AD ALEDOS
QVOTANNIS TRES ADOLESCENTES THEOLOGIÆ
STVDIOSOS QVA AD EXTRVENDAS NOVAS
IIAS ÆDES VNA CVM VNIVERSA SVPELLECTILI
LIBRARIA ALMÆ MATRI ACADEMIÆ LEGAVIT.

over the gateway within the second court, where it still stands.* During Mr. Boyd's connexion with the University, it prospered greatly till at the era of the Restoration it boasted (besides a Principal) eight Professors, a Librarian, a tolerable library (to which George Buchanan contributed largely) and an increased number of bursars and students of all ranks. The buildings were also rebuilt in a more enlarged and elegant fashion than they had formerly been.

In 1636 Charles II. endeavoured to force Episcopacy upon Scotland without distinction of persons. Mr. Boyd, though at first dissenting from the principles of the Covenant, and always a strong Royalist, was induced at length to give them his adhesion. The ascendancy acquired by the Independents after the execution of Charles I. was a sad disappointment to the hopes of the Scotch Presbyterians, and largely affected the fortunes of our College. Cromwell, although tolerant in religious matters, could not brook the Scotch loyalty to Charles II., and in order to chastise their monarchical pride, marched into Scotland in 1650 at the head of a large army. After the disastrous battle of Dunbar, in September of that year, the Protector obtained possession of Edinburgh, and shortly afterwards "*came peaceably*," we are told, "*with his whole army and cannon*, by way of Kilsyth to Glasgow." The ministers

---

* " By an entry dated May, 1658 (No. 15 of Clerk's Press, p. 214). it appears that there were given out for Mr Zacharias Boyd's statue, with the compartment in whyt marble, and the wryting tabell in black, twenty-five poundis sterling "—*Deeds Instituting Bursaries*, &c., pp. 39, 40.

and magistrates all fled, with the exception of stout old Zachary, who stood by his post, and as an old chronicler has it, "railled on the invaders to their very face in the High Church," where Cromwell went in state one Sunday forenoon to hear him preach. "The fantastic old gentleman," as Carlyle designates the venerable preacher, chose for his text the 8th chapter of Daniel, and improved the occasion while he relieved his mind by inveighing in no measured terms against his august hearer, drawing a vivid parallel between him and the rough goat mentioned in his text, very much to the latter's advantage, and calling the Protector and his followers "sectaries and blasphemers." On leaving the church, Cromwell's secretary, fiery Mr. Thurlow, "whispered him leave to pistol the old scoundrel." "Tuts!" replied the General, "you are a greater fool than himself. We'll pay him back in his own coin!" He accordingly invited his reverend foe to dinner, which was of the scantiest character, and concluded with a prayer, which lasted for several hours, "even," as an old writer has it with a sort of sympathetic sigh, "even until three in the morning." Of Zachary's pulpit utterances many stories are told, of which the following is not the worst:— Finding that several of his hearers left the church after the forenoon service, in order to escape further infliction, the preacher made use of this expression in his afternoon prayer—"Now, Lord, thou sees that many people do go away from hearing the word, but had we told them stories of Robin Hood or Davie Lindsay, they had stayed, and yet none of these *are near so good* as the word that I preach."

Cromwell contrived to leave his mark on the University, as he did on most things with which he had to do, by appointing one of his favourites, Mr Patrick Gillespie, to the Principalship, to the grievous chagrin of Zachary, and "most pairt of the facultie." The former seems to have devoted the last three years of his life mainly to the business of the College and the revision of his poetical works. Concerning the latter many absurd misrepresentations are current, to show the unfairness of which we give the following specimens of verses popularly attributed to Zachary, along with the verses which he actually wrote:—

PARODIES.

There was a man called Job,
   Dwelt in the Land of Uz;
He had a good gift of the gob,
   The same case happen us.
                Colvil.

Job's wife said to Job,
   Curse God and die;
Oh no, you wicked scold,
   No, not I.

Jeshurun waxed fat,
   And down his paunches hang;
And up against the Lord, his God,
   He kicked and he flang.

TRUE READINGS.

In Uz a man cal'd Job there was,
   Both perfect and upright;
Who feared God, and did eschew
   Evill even with all his might.
         Garden of Zion, vol. ii. p. 2.

Then said his wife, Retain'st thou still
   Thine old integritie;
What meanest thou, O foolish man,
   Now curse thou God and die;
But he again said unto her,
   His witlesse wife to schoole,
Thou speakest now thou knowes not what,
   Thou speakest like a foole,
         Garden of Zion, vol. ii., p. 8.

But Jeshurun, who should have beene
   Most righteous, did kick;
Thou art exceeding waxed fat,
   Thou art also grown thick;
Thou covered art with fatnesse; then
   His Maker he forsook,
And of his sure salvation's rock,
   No care at all he took.
         Garden of Zion, vol. i., p. 67.

	JACOB TO RACHEL.
And Jacob made for his wee Josie,	Yea, for your sake, this little Joseph more,
A tartan coat to keep him cosie;	I love than all that born were him before;
And what for no, there was nae harm,	. . . . . .
To keep the lad baith saft and warm.	Him I doe count from Heav'n to be our lot;
	Let us him make a particolour'd coat.
	Zion's Flowers, MS. p. 403.

	OF PHARAOH.
And was not Pharaoh a wicked and harden'd rascal,	Because this King thus hardened his heart,
Not to allow the men of Israel with their flocks and herds, their wives and their little ones, to go a forty day's journey into the wilderness to eat the Pascal.	Often great plagues his Kingdome felt the smart.
	Garden of Zion, vol. i. p. 53.

In February, 1653, there is an entry in the Records that Mr. Boyd "wes sicke," and unable to attend a University meeting; in March following he died. All honour to his memory, which should ever be held sacred by all to whom the honour of Glasgow College is dear; for he was a man who though austere, as befitted the character of his age, was yet kindly and generous, and who with some failings bore a high character for scholarship and uprightness, and proved so true a friend to this University when it stood most in need of friendship.

About this time the buildings were undergoing great changes. During the course of about thirty years from 1630 the new buildings appear mostly to have been erected, chiefly under the principalship of Gillespie (1652-60). Mr. Baillie seems to have taken great offence at the Principal's proceedings. "For our College," he writes in a letter to Strang, 1658, "we have no redress of our discipline and teaching. Mr. Gillespie's work is building and teaching: with the din of masons, wrights, carters, smiths, we are vexed every day. Mr. Gillespie alone, for vanity to make a new quarter in the College, has cast down my house to build up another of greater show, but far worse accommodation. In the meantime, for one full year I will be and am *exceedingly incommodate, which I bear because I cannot help it*, and also because Mr. Gillespie had strange ways of getting money for it by his own industry alone. An order he got from the Protector of 500 pound sterling, but for an ill office in the country. His delation of so much concealed rent yearly of the crown, also the vacancy of all churches wherein the College had interest; this breeds clamour as the unjust spoil of churches and incumbents —upon these foundations are our palaces builded, but withal our debts grow, *and our stipends are not paid*, for by his continual laying our rent is mouldered away." Mr. Baillie also complains bitterly of the Principal's "pulling down the whole forework of the Colledge, the high Hall and Arthurlie, very good houses, all newly dressed at a great charge." So much for worthy Mr. Baillie, who only bore with the high-handed Principal "because he couldn't help it."

The restoration of Charles II. in 1662, struck a severe blow at the prosperity of the University, by depriving it of the best source of its revenue—the Bishopric of Galloway. The merry monarch who thought that Presbytery "was not a religion for a gentleman" reestablished Episcopacy in Scotland, and overthrew the Presbyterian Church. The putting in force of the Royal Edict was en-

trusted to Lord Middleton. His Lordship was a man of
profligate manners, and had gathered around him in his
"jovial Parliament" (as Scott terms it) a troop of roy-
stering dare-devils, attended by trumpeters, macers, and
kettle-drums. A bacchanalian ovation awaited him wherever he went and especially at Paisley, Dumbarton, and
Hamilton he was right royally entertained. "Such who
entertained the commissioner best," says the matter-of-fact
Wodrow,"had their dining-room, their drinking-room, their
vomiting-room, and sleeping-rooms, when the company
had lost their senses." At Ayr "the devil's health was
drunk at the cross at midnight, and so the dissolute crew
staggered onward on their way to Glasgow." Middleton
held his Council in the noble old fore-hall of our College,
looking out into the High Street. The hall remains iden-
tically the same to-day as when its rich old wainscotted
walls rang with the excited voices of his lordship's "drunken parliament," of whom, "all present" we are told,
"were flustered with drink, save Sir James Lochart of
Lee." Bishop Burnet mentions that the Duke of Hamilton, who was a member of the council, informed him
that "they were all so drunk that day as to be incapable
of considering anything that was laid before them, and
would hear of nothing but the executing the law without
relenting or delay." From this council issued the celebrated Act of Glasgow, whereby nearly a third of the
ministers of the Presbyterian church were thrust from
their charges at a moment's notice, and out of its decree
arose the conventicles and field-preachings throughout
the country, which afterwards were so often assailed

by the troopers of Claverhouse and Dalzell, together with the consequent train of finings, imprisonments, and torturings.

So impoverished was the University, owing to these and other causes, that a large debt was contracted, and three of the professorships (one of theology and those of humanity and medicine), fell into abeyance. So things continued till the time of the revolution, when the College again began to revive from the state of depression in which it had so long remained. In 1693 each of the Scotch Universities obtained a gift of £300 a year out of the Bishop rents of Scotland, and the number of students who matriculated in Glasgow was greatly increased. In 1702 those attending Theology, Greek, and Philosophy amounted to 402.

We have now, as minutely as the limited space at our disposal will admit of, traced the history of our College from the year of her foundation to the beginning of the eighteenth century. It is not our purpose to follow any further her varying fortunes through times of prosperity and depression, or in any way to deal with what is matter of recent history. What has befallen her during the last century and a half—her rapid growth—her increased fame—the great and wise men who have filled her chairs and studied within her halls—down to the last changes in her system, and the late magnificent response made by the nation to the appeal of her professors for aid—these and such like are they not chronicled in recent pamphlets, and recorded in the pages of the College Calendar? Some years ago a great historian addressed a large and eager crowd of students in the common hall of this University. It was his inaugural speech on being installed Lord Rector, and after rapidly reviewing the history of the College the orator wound up his address with the following brilliant peroration.

"I trust, therefore, that when a hundred years more have run out, this ancient College will still continue to deserve well of our country and of mankind. I trust that the installation of 1949 will be attended by a still greater assembly of students than I have the happiness now to see before me. That assemblage, indeed, may not meet in the place where we have met. These venerable halls may have disappeared. My successor may speak to your successors in a more stately edifice, in an edifice which, even among the magnificent buildings of the future Glasgow, will still be admired as a fine specimen of the architecture which flourished in the days of the good Queen Victoria. But though the site and the walls may be new, the spirit of the institution will, I hope, be still the same. My successor will, I hope, be able to boast that the fifth century of the University has even been more glorious than the fourth. He will be able to vindicate that boast by citing a long list of eminent men, great masters of experimental science, of ancient learning, of our native eloquence, ornaments of the Senate, the pulpit, and the bar. He will, I hope, mention with high honour some of my young friends who now hear me; and he will, I also hope, be able to add that their talents and learning were not wasted on selfish or ignoble objects, but were employed to promote the physical and moral good of their species, to extend the empire of man over the material world, to defend the cause of civil and religious liberty against tyrants and bigots, and to defend the cause of virtue and order against the enemies of all divine and human laws."

Twenty years have barely elapsed since these words were spoken, yet a few months more will witness the realization of Lord Macaulay's prophecy. The rich old orchards, with their tempting fruitage and sunny slopes—the shady avenues, where learned Professors loved to walk and meditate—the cluster of mighty trees, in whose widespreading branches flourished a thriving colony of hoarse-throated crows—all these have long since passed away. The Molendinar no longer wimples seaward fresh and pure, nor is the upper green sacred to flowers and science, only a few barren trees remaining—sad remnants of its former glory. Those buildings, which the old chronicler thought "like unto a king's palace," seem to our modern eyes rather mean and dingy, and the halls where philosophers, scholars, statesmen and poets have taught and spoken will in a year or two echo with the voices of bustling officials, and the noisy pens of railway clerks. Confident though we are that the future prosperity of our College will as much exceed that of its past as the new buildings exceed the old in architectural beauty, we cannot help casting a lingering look of fond regret on those old halls, so soon to be swept away. To us, in common with the majority of our readers, these halls and courts are associated with happy reminiscences of olden times, when arm in arm with some friendly class-mate we strolled through the old quadrangles, never dreaming of the changes so soon to come. In anticipation of these changes we have written this hasty and imperfect sketch, a humble but loving tribute to the memory of our College.

NOTE.—It may be interesting to many of our readers to trace the steps by which the grounds of the Old College have been acquired.

The first portion, acquired by gift from Lord Hamilton as mentioned in the text, is described as "quoddam tenementum cum pertinenciis unacum quattuor acris terrarum montis columbarum prope torrentem de Malyndonore contigue adjacentibus, quod quidem tenementum jacet in Magno Vico descendente ab ecclesia Cathedrali Glasguensi usque ad crucem Fori ex parte orientali ejusdem inter locum Fratrum Predicatorum ab australi parte et terram Domini Thome Arthurle Capellani a parte boreali." This land comprehended two portions, first, the site of the original building, consisting of two courts, and covering about half an acre; and second, a garden of nearly four acres in the low part of the green, adjoining the Molendinar on the east, Arthurlie's lands on the north, the Friars Lane or Blackfriars Street on the south, and the Muyr Butts on the west. The two portions of ground were not adjacent to each other—although of course there must have been means of access to the garden—because in 1615 the Bishop of St. Andrews mortified to the College "a tenement lying between the College and its gardens." This tenement *may* have been identical with the Muyr Butts, and have extended all the way along the west side of the four acres. Between the Butts and the grounds of the Blackfriars preachers there was at one time a private lane or alley which led from the Friars Lane to the back of the College buildings.

The next acquisition was the gift of Sir Thomas Arthurlie, mentioned in the text, a long narrow strip of ground of about two acres adjoining the College on the north side. It extended along the Vicar's alley (the New Vennel) from High Street to the Molendinar. The front portion of this ground is now occupied by the Professors' Court. Arthurlie's lands cannot, however, have embraced the whole of 'the new court,' because in 1632 "the few males and superiorities of the tenement of land and yeards lying betwixt the house belonging to David Rob and the New Vennel" were purchased from the Laird of Bedlay by Charles Morthland, Professor of Oriental Languages, on behalf of the College, who was also instructed to buy the property of the said tenement. It is stated in the same minute that six of the Professors' houses stood on this piece of ground. The portion last acquired seems to answer to the description of "the Paidagog or Colledge yaird," and the portion of Arthurlie's lands lying betwixt it and the College to the description of "the Auld Colledge Yaird," which at one time supplied the learned inmates of that august institution with Kail.

The Chapter House and ground formerly belonging to the Friars were bestowed on the College in the time of Queen Mary. They are described as "the Manss and Kirkrowme of the Freris predicatoris within the citie of Glasgow—with threttene aikers of land lyand besyde the samyn citie." The Friars predicatores were the Dominican or Black Friars, who are said to have been called the Friars Preachers on account of their frequent preaching. The Chapter House was nearly 200 years older than the College. It was succeeded by the College Kirk, which was afterwards transferred by the College to the town in 1635. In 1618 the Chantry of St. Mungo, which we presume was a chapel set apart for the praise of that saint and had been connected with the old Chapter House, was acquired by purchase. It fronted the High Street and stood close by the site of the Principal's house. The chantry ground was retained and still forms part of the College grounds.

If we can put any reliance on the descriptions in the Title Deeds, the gardens round the chapter house were at one time of the most luxuriant description. This is at least suggested by the name of "the Paradise yards," which, along with "the West Freir yarde, the Colhouse and Cloister Knot yardis," all lay "conjoinit with the greit orchart, betuix the samyn and the kirk callit the Blackfriers' Kirk." The College was wont to let the orchard, as appears from the old rent-rolls, and we get some notion of what the ground produced from a note appended to a document entitled "The Fencing of Muyr Darnlye and Cruxtown, Colledge and Pedagog," to the following effect, "the fensing of the *quheat, peis, beinis,* grouand upoun the land in Dowhill maid the penult of Merche before Mr. Hew Fullarton at the Mercat Croce." This document seems to us to have been a kind of judicial allocation of the produce of the College garden between three tenants—or rather three purchasers of the produce, because no rent is entered in the Rental of that time as derived from the garden, though it was let on lease shortly afterwards.

The "threttene aikers of land besyde the citie" must have lain beyond the Molendinar. That portion of the green amounts to more than seven acres, and the property of the College beyond the wall of the green on the north-east extremity of it amounts to about six acres. The latter part has been feued for public works and the like. Taken together these two portions rather more than account for Queen Mary's gift. "The high green," in which the observatory long stood, was used as a private garden where the Professors might pursue their meditations undisturbed in the open air. This was also probably the "great garden for Botany and a Physic garden," which in 1704 was improved and enclosed with a wall. The whole green was enclosed with a wall about the same time, for in 1696 the University bought from the Minister and Session of the Barony Parish "part of the five-shilling-land of the Dowhill," called "the Grassum Lands," at the price of 1184 merks Scots, "the said Universitie being about to enclose the haill lands of the Dowhill in a park which they cannot convenientlie doe without enclosing the said Grassum lands." The Grassum lands must therefore have lain between the high green and the low green on the sloping banks of the Molendinar, where there was, and still is, a grove of trees. The name indicates that these lands were considered available for feuing purposes, and the probability of their having occupied this position is heightened by the fact that about the same time the University purchased some feus in the same line at its southern extremity.

We have now accounted for the whole ground connected with the College, and shown, in sufficient detail, how and when it was acquired. We feel disposed to wind up with a reflection. Often have we heard of the 'grand uncertainty of the law,' often have we felt the delights of casuistry, but we never were more bewildered by contradictory statements, never more convinced of the vanity of conjecture, than in the case of the Muyr Butts. Did they ever exist? If so, where did they lie? What were they? Why were they called *Muyr Butts*? and why *Butts?* When the Editors are made Lord Rectors of the University, they will be happy to present with a gold medal any enterprising young historian who will give a satisfactory answer to these simple questions. Our own opinion is that the Muyr Butts were set apart for the practice of archery, and occupied the position we have indicated above.

OLD ALICE.

They told me—they who went to see the play—
"Old Alice" was the part they liked the best,
Played with simplicity which hid true art,
Yet with a touching emphasis that made
The louder—more pretentious style—seem poor.

I went one night, but had forgot their comments,
When, ere I knew, "Old Alice" quietly moved
Into the scene. O time and change! 'twas *she*
Who in the dreamlike past of far off days
Played all the youthful queens and every form
Of unimagined loveliness; 'twas she to whom
Age seemed impossible, decay a jest,
Whose radiant forehead and whose lips of love
Made havoc with all hearts and most with mine!

"*Old Alice!*" what has happened in those years
That men should call thee so out of thy name?
Comes but to me that vision of thyself,
Treasured so long, not knowing thou wert old,—
Comes but to me strange wonderment to trace
Bright memories in those altered lineaments!

Yet now I look again thou art not old,
For into autumn thou hast brought with thee
The gleamy warmth and the ethereal grace
Of summer hours,—and if thy bright day wanes,
A tender moonlight is around thee still
Silvering the evening cloud with gentler ray!

Henry Glassford Bell.

GREEK ETHICS.

"I ASKED him why those slain in battle were allowed to remain unburied?"

He said it had always been the custom, but that he could not explain it.

"But," I replied, "why should you disturb the bones of those whom you have already buried, and expose them on the outskirts of the town?"

"It was the custom of our forefathers," he answered; "therefore we continue to observe it."

"Have you no belief in a future existence after death?

Is not some idea expressed in the act of exhuming the bones after the flesh is decayed?"

"Existence after death! How can that be? Can a dead man get out of his grave unless we dig him out?"

"Do you think man is like a beast that dies and is ended?"

"Certainly: an ox is stronger than a man: but he dies and his bones last longer: they are bigger. A man's bones break quickly: he is weak."

"Is not a man superior in sense to an ox? has he not a mind to direct his actions."

"Some men are not so clever as an ox. Men must sow corn to obtain food, but the ox and wild animals can procure it without sowing."

"Do you not know that there is a spirit within you more than flesh? Do you not dream and wander in thought to distant places in your sleep? Nevertheless your body rests in one spot. How do you account for this?"

Commoro laughing, "Well, how do *you* account for it? It is a thing I cannot understand: it occurs to me every night."

"Have you no idea of the existence of spirits superior either to man or beast? Have you no fear of evil except from bodily causes?"

"I am afraid of elephants and other animals, when in the jungle at night, but of nothing else."

. . . .

"Do you see no difference in good and bad actions?"

"Yes, there are good and bad in men and beasts?"

"Do you think that a good man and a bad man must share the same fate and alike die and alike end?"

"Yes: what else can they do? how can they help dying? good and bad all die."

"Their bodies perish, but their spirits remain, the good in happiness, the bad in misery. If you have no belief in a future state why should a man be good? Why should he not be bad if he can prosper by wickedness?"

"Most people are bad: if they are strong they take from the weak: the good people are all weak, they are good because they are not strong enough to be bad."

Most readers of the dialogue in Sir Samuel Baker's book, from which the above sentences are taken, will admit that the savage Commoro has the best of the argument, but his position represents the very crudest stage of Ethics, a stage further back than that to which we are referred by the earliest traditions of any civilized people. The sentiments and the practice of barbarous tribes are like fossilized remains of a pre-historic humanity in which "the traces of primæval man appear," unless indeed they point to a falling away by isolation or a degeneration of the original type. Morality, as we find it in the oldest Hebrew and Oriental records, is already raised above the bare idea of individual strength—might is right, in the most superficial sense—by the influence of family ties and a trace of some religious or superstitious reverence. Morality in this form may be said to be born with man, and, as far back as we can read, it has advanced beyond the trenchant brutality of Commoro, although in utterly sceptical or disorganized periods of social life, from the date of the Peloponnesian war to that of the French Revolution, and in the practice of the worst kind of men in all ages, it is apt to revert to that brutal type. But ethical speculation, properly so called, begins with Greece. The contemplative thought of the East was all wrapped up in her mythology. There was no step towards the gradual disentanglement of the different lines of investigation which forms so great a part of the history of the Hellenic mind. The East is in the main a majestic unity without the capacity of development, for all growth starts from some friction of ideas. The germs of art, philosophy and government cluster round her religion and do not fructify. Her sciences are buried in a mysterious worship. Her morality is confined to precepts of submission. The motionless Theocracy of Brahminism and the self-annihilating idealism of Buddha end in the same stagnation. India is dominated by priests without prophets, and by schoolmen without science. In Greece first we have progression, activity and change: by her geography and the mixture of races on her soil, she is predestined for variety and freedom. The spirit of the East is the absorption of man in nature, that of Greece is "individuality conditioned by beauty." At the dawn of her civilization heroic fables take the place of a rigid dogma. Her Polytheism from the first contains more hope for the future than Orientalism, the conquest over which is typified in the overthrow of the Titans. The merely natural powers, symbolised rudely in Fetichism, more abstractly in the old Persian faith, are, at an early date, subordinated to those which regulate and preside over human intelligence. Athene restraining the wrath of Achilles is already divine wisdom imposing a curb on the "passionate heart."

I. It is an anachronism to look for an ethical system in Homer. There is endless matter for study in his writings but no philosophy. What we find mainly is a representation of the era of bodily nature, pictures of a time when manners plain and fierce were only tempered by a love of beauty. Everything is concrete; there are ideas of excellence, transcending those of Commoro, but still generally associated with ideas of strength, of nobility and meanness, of truth, of courage, of reverence for the aged and for the gods, with a lament over the fact that men have become more unlike them; but there is an uncertainty about the rules of right and wrong. Physical and moral qualities are confused: more deference is paid to a swift foot, a loud voice, a broad chest, than to self-command or justice. The Iliad turns on slighted honour, and Achilles, the finest model of offended chivalry, hates a lie more than the gates of hell, but Ulysses, the chief of all knights errant, is lauded for his ingenious wiles. Homer has not arrived at the conception of law as distinct from an isolated command, and in his account of the divine attributes he is inconsistent. The jars of good and evil lie at the door of Zeus, even while he protests against men laying to this charge the fruits of their own recklessness.

Hesiod's Bœotian pastoral depicts, with inferior genius, a state of society in advance of Homer's, a society in which a half instinctive half patriarchal code of ethics is recognized. A sort of wisdom about life is beginning to grow up in the shape of proverbs and maxims, mostly prudential, partly sentimental. Hesiod and the seven sages (living at a time when the aristocratic element was beginning to succeed the old hereditary monarchies, and men's minds were groping their way, by aid of words, figures and fancies borrowed from the remnants of nature-worship on the one side and a half historic belief in gods and heroes on the other, from the world of sense to the world of thought), are the main sources of those simple lessons, many of which were employed by the later philosophers as texts to expand into an ampler meaning. Among those golden sentences were, μηδέν ἄγαν, γνῶθ σεαυτόν, χρὴ πρός τὸ τέλος σκοπεῖν, πλέον ἥμισυ παντός, with several others quoted in Plato, *e.g.*, "The flocks of the just bear him fleeces, his trees bear him fruit." "Help your neighbour and he will help you." "Virtue is seated on a pleasant sward, but at the top of a steep rock to which a narrow path ascends." Much of the teaching of the gnomic poets is, like that of Solomon, in the same tone. The sanctity of an oath, the power of time, the charms of friendship, the respect due to parents, the authority of law and the certainty of retribution, were their prevailing topics expressed in γνώμαι or aphorisms from which they derived their name, and which were engraved on obelisks and erected in Athens by the Peisistratidæ. To know those simple prudential maxims in their poetical form constituted a great part of the μουσική of Greece. If a Greek were asked what justice was, he would naturally reply by quoting a line of Simonides or a verse of Solon.

This morality was tolerably accurate but superficial. In Hesiod, however, and the best of the gnomic poets, there are traces of a deeper element. Among the veins of thought that traverse the old literature of Greece two are conspicuously opposed. The one represents our favourite modern ideal of the fresh Hellenic mind. Inspired by light air, bright suns and blue seas, it sings of "the dancing stars and the dædal earth."

> "Ver ubi longum tepidasque præbet
> Jupiter brumas."

Its mottoes are "Carpe diem," "Vivas in amore jocisque." This spirit, which pervades the more joyous myths, Homer's hymns, Anacreon's lyrics, the elegies of Mimnermus, the odes in Theocritus, is that of men ἀκηδέα θύμον ἔχοντες, with minds untouched by the pale cast of thought, but with senses, like those of children, alive to every impression of "this fair round world." On the shore they heard "old Triton blow his wreathed horn:" at dawn they saw the steeds of the rosy-fingered Eos

> "Arise
> And shake the darkness from their loosened manes
> And beat the twilight into flakes of fire."

To them, "fleeting the time carelessly as in the golden age," beauty was truth, truth beauty, that was all they knew on earth, and all they cared to know. They made and worshipped the statues of Aphrodite, and enshrined at Cyprus the religion of pleasure which was afterwards buried beneath the ruins of Pompeii.

But, alongside of this strophe of exuberance, there is, almost from the first, an antistrophe of regret: in the earliest Greek poetry there is an occasional undertone, the feeling of imperfection and decay which darkens, like a deepening shadow, as we advance from the morning to the evening of the world. Even Homer looks back to his golden age: he anticipates the regrets of Sir Thomas Malory in the fifteenth—of Mr. Froude in the nineteenth century of Christendom: for the godlike force and freedom of the race have passed, we are assured, before the ten years war at Troy, and now on earth there breathes not nor creeps a more unhappy thing than man.

"Οὐ μὲν γάρ τί πού ἐστιν ὀϊζυρώτερον ἀνδρὸς,
Πάντων ὅσσα τε γαῖαν ἔπι πνείει τε καὶ ἕρπει."

In Hesiod this idea of diminished strength is refined into that of a fall from innocence and virtue. He complains of living in an iron world, faithless and full of ills, "Πλείη μὲν γὰρ γαῖα κακῶν, πλείη δὲ θάλασσα," over which there wander 30,000 spirits to punish unjust deeds. Theognis, the most melancholy of the gnomic poets, declares "It were better for men not to have been born at all, or if born the next best is to go as soon as possible to Hades," and Hades in his mind was a gloomy realm.

"Οὐδεὶς ἀνθρώπων, ὃν πρῶτ' ἐπὶ γαῖα καλύψῃ
Εἴς τ' Ἔρεβος καταβῇ, δώματα Περσεφόνης,
Τέρπεται οὔτε λύρης οὔτ' αὐλητῆρος ἀκούων,
Οὔτε Διωνύσου δῶρ' ἐσαειράμενος."

Simonides, perhaps the most cheerful, confesses "It is hard for man by nature full of imperfections to be good," and again "like leaves so is the race of man." Already, by the opening of Pandora's box, "poor humanity" seemed beaten down and maimed and wasted. A sadness had come upon the air and on "the murmur of the falling floods," and its reflection in the poets, historians and philosophers of the time has descended to us, with the more jubilant lyrics of Ionia, "immortal age beside immortal youth."

This melancholy culminates in the fragments of Heraclitus and the Eleatics. Life with the former is a stream, and the world a series of dissolving views. There is a law controlling its changes to which the sun and the sea and the seasons must submit, man with his clouded vision, who can catch truth only from afar, who is an ape to the gods, must learn to obey their will. The attacks of Xenophanes on the anthropomorphism of the older poets connect him rather with the progress of theological than of ethical thought, and his philosophy contained the germ of the sweeping pantheism—so destructive to ethics —which was developed by his successor in the same school. With Parmenides "all is one" in a sense which excludes the individuality and responsibility of man, and carries us back in practice almost to the fatalism of the East. He speaks of birth as mournful, "στυγεροῖο τόκου καὶ μίξιος ἀρχή," and of mankind as ephemeral waves lifted for a moment, and that only as in a dream, from the bosom of the infinite sea. The Eleatic sages were overwhelmed by the weight of their own conceptions, and their poems are dirges over human ignorance uttered in a mournful voice from their intellectual thrones.

Meanwhile another system, which left more room or liberty, had developed itself in Magna Græcia. The philosophy which Pythagoras brought from Samos and planted in Italy had a greater effect on Greek thought than that of any other Pre-Socratic school, and this in spite of the fact that its details were, in many respects, opposed to the national spirit: but its ethics, as far as they have come down to us, are still crude and rudimentary. They are theoretically based on the fundamental dualism from which the συστοιχία of the world is developed. The assertion that Good belongs to the column of Order, Unity or Definiteness, Evil to that of Disorder, Plurality or the Indefinite, is the first explicit recognition of an idea which never lost its hold of the Greek mind. Consistently with his mathematical view of the universe, moral, mental, and physical, Pythagoras adopted the only view of justice which is capable of being expressed by numbers: it is an equality, an ἰσότης, and the just man, τετράγωνος ἄνευ ψόγου, is a square without reproach or blot. Injustice is the disturbance of the balance which the moralist has to set even by the ἀντιπεπονθός, "the good old rule, the simple plan," of an eye for an eye and a tooth for a tooth which belongs to the infancy of every civilization. Similarly friendship was defined as an equality of communities, and the rubric πάντα τὰ φίλων κοινὰ was adopted. If the golden verses are Pythagorean some of their practical precepts are remarkable. "Avoid hatred—never hurt others—bear wrongs with patience." "Discord born with mortals wounds them mortally, we should flee from it and give it place." "Men are the artizans of their own misfortunes." "Do not abandon yourself to sleep before examining three times the actions of the day." The Metempsychosis was a logical deduction from the view of the soul as incorporeal and yet requiring a body as a garment; it may have been suggested by some of the mysteries which undoubtedly left some impression on early Greek morality. Those of Orpheus and Eumolpus appear to have taught the doctrine of a future life, of rewards and punishments, and the need of an expiation for guilt, all which ideas are prominent in Pythagoras. But his system, like these mysteries, was framed too much on the Oriental model to keep its place as a whole in the heart of Hellas. His half theocratic society pushed its rules to the verge of tyranny; its castes, its secrecy and its vows of obedience were adapted to make believers rather than philosophers. The destruction of the Pythagorean political institute, which Plato vainly endeavoured to revive, may be taken as a symbol of the expulsion of the eastern element which up to that time still clung about the mind of Greece.

Democritus, the most illustrious exponent, if not the founder of the Atomistic philosophy, opposed to the pre-existing idealisms a complete system of sensational morality, which again advanced on that of Pythagoras in giving, however inconsistently, a higher place to the independent action of the individual. Many of its practical maxims, as "Temperance sharpens pleasure," "Courage is spoiled by its excess," "Never wish for anything absurd," are commonplace; others are more suggestive, as "When thou art alone act as if in a crowd, respecting thyself," "Good turns to evil in ill-regulated minds," "τὸ μή ἀδικειν το μή ἐθελειν." "In the whirl of necessity man is only half a slave." The spirit of mystery driven from Greece proper found a refuge in Sicily, and took form at a somewhat later date in the motley rhapsodies of the eclectic poet and sage Empedocles. In his scheme of the universe the Pythagorean dualism reappears in the two powers, Love and Hate, and the notion of two worlds, that in which we at present dwell, marred by ignorance and strife, and that from which we have lapsed, the realm of truth and rest: the Eden, the Elysium, the Faery Land of fancy. As the penalty of former guilt, man is doomed "τρίς μυρίας ὥρας ἀπὸ μακάρων ἀλάλησ-θαι," but when he has passed through many stages of existence, lived a course of ascetic lives, "ransacked the ages, spoiled the climes," and purified himself as through fire, he may be permitted to return to them. This idea of a fall—a perpetually recurring myth to which we are recalled by Empedocles—is really an evidence of intellectual progress. It is not dreamt of in the philosophy of Commoro: for the sense of the imperfection of life is the shadow cast by a higher idea of perfection, it is, as Carlyle expresses it, "the inverted image of our nobleness: the depth of our despair measures the height and capacity of our hopes." This feeling which in modern times has become intensified in proportion as our standard of excellence has been raised, wrought on the

Hellenic mind for both good and evil. The result was good in so far as it led the Greeks to think more lowly of themselves, to recognise the truth involved in their "παθήματα μαθήματα," to dare all things, and be confident of nothing, knowing that prosperity is fickle, and that easy virtues are prized neither by gods nor men. The result was evil when it tempted them to arraign Heaven or to acquiesce in Fatalism. All Pre-Socratic literature which touches on moral questions is tainted with those errors. Hesiod's Zeus sits on his throne guarded by force and jealousy. The sublime morality of Œschylus is darkened by the omnipotent presence of a Destiny which brings down its retributions on guilt, but not always on the guilty. He has so handled the great myth of Prometheus as to make it appear that God is the enemy of man, for, we are told, He kept them underground in sunless caverns, till the fire-bringer saved them and became the proto-martyr of the race. Prometheus is the "vir justus et propositi tenax" against the "vultus instantis tyranni," the type of the reformer of every age, renewing himself in successive avatars in the prophets and teachers of Hellas, Judea, and Christendom.

The poet Pindar represents Greek mythology in it's purest form, not yet deliberately rationalised but harmonised and filtered by life into a medium of instruction. He declares that he will say nothing of the gods but what is good, that they are the authors of every perfect gift, without whose countenance nothing can prosper, that they are changeless, and their will is fate τὸ μόρσιμον Διόθεν Πεπρωμένον ἐκφέρεν, and yet even Pindar speaks of their envy. The ruling idea in what we may call the Religion of Herodotus, is the inevitable chastisement of everything which passes the bound of moderation. All excess, too much happiness, too much pride, too much cruelty, or too much greatness, calls down an arbitrary Nemesis, which, acting on a gigantic scale like Thrasybulas and Tarquin, lops off the heads of all the tall poppies "ὑψιφρόνων τιν' ἐκάμψε βροτῶν;" it is a process of theological ostracism keeping the lives of men within limit, like the voices of a chorus. "Mark," the historian, puts into the mouth of Artabanus, the counsellor who stands by the throne of Xerxes like the slave in the Roman car, "Mark how the God—ὁ Θεος—dashes down animals of surpassing size, and does not suffer them to make a vaunt of their strength while he leaves the little ones unharmed! Mark how his bolts are launched against the tallest trees! He delights in laying the exalted low, and has smitten and destroyed with terror many a mighty host, for God permits no one but Himself to call himself great."

With this reference we may close our survey of the mythological aspects of early Greek morality. The reflex partly of national, partly of individual feeling, they exhibit all the inconsistencies of a transition stage of thought, when the more primitive polytheism of Homer's time was beginning to give place to abstract views of man and nature; what is true in them has been absorbed in the religion, what is false lingers in the superstitions of our own day. Of the practical life of the Greeks during this period we have few details; such as there are, point to a gradual softening of the manners of the heroic age, to a gracefully sensuous rather than a grossly sensual existence, seldom ennobled by very lofty examples or disfigured by atrocious crimes, to a gradual merging of the .idea of the family in that of the state. In the infancy of science there are few distinctions. We have seen Ethics formalised and stiffened by mathematics on the one side, and merged on the other in a mystic theology: it was also confounded with Law, and this confusion prevailed so long that moral were never clearly separated from positive obligations till the time of the Stoics. With us ,Law is commonly regarded as a gradually inducted standard, bearing the authority of a long experience, but requiring to be administered or even modified with reference to the requirements of each successive generation. The Greeks, like the Hebrews, were more accustomed to regard it as a sort of inspiration, or divine ordinance issued for the regulation of their lives. Their legislators Solon, Lycurgus and Xarondas were ministers of the decrees of Themis This idea, together with the prominence given to the fact of citizenship by the smallness of their states, helped to elevate valour and loyalty above the other virtues and fostered the habit of referring to written law as the supreme sanction of morality. The first clear recognition of the insufficiency of this standard, and of the possible conflict between the higher and lower law, is the famous answer of Antigone to Creon. "Those laws of thine were ordained neither in Heaven nor by the justice of the nether world; nor have they any power to override the unwritten and immutable decrees of God—ἄγραπτα κἀσφαλῆ θεῶν νόμιμα." Sophocles is perhaps the most modern in spirit of the Greek poets, the life of his dramas is at once more complex and more refined than that represented in the pages of his predecessors, he dwells more on the delicate play of the affections and appeals throughout to subtler sentiments—his women come nearer to our hearts than those of the medieval Romances, and we have, particularly in the "Coloneus," frequent instances of that emotional interpretation of natural scenery which is comparatively rare in ancient art. He was not wholly unaffected by the traditions of the era that was passing, for his religion is pervaded by the sentiment of the Herodotean Nemesis: but with him the innocent who fall protest their innocence, in his scheme of life the energy and will of man wrestle with the irony of Fate, and the higher principles which he maintained had to fight for their acknowledgment with the sceptical tendencies of his own and the next generation.

II. There comes a time in the history of men and nations when the hereditary beliefs of life are put on their trial: the canons of taste, religion and morals which have been hitherto accepted blindly are revised in a spirit of antagonism, all formulæ are questioned, old errors and old truths are thrown overboard together: there is a reaction of incredulity and irreverence. Such were the phenomena which introduced the second stage of Greek thought in the middle of the fifth century, B.C., and of this spirit the Sophists were the accredited exponents. Like the Tyrants who preceded them in the political world, they were conductors of a transition; they replaced the poets and rhapsodists in their influence on the national mind and fore-ran the more systematic philosophers of real life. Before their era philosophy had stood apart in the "*fallentis semita vitæ.*" It was developed in little schools in remote corners of the Hellenic world. Now, for the first time, the pressure of a great foreign war had done what common councils and feasts had failed to do in making Greece a nation. The thought of Pythagoras and Thales became her thought, and in Athens, the Prytany of wisdom, the insufficiency of their isolated and abstract views of the universe was made apparent through their mutual contradiction. The scepticism which had been fructifying in the heart of the old mythology pervaded the epoch of the Sophists,—all the previous speculations had been leading up to it. The condition of mind of Adeimantus, in Book II. of Plato's Republic, was the natural result of the preceding argument which is an epitome of the tentative and conjectural stage of Greek ethics. The early gnomes had been found wanting. The philosophies had clashed. The laws had lost their majesty. The rites of expiation were bought and sold. The tears of Heraclitus and the laughter of Democritus expressed the same despair. One thing remained the art of life, good management, prudence and the proper use of words in influencing men. Eloquence was power: truth itself a mode of speech, ὀυ φύσει ἀλλὰ νόμῳ, to each man,—as Horne Tooke long afterwards asserted—that which he trowed.

This popular creed the Sophists echoed and adorned. The charge that they had a set purpose to corrupt the manners of the age is not worth refuting. They had no more an intention to corrupt than Mr. Hepworth Dixon has, but it was a corrupt taste that made their fortunes. The same charge might with equal fairness be brought against much of the newspaper literature and many of the popular preachers of our own day. Precisely in the spirit of "The Times" Protagoras applied to morality the doctrine of the perpetual flux. He boasted that he could make the worse appear the better, only because he recognized no permanent difference between better and worse. In his famous maxim πάντων μέτρον ἕκαστος, involving the doctrine that everything exists in relation, and must be judged according to its circumstances, there was an element of truth: it called attention to the subjective side of knowledge and led to a critique of cognition: but Protagoras himself misapplied it, and resting in sensationalism, became a sceptic in metaphysics, and in ethics substituted interest for principle. The Sophists generally were the first to start ἀπόριαι in morals, and by so doing paved the way for the discussions of Socrates and Aristotle, but they were themselves satisfied to raise doubts without attempting to lay them. It has been said that Plato parodied their dialectic, which was a product of liberty. It is true he fails adequately to estimate the services they rendered to practical logic, grammar, and criticism, but he is right in considering the bold fluency of their superficial answers as alien to the spirit of a genuine philosophy. In their love of brilliant paradoxes they again reflected their age: an age from which the old blind reverence had vanished without leaving a higher reverence in its place. The following sentences of Aristophanes' remind us of Voltaire: "The clouds are goddesses, and all the rest is nothing;" "If Jupiter will not listen to reason, let us declare war against him;" "If Justice exists, why has not Jupiter been punished for locking up his father."

There is a sense in which Thucydides, the greatest historian of Greece, may be said to have been her greatest Sophist. A sceptical critic of tradition, he replaces the religious element in the work of his predecessor by maxims of expediency and worldly wisdom; and the only law at which he arrives in the evolution of events is a generalization of human caprice. The Peloponnesian war, which ruined Greece politically, had a bad effect on her morals in re-establishing the rule of force and the worship of success, always dangerously captivating to an impetuous people. When the states were rending each other like hungry vultures they lost what faith had hitherto been left in the desecrated shrines; all the bonds that had made them one, τὸ ὅμαιμον το ὁμο-γλώσσον, τὰ ἤθη ὁμοτροπῆ, τὰ κοινῆ ἱδρύματα θεῶν, were forgotten. As during the French Revolution, the spirit of equality was exaggerated into a disdain of all law but the will of the majority. Men transferred the names of the virtues and vices; seeing good only in pleasure and evil in pain, they were possessed by a passion to enjoy and a fury to dominate. The historian himself, who recoils in horror from the excesses of the Corcyrean massacre, narrates the no less iniquitous affair of the Melians with unblushing calmness. The times were acting out on a large scale the spirit of the old Dorian song, "My riches are my sword, my shield, my lance, these are my titles to be lord and king."

In the darkest days of Athens, when their lawlessness and pride had brought upon her people the Nemesis of the thirty Tyrants, there appeared among them a prophet who made a last attempt to reform their manners, to bring them back to purer standards, to give them firmer bases of belief, to enthrone again the ancient virtues on conscience and on reason, and to do this by a league of honest citizens rather than of philosophers. Who shall reproduce the real SOCRATES of history, the warrior of Delium, the solitary nonconformist who stemmed the tide of popular indignation after Arginusæ, the old man with an exterior like Silenus, a heart full of the gods, who went about teaching and preaching in the streets of the "Violet Crown;" who shall separate him from the great tragic and comic actor in the most sublime series of ancient fictions, who wears the cothurnus in the "Apologia," the sock in "the Banquet," who is known to us as Plato's mask? Our only guide in this attempt is a comparison, and in Xenophon and Aristotle the imaginative and ideal side of his character is wanting: but they agree in their accounts of his moral teaching, his irony, his interrogative method, his use of parables, his belief in a divine mission and his attitude toward the Sophists. He went with them in abandoning speculations, $\pi\epsilon\rho\grave{\iota}\ \tau\hat{\eta}s\ \ddot{o}\lambda\eta s\ \phi\upsilon\sigma\epsilon\hat{\omega}s$,— the study of nature—for the study of man. He admitted that the earlier thinkers had let go the reins of thought, that they had neglected to test their instrument, that their systems were dissolved in a maze of obscurity. Philosophy must be brought down to earth and carried "home to men's hearts and bosoms." The search in which Thales and Parmenides had gone astray, which the Sophists had resigned, must be renewed under better auspices. The self-satisfaction which filled up the void of wisdom with words must be exchanged for a confession of ignorance. Before proceeding one step on the way to knowledge we must know what we know and what we do not know at starting. Socrates made the old maxim γνῶθι σέαυτον the foundation of a new psychological method, and turned to a different use the principle of Protagoras. Like the Sophists he started with a σκέψις: but it was not the scepticism which is predetermined to deny: it was rather, like the Cartesian doubt, the spirit which proves all things and holds fast by that which is good; a negative in answer to a negative the result was positive. While endeavouring to reestablish the old reverences, he held himself bound to the higher when it came into conflict with the lower law. "If you were to offer to dismiss me on such conditions I would exclaim, O Athenians I regard you with the utmost respect and affection, but I shall obey God rather than you." To all mere rules of expediency he opposed a firm belief in the ἄγραπτα νόμιμα θεῶν, and their reflection in a single standard of right, inherent in and recognizable by the mind. Behind all physical phenomena he held, with Anaxagoras, the unity of a supreme power governing the world and directing all things for the best. Behind all "passions, thoughts, desires," and all the complexities of human life he maintained the internal presence of the same deity. He erred, as Plato did after him, by failing to recognize the will as a distinct factor of action. His rubric Ἐπιστήμη ἡ ἀρετή, virtue is knowledge, is in one point of view the assertion of a rational morality, as a science and not merely an art, in opposition to the idea that freedom consists in acting at random. It implied that the highest functions of the soul work harmoniously, that the laws of the good, the true and the beautiful meet if we trace them far enough. But Socrates did not appreciate the force of the truth enunciated first by Aristotle, that one may see the right end and yet reject the right means to attain to it. "*Video meliora proboque deteriora sequor.*" The knowledge of good and evil was to him the tree of life and "*eritis sicut dei*" was in his mind no satire. Before his age, he was yet a Greek, and a taint of intellectual assumption went along with his modesty. His sympathies though intense were limited. His practical morals were simple: his temperance was the ability to endure hunger and cold and thirst, his justice an obedience to written and unwritten laws. Happiness being among his ends of life, he was not a Stoic, though we can trace the germ of Stoicism in his death and his frequent injunction that we should make ourselves independent of circumstances. There is a true way of interpreting this, there should be a citadel in the mind unshaken by the waves of fortune. There are two false ways: when we float down the stream of life singing with our English Anacreon "gather ye roses while ye may" or when we stand apart from other men "in impotence of fancied pride." The Cyrenaic—among the imperfect schools that sprang from Socrates—took the first of those false views and lapsed into a crude Epicureanism. Their motto "μονόχρονος ἡδονή," "μὴ προκάμνειν," was, in an irreligious sense, take no thought of the morrow, let us eat and drink and die. The Cynics took the second, and holding that virtue was αὐτάρκης πρὸς εὐδαιμόνιαν, mistook self-confidence for virtue, abandoned their duties to their fellows, wrapped themselves up in an embittered wisdom and ended in approximating to the life of the brutes. Diogenes the Cynic was a maimed parody of Socrates: half Mentor, half Thersites, he went barking through the city which patriots were trying in vain to save from Macedon.

PLATO was the heir of all the ages of Greek thought up to his time, and he gave to that thought its highest expression. He fused down and remodelled the polytheistic poetry of Greece in his apologues and his myths. From the Ionic school he borrowed part of his cosmology. He applied the Heraclitean flux to his theory of phenomenal existence. He took his immutable ideas from the Eleatics, dipping the colourless abstractions of Parmenides in an ethical dye and endeavouring to bridge over the gulf that separated them from life. From Pythagoras he derived his belief in the omnipresence of the laws of number, his notion of a philosophic polity and his conception of order as the standard of the moral and mental universe. In his earlier dialogues the

Metempsychosis appears in connection with the ἀναμ-νῆσις of a past existence: in the Gorgias and Republic it is refined into a faith in immortality. Plato's ethics are on one side connected with his metaphysics as presided over by the Supreme Idea, his loftiest abstraction. On the other they are closely interwoven with his politics. His perfect man is the perfect ruler of his ideal state. In many respects his morality is singularly modern: the highest thoughts of Œschylus, Pindar and Sophocles pass into it freed from their former limitations. He has discarded the crude notions of the Nemesis, of retaliation, of external motives generally and without seeking, as the Neo Platonists did, to annihilate the body, he places it in constant subordination to the soul. In the "Republic" he tells us that God, simple and true without change or shadow of turning is the source of good only, never of evil, but that the wicked need chastening and owe gratitude to the Deity for its remedial power. "As for the just man if he fall into poverty or disease or anything that seems evil, we must know that all these things work together for good to him whether he be dead or alive: for he who exerts himself to practise justice and virtue and so become like the gods is never by them neglected." In the Theatetus he declares "Evil is necessary but with the Gods there is no evil: therefore we ought as soon as may be to take flight to their company, the means of flight being unceasing efforts to become like them." In the Crito and again in the Republic he protests against returning evil for evil, as "justice can never consist in doing an injury to any one." In the Symposium he says "Men are willing to have their feet and hands cut off if these seem to them to be evil, for what they love at heart is good. Lovers not only men, but even women, are ready to die for one another." In the Phædrus we have this, of a former life, "Being initiated and beholding visions perfect, simple and happy in the pure light, pure ourselves as yet unclothed with this body which we carry about with us, the source of wars and strife, to which we are bound as an oyster to his shell," and in the Laws the following, "Self conquest is the greatest of victories—τὸ νικᾶν ἀυτὸν ἀυτὸν πασῶν νικῶν πρώτη τε καὶ ἀριστή—for there is a war in our members against ourselves;" "Ignorance is an evil, but bad cleverness is worse;" "The cause of all our blunders arises from our believing that it is right to love ourselves;" "Let no one speak ill of another." Reading such passages as these we are apt to say that ages before the introduction of Christianity Plato was almost persuaded to be a Christian: but like Homer he is uncertain and contradictory. His Theism is still tinged with mythology; even his God is not master of the Fates. His psychology is defective in failing to take account of the will or to discriminate sufficiently between the moral and the purely intellectual parts of our nature. The range of his sympathy like that of all the Greeks is limited to Greece. No one makes a more contemptuous or more frequent use of the word barbarian. It has not even occurred to him, that slavery needs a defence, or that men and women of every rank may have equal rights.

III. ARISTOTLE—whose writings introduce the third stage of Greek ethics—was to all intents a pupil of Plato. He borrows illustrations from his master almost in every page, and accepts with little or no modification many of his leading ideas. They are at one in their conception of the Chief Good as something self-complete, τέλειον καὶ αὐτάρκες, in their intellectual views of virtue, in the importance they attach to education, in their manner of regarding Pleasure ·and Friendship. But after this begins a contrast. Their styles of writing are opposed, in place of dramatic effect and poetical allusion we find in Aristotle definite logical formulæ and a regular system. He first marks off the sciences from one another, and assigns to them their separate provinces and methods. In the sphere of speculation he is more transcendental than his predecessor: his metaphysics having no connection with real life. In the field of practice he is more definite, more ready to enter into details, and more willing to be guided by circumstances or by opinion. Aristotle's politics are more modern than Plato's: his theology is less so. He has cut the Past and abandoned the attempt to reconcile a philosophical belief with the traditions and instincts of ordinary men. When he talks of the Greek Gods it is a mere *façon de parler:* his own Supreme Deity is a power almost without personality, νόησις νοήσεως. He removes the Platonic basis of morality in religion, and substitutes another founded partly on the nature of the human mind, partly on the good of society. His Psychology distinguishes more clearly the different faculties, gives greater prominence to the force of habit, and separates the will from the reason, though owing to his still confusing it with Desire he is only able to raise without being able to settle the question of its freedom. He distinctly asserts the superiority of the moral to the written law, "'Ἔτι κυριώτεροι κἁι περὶ κυριωτέρων τῶν κατὰ γράμματα νόμων ὁι κατὰ τὰ ἔθη ἐισίν," but his views regarding the ultimate foundation of the former are still fluctuating. His Ethics are the porch to his Politics, and in the latter he fails to advance beyond the conception of a well regulated Greek state, limited in extent, and still upheld by the institution of slavery, for which, however, he thinks it necessary to apologise. He inherits from Plato, and helps to perpetuate, the erroneous political and moral economy which regards the prosperity of one nation as a deduction from the prosperity of another, a view which, under the name of the balance of power, still formularizes the selfishness of our own day, and which, only a few years ago, helped to intensify our insular distrust of the great western war of liberation. While admitting that various forms of government are adapted to various stages of civilization, he still appeals to the lawgivers of his race with an exaggerated confidence. His virtues are all more or less political. They are controlled by the idea of limitation, which presided over Hellenic thought in all its phases from the time of Pythagoras to that of Zeno. Their motive is the καλόν, a conception which is, like the law of honour in the age of chivalry, partially moral, and largely æsthetic: their end ἐνδαιμονία, an exalted standard, but still a standard of happiness, into which duty in the modern sense of the word scarcely enters. Let us take as a compendium of Aristotle's view of life his description of a perfect character—the magnanimous man—in whom he tells us all the virtues, temperance, courage, liberality, justice, and wisdom are combined in a κόσμος. "At the extreme of greatness he holds the mean in acting with regard to its conditions. He aims at the highest honour, and receives it calmly as his due. Dishonour cannot touch him, nor fortune, fair or foul, disturb his equanimity. Little distinctions—as the prizes of wealth and petty power—he contemns, and cares not for them to run into little dangers, but for a great end he is prodigal of life itself. He likes to grant, and dislikes to receive or to be reminded of favours. If any one lays him under obligation, he will over-repay the benefit, and so regain the superior place. He will play second-fiddle to no man. To those in rank his glance is stern and high : to the lowly he waives a little of his claim. Fearless and true he knows no concealment, save in irony, and is open alike in his love and hate. He flatters not nor bears a grudge, for 'tis beneath his dignity to remember evil. He is no gossip, nor cares he to enquire after blame or praise. He always prefers honour to gain. His gait is slow and stately, his voice is deep, and his enunciation deliberate."

There are heroic elements in this Athenian beau-ideal who speaketh no evil and murmureth not, but there are others almost mean, almost ridiculous. What self-complacency, what contempt, what a strut, what an amount of "leather and prunella" there is in this high-souled man! He hates to be reminded of favours. He will have the superior place. His voice is deep and his enunciation deliberate! How many of his characteristics are to be found in Milton's Lucifer. Let us turn to this other model in old Decker's play—

> " The best of men
> That ere wore earth about him was a sufferer,
> A soft, meek, humble, patient tranquil spirit
> The first true gentleman that ever breathed."

Or even look back to Plato's King who is called a stargazer and a babbler by the multitude, whose heart and treasure are laid up in Heaven, whose vision is bent away from earthly honours towards the celestial city ἐν λόγοις κείμενη, who is content if he can live "*integer vitæ scelerisque purus*," and be ready, when his hour arrives, to obey the voice that calls him home. Aristotle's moral theories are real but seldom exalted, they are unprogressive and devoid of aspiration. Intemperance he tells us is wrong, because it breaks its bounds, but he does not tell us by what law these bounds themselves are fixed. His measure requires a measure. Why is the mean right? Where is the mean in truth, in justice, in purity? These questions he cannot answer. Some virtues he does not recognize at all. Humility, such humility as that of Chaucer's Griselda—he affirms to be a worse extreme than vanity. His treatise on friendship is a masterpiece, but it is the friendship of free Greek citizens from which handicraftsmen, slaves, foreigners and women are excluded. He has no thought of a philanthropy stretching like a golden chain around the race. He has left for our admiration a lucid system, cut out in clear straight lines, strictly beautiful, like the Parthenon, but it is roofed in and lit by terrestrial lamps. Plato's is more vague, but it displays afar "the cloud-capped towers, the gorgeous palaces" and glimpses of the stellar spaces through the cloud.

Plato describes the soul, Aristotle the understanding, Theophrastus the dresses of men. The thinkers of all ages are constantly parodied in their schools. The followers of a great teacher in trying to make him more consistent, generally contract the scope of his philosophy and take away half its life. So the Pythagoreans dealt with Pythagoras, the later Eleatics with Parmenides, the Cynics and Cyrenaics and Megareans with Socrates, the Cartesians with Descartes, Condillac and Helvetius with Locke. So Mr. Mansel has handled Kant. So the Academicians and the Peripatetics dealt with Plato and Aristotle: the former degraded the Idealism of their master into a phantastic Symbolism: the latter preserved the sensational and materialistic elements of Aristotle's system and rejected all the rest. The morality of the one school became purely abstract, of the other purely utilitarian. Theophrastus the author of the characters exclaims, in the despair of a new scepticism—"We throw away the pleasant things of life for the sake of fame laboriously earned but sterile in results: death overtakes us when we begin to live: be happy then by ceasing to philosophize."

The school of EPICURUS, however, proved that a system of thorough-going materialism was by no means incompatible with an enthusiastic zeal for Philosophy. The praises of this Queen of the ancient world have never been so sublimely celebrated as by one of his most consistent followers

> "who denied
> Divinely the divine and died
> Chief poet upon Tiber side."

Epicurus, adopting the physics of Democritus, elevated the morality of Aristippus into an Eudaimonism so refined that, in nine cases out of ten, it would lead to the same practical results as the law of duty. The ἡδονὴ καταστηματική which he makes his aim is the peace of mind resulting from an equilibrium of the whole nature, in which there is

> "Nothing to mar the sober majesties
> Of settled sweet Epicurean life."

His sage is temperate because he is wise, the care of his own calm will impose self-restraint and goodwill on his life; when men hurry to and fro, he looks down and smiles in secret on "clanging fights and flaming towns." Contented with a dinner of herbs, he can command in his little garden a realm of tranquil thoughts grand as the poet's palace of art, in which he abides with all the personal and half of the social virtues : when death, the end of all, arrives he will receive it as the embrace of a "passionless bride." His brain is full of moderate aspirations, and in his dreams these are embodied in images μεγαλῶν ἐιδωλῶν καὶ ἀνθρωπομόρφων which he calls divine. But these exist alone as visions or "they lie beside their nectar careless of mankind," for the gods of Epicurus are themselves Epicureans.

> "Omnis enim per se divom natura necesse est
> Immortali aevo summâ cum pace fruatur
> Semota a nostris rebus sejunctaque longe ;
> Nam privata dolore omni privata periclis
> Ipsa suis pollens opibus nihil indigna nostri
> Nec bene promeritis capitur nec tangitur irâ."

The Lucretian Ethics are not wholly indefensible; most ordinary lives even now run far beneath their level, but they are deficient in philanthropy and devoid of faith. To the philosopher they are the apotheosis of a refined and elevated selfishness; to the many their theories are "glorious insufficiencies," their practice was inevitably degraded into the worship of pleasure. Let us contrast with the above hexameters the following extract from the hymn of the Stoic Cleanthes, that hymn to Jupiter which has been called the most devotional fragment of antiquity.

> "All deformities
> Their proper nature lose in wisdom's plan,
> Merged in the bland disposal of thy love,
> Which tempers evil to a higher good ;
> Do thou dark Dweller in the clouds correct
> Our wandering wishes, counteract their end,
> Protect us from our own insanity,
> And chase the perilous darkness of the soul."

Here we have more of the celestial light and the belief in a Providence: but, as the Epicurean doctrine inclined to

Atheism, there is a latent Pantheism in the Stoic and a fatalistic tendency. "Lead me Zeus and Destiny," is the prayer of Epictetus—"whithersoever I am appointed to go I will follow without questioning: even though I turn coward and shrink I shall have to follow." The STOICS made a step forward both in practical and in speculative Ethics. Their psychology gave a fresh prominence to the discussion of the human will, and on this subject they arrived at a theory of determinism, similar to that which has been recently revived. They approached the conception of duty. Their scheme first transcended nationalities, and the extent to which it ignored artificial distinctions appears in the fact that one of their sages was a slave. Their rules of life were lofty if one-sided. Their wise man, like Plato's philosopher, has put pain and pleasure and all the accidents of a day beneath his feet. King, priest, and prophet by divine right, living in just conformity with nature, or, as Clarke expressed a similar modern thought, with the eternal fitness of things, he is such "ut nec tabescat molestiis, nec frangitur timore, nec sitienter quid expetens ardeat desiderio, nec alacritate futili gestiens deliquescat." The two great maxims of Stoicism Ανέχου and Απέχου; bear up against sorrow, sin and death; keep your soul unspotted and make your mind a kingdom to yourself, are the heroic refrains of great moralists in all ages from Cleanthes to Fichte. But with a semblance of nobility, it is false through the exaggeration of a narrow view. To become strong the Stoic destroyed the sources of vitality, as the despot destroys the freedom he cannot rule and calls the solitude peace. His conception of Order was extinction of a full third of our nature. The Puritan of antiquity, he set up an aristocracy of character as exclusive as the aristocracy of race and birth which he had demolished, and prided himself on his monopoly of Reason as the modern Calvinist on his monoply of grace. His Abstinence, like that of all ascetics was, even when, as it seldom is, consistent and sincere, apt to become a Stylites pillar of self-glorification. Cato's conceit, like that of Artisthenes, shone through the rags of his tunic as he strutted across the Forum. Stoicism was a bridge between ancient and modern thought. It first maintained, in opposition to the view of Aristotle, "there are many things diviner than man," the view of Kant "the only great thing is his moral will." In it first the soul as distinct from the intellect tried to probe the mystery of existence. But, like Monasticism, it taught its followers to think too much about their own souls, and, like Neoplatonism, degenerated into a "*meditatio mortis*." Nevertheless the old Stoic trying to live again the life of an imaginary republic under the regime of Commodus and Petronius Arbiter was a noble protest against luxury, scepticism, sycophancy and corruption. Pagan morality dies grandly with Marcus Aurelius, nor has Christian morality, on one side at least, gone far beyond him. Let us open his book, "One man, when he has done a service to another is ready to set it down to his account as a service rendered. Another is not ready to do this, but still in his own mind he thinks of the man as his debtor and he knows what he has done. A third does not even know what he has done, but he is like a vine which has produced grapes, and seeks for nothing more after it has produced its proper fruit;" again "When thou hast assumed these names—good, modest, true, rational, equal minded, magnanimous, take care that thou dost not change them, fix thyself in the possession of them and abide in them as if thou wast removed to the Happy Islands." "What an affinity," exclaims Mr. Arnold who has quoted these sentences, "What an affinity for Christianity had this persecutor of the Christians, its relieving tears, its happy self-sacrifice were the very elements for which his soul longed: they were near him, he touched them, he passed them by. Could he have read the Sermon on the Mount what would have become of his notions of the *exitiabilis superstitio* of the Christians? Vain question: yet the charm of Marcus Aurelius is that he makes us ask it. We see him wise and just, self-governed, tender, thankful, blameless: yet with all this agitated, stretching out his arms for something beyond—'*tendentemque manus ripæ ulterioris amore.*'"

IV. This well-balanced yet eloquent appreciation is the more valuable because of its contrast with criticisms of a different stamp. It is a common practice to steal the best thoughts of the ancients, and then to revile their authors and disparage the ages in which they wrote. We abuse our hosts when drunk with their own wine. Moral corruption doubtless prevailed widely among the nations of the Pagan world, but it prevails widely among ourselves, and we have no evidence to show that the general practice of the Greeks fell further short of their theories than that of England or France does of the standards which they have agreed to uphold. To rake among the kennels* of the lower empire for abominations in evidence against the philosophy of Plato and the Antonines is no less preposterous than it would be to appeal to the story of the Levite's wife as an example of the inefficacy of the Jewish Decalogue, or to point to the monstrosities of medievalism, the disgraces of the Papacy, the horrors of the Inquisition, or the immoral carnivals of Munster and Oneida Creek as a reproach to the creed of Christendom itself. It does not, however, follow because the average manner of life at Athens was probably on a par with that of Paris or New York, that Ethics have remained stationary. Mr. Mill indeed complains that "our modern morality is in great part a protest against Paganism," that "its ideal is negative rather than positive," and that "in some respects it falls below the best morality of the ancients." This is partially correct. Owing to the greater complexity of our civilization some of the ancient virtues have fallen into abeyance. These are mainly such as were fostered by the patriotism of a small Greek state, as Friendship, Liberality for its own sake, a comparative scorn of mere money-making, the disinterested regard for the Commonweal and the love of Simplicity which characterises the best days of the Roman Republic : to which we may add the love of Speculative Truth which grew in part out of the free discussions of the schools, and was repressed when their influence was superseded by

* See the article on Heathenism, Judaism, and Christianity in the *North British Review* for Dec., 1867.

that of authoritative dogmas. With ourselves too much is apt to be made of obedience to certain restrictions, what Heinrich Heine calls "melancholy abstinence from the joys of this beautiful life," too little of participation in its active duties. There is too much talk about self-sacrifice, too little practice of self-reliance. The sloth of old age is the accompanying drawback of its decorum, and the temptations to hypocrisy and moral cowardice often increase as those to excess diminish. Men have become less like tigers more like sheep. On the other hand we have made in some directions a great advance. "Another race hath been and other palms are won." Our Ethics though still prone to be Stoical in theory, Epicurean in practice, are animated by new aspirations and sustained by firmer hopes. History and Science have in many respects enlarged and elevated our morality. A broader freedom, a deeper sense of veracity and honour, regard for purity, and consideration for weakness, came from the German forests to renovate the stagnation of the Italian plains, to help to destroy slavery and begin to raise woman, for the first time, to her rank in the scale of society. Physical discovery has at a later date thrown fresh light on the laws which regulate the health of body and mind. It has also impressed us with the idea of progress—" the thoughts of men are widened with the process of the suns"—an idea everywhere contrasted with the finality which everywhere marked the theories and the practice, the science and the art of the ancient world. For the Parthenon, the Apollo Belvidere, the Antigone, Aristotle's Ethics, it has given us in exchange Gothic Cathedrals,

Raphael's Madonnas, Shakespeare and Dante, Wordsworth listening to the "mighty waters," Kant's apostrophe to the stars, a sense of incompleteness, combined with a faith in expansion without end.

> " To day's brief passion limits their range,
> It seethes with the morrow for us and more."

Much is also due to the influence of Religion. Morality is not indeed necessarily based on any particular creed. The near approach to identity in the practical precepts of Buddism, of the Talmud, of Christianity, of Plátonism, and of the Pantheism of Spinoza, establishes the existence of ethical standards, independent of, and compatible with very various forms of belief: but neither are they entirely unrelated: for their spheres intersect although they do not coincide. A low morality is almost certain to accompany a degrading superstition, and we need not look for high standards of life among the fellow savages of Commoro or the image worshippers of Naples. The undogmatic Christianity of the Gospels is the great lever of modern Ethics. By indefinitely extending their arena, and setting forth motives of action, at once lofty and generally appreciable, it offers to do for the whole world what the schools only professed to do for their selected followers. The cardinal difference between ancient and modern moral systems is the comparative exclusiveness of the one, the universality of the other. The Platonic virtues in their highest form can only be understood or fully practised by the golden race who minister in the temple of his Hellenic state. The Aristotelean magnanimity and magnificence are prerogatives of a well-educated Athenian citizen. Stoicism, which broke down the walls of race and rank and wealth, was still fenced with intellectual pride, and the capacity of rightly interpreting its precepts was confined to a few. Ancient morality was more or less artistic: it regarded a perfect life as the blooming of natural excellencies, the development of natural powers like heat and light, rarely as obedience to a law, and, with both good and bad results, dwelt on the quality of the action rather than the merit of the actor. It preferred a constitutionally noble nature to the self conquest that is the result of an internal combat, the "beautiful disdain" that recoils from evil as from ugliness to the sainthood that subdues "the world, the flesh, and the devil." Christianity in giving prominence to the latter conceptions added to ethics the side which is most capable of being brought to bear on the mass of men. It first announced a Heaven willing to stoop to feeble virtue and "lit up morality," with an inspiration in which all may be partakers. The Religion of Pleasure was for the wise; the Religion of Pain was for the strong: the common end of both was Egotism. The Religion of Love, transcending the old barriers of family and tribe and nation, is for all who are "toiling, rejoicing, sorrowing" on the highways and byeways of life: it addresses itself, not to contemplate, but to aid "the strife of poor humanity's afflicted will." To the old philosophers a future world assumed at best the form of an alternative. Plato himself was half conscious of the invalidity of his proofs of its existence, and felt the want of a raft to float him down the sea of his thought. Glaucon in the Republic is made to wonder at the new revelation—Καὶ ὃs ἐμβλέψαs μοι καὶ θαυμάσαs εἶπε. Μὰ Δί οὐκ ἔγωγε. Aristotle reduces it to a vague impersonal perpetuity of the pure reason. "Death," writes Seneca, "is the one port in a stormy sea: it is either end or transition, it is either a gain or nothing." The last words uttered on human destiny by the expiring classic schools are the expression of a doubtful hope. "It is pleasant to die if there be gods; and sad to live if there be none." That it is possible to live a noble life on the stern conditions of this creed, the names of many philosophers and some of the most lustrous pages of biography amply demonstrate. Warriors and patriots have always been found to die τοῦ καλοῦ ἕνεκα. The man of leisure and far-ranging thought in the ancient world might find consolation for the violence done to his affections in speculation, and the belief that in some shadowy manner he was θεοφιλέστατοs. The modern Physicist may reflect that he will be remembered as having done something to extend the knowledge of those majestic sequences which will continue to uphold the universe when he is "blown about the desert dust or sealed within the iron hills." The Comtist may claim a more disinterested satisfaction on his philanthropic faith that while "the individual withers the race grows more and more." The Transcendentalist has his moments of exaltation in the sense of his communion with the soul that breathes through "all this mystic frame." But their theories seem devised for a world from which want and misery and shame have been cancelled. To the millions who live on common hopes and fear they "whisper of the glorious gods and leave us in the mire." The doctrine of Immortality has been a gradually growing belief, but it has received from the Gospels a new and more distinctly expressed authority.

Finally, Ethical systems are to be judged not solely by the substance of their precepts, but by the mode in which they are urged on our acceptance. All genuine philosophers have agreed in regard to the main principles of morality. They would probably agree in condemning the gratification of private revenge. Plato would say, "The philosopher will not think of such things: it is not just to return evil for evil." Aristotle, "It is beneath the dignity of the magnanimous man." Epicurus, "It is not worth my while to disturb my own repose." Zeno, "Anger being one of the παθῆ, and not conformable to Reason, is to be subdued." Bentham, "It is for the greatest good of the greatest number that the vindication of justice should be solely committed to the public laws." But Christ says, "Not until seven times but until seventy times seven thou shalt forgive thy brother." Christianity thus quickens our sense of goodness by a glow of emotion: it makes utility beautiful by shedding around it a celestial ray. It has deepened the basis of the ancient virtues and it has added others. The Charity that is not puffed up; the Benevolence that covers our relations with "man and bird and beast;" the Mercy that softens Justice as with a gentle rain; the Humility of which the Cross is the Crown; Duty recognised as the "Daughter of the voice of God," belong by the best right to the Religion of Love.

We do great wrong to the wise and brave of the Past, the foundations of whose fame are "built below the tide of war," when we make of their achievements and their thoughts mere platforms for our own complacency : but we do them no wrong when higher still, above the violets of the Acropolis, we rear the blossoms of Paradise, the plants and flowers of light.

J. N.

TO ELIZA.

THE sun shines fair on sea and land,
   The birds sing blithe on ilka tree,
And thro' the gouden sheaves o' corn
   My true love comes a' wooing me;
And sang o' bird, and shimmer o' sun
   Are sweet to hear, and fair to see,
     Sweet to hear and fair to see!
A bonnier world there couldna' be!

The sun shines fair on sea and land,
   The birds sing blithe on ilka tree,
But thro' the gouden sheaves o' corn
   My love shall come no more to me.
And sang o' bird, and shimmer o' sun,
   I canna' thole to hear or see.
     Misery, oh misery!
This world is all too bright for me!

CUI BONO?

I.

The big rain beats upon a weltering sea
   That maketh moan along the barren shore,
   Round cliff and headland do the fierce winds roar,
And toss the tremulous spindriff far alea.
Far up the heights the screaming sea gulls fly,
   They wheel and charge, and beaten back re-form,
   And wage fierce gladsome battle with the storm.
Not so one "poor wee" bird whose sharp small cry
Proclaims the agony of its timid heart,
As now with many a furtive little start
It feebly strives the windy heights to soar;
The rude wind blows it back upon the shore,
Where beat upon by storm and rain it lies,
And lets its life out in small plaintive cries.

II.

So 'mid a hurricane of doubt and fear,
   And sins that mar, and pleasures that make sad,
And empty longings that bring sad death near,
   And want of faith that driveth strong men mad,
I strive in all th' impulsiveness of youth
   By many vows, and broken sobs and sighs,
To win the shining Table-land of Truth,
   And cleave a path thro' unbelief and lies.
   Ah! foolish heart that in the effort dies!

And weak resolves that have not strength to reach
   The calm, still height, but by each sudden gust
   Of shameless passion that hath end in dust,
Are blown back beaten on the barren beach !
Oh Lord ! look down in pity—Lord ! look down,
   And with thy smile chase all the storm away,
   And give me faith to see the perfect day,
And give me strength to win unto the crown.
Look down in pity, Lord ! dear Lord ! on me,
   Poor erring thing whom little doubts appal,
   Weak heart that hath not any faith at all,
But gropeth feebly in the dark for Thee.
Nay, rather, Lord, forgive me that I pray
   Who am so worthless and so weak withal,
     In pitiful low depths of shame I bow,
     Poor thing of faint resolve and brittle vow,
   I cannot, dare not pray to Thee at all,
     Too great, O God ! too great and good art Thou !

HEINE.

HEINE was born on the 1st of January, 1800; he used to say that he was the first man of his century. By birth he was a Jew; by education a Roman Catholic ; by choice a Protestant. The first fourteen years of his life foreshadowed his mission as the reconciler of French and German thought. He was born at the German town of Dusseldorf on the Rhine, but it was under the government of France and filled with French grenadiers, two of whom will not soon be forgotten. The life, thought and language of France were as familiar to him as the habits and language of Germany. The circumstances of his early life were fitted to foster his natural republicanism and his natural admiration for a great Frenchman like Napoleon. His youth was spent partly in Hamburg with his friends; partly at the universities of Bonn, Berlin and Gottingen where he took a degree in law, a science which he hated as much as he knew it little. Indeed, his time was not spent in study but in writing poetry, quarrelling with his friends, fighting duels and falling in love.

In 1823 he published two tragic and a good many lyric pieces which were received with the coldness usually accorded to the works of youthful poets. The next six years of his life were spent in travel through Germany, Italy and England;—and at intervals he published his *Reisebilder*, Pictures of Travel. These writings founded his fame; they were in the mouths of everybody, and for a time at least sunk into the hearts of young Germany. For a time too he edited a newspaper, giving pretty free vent to his republicanism; so unreservedly indeed that in 1830 he had to leave Germany. He went to Paris where he spent the rest of his life.

I said that he was a Protestant by choice, and it is true so far, for he was baptized when twenty-six years old, and was always a fervent admirer of the religion of Luther and Hegel :—an admirer but not a disciple, for his was at heart a classical spirit, and he ought to have lived in the days of Sophocles and Phidias. His utter failure would not have been so noticeable then;—it would have been more easily excused. But we must take him as we find him, and we find him a legitimate but prodigal son of the nineteenth century. It was his mission to take up the sword of Goethe;—to free thought, life and style from tradition and convention, and to recall or at least to institute an era of natural life. He had no admiration for the life of the Middle Ages;—still less for any echo or imitation of them, and like Goethe escaped free from the infection of the sentimental school. But he had none of Goethe's self-command;—none of his weight of character;—none of his patience to let thought work its way slowly into the minds of men, and patience it has been well said is the greater part of genius. In both prose and verse he expressed his republicanism so freely, so wittily and so personally against every German government, that at the age of thirty he was an exile. From that time, while he loved his native land, he was embittered against her, and she was embittered against him. He first abused his influence, and then lost it. France was the land of his idolatry, but France cared little for a German and an exile.

His greatest charm is his style both of prose and of verse. The beauty of his language is unfailing. His matter is often true, sometimes untrue; often new, sometimes old in a gayer dress; often moral, frequently the reverse; often deep and elevating, often superficial and grovelling; but never dull, never the same, never provokingly orderly. When you think you have him in both hands, he is laughing at you from round a corner;—when you think him a mile off and walking in the other direction, he is staring you full in the face. As his philosophy was to find a harmony between spirit and matter, his style is a kind of proof of its possibility. It is as if the words contained the thought pure and unalloyed. He is among masters of the pen what Corregio is among masters of the brush. A rounded grace of form and outline, the joy of life, the very divinity of sensuousness, but alack his Leda, his Europa, and his temple of Venus are more satisfying than his Madonnas or his Holy Night. We read that the Père Bouhours (who was the Père Bouhours?) propounded to himself the deeply witty question : "Si un Allemand peut avoir de l' esprit?' We may now ask ourselves if anyone else may be said to have "esprit," if there is any "esprit" left when thirsty Heine has sipped so much away. For this is what he did; he made esprit not the relish but the food and drink of life. His morals were vicious ; his heart was bad ;—esprit is all he shows in full perfection. But is God dead because Heine is licentious? is Christianity a myth, because Heine has no love, sympathy, or self-respect? But perhaps we ought not to judge him ;—

> "Dort oben giebt es einen andern Jury,
> Als hier in Gross-Britannien."

> "Up there is sitting quite an other Jury,
> From ours in good Great Britain."

At any rate, while we lament that his life throws discredit on philosophy; when we turn with Matthew Arnold to the chamber in the Rue d' Amsterdam, and hear the ghastly consolation of the Philosophy of pleasure;—"God Aristophanises; he is a greater master of satire than even Henry Heine," we ought not to forget that he lived through the following thought. The passage I have translated occurs in one of his tragedies, his earliest productions, wherein his later excellencies and failings appear in broad features. The taste for the horrible is found everywhere, but reaches its highest point in the closing scene of William Ratcliff, where it is inhuman. Yet perhaps he never wrote anything more simple, more witty, or more touching, than the scenes in the (Diebesherberge) Robbers' Inn only a few pages before. The following lines are from his other tragedy Almanzor; which is not on the whole so good. It was his first effort, and the language is more bombastic than noble, more pointed than witty. The scene is in Spain;—the time is after the conquest of Granada and consequent introduction of Christianity. The heroine has become a Christian, the hero has not. He has told her his horror at seeing the rites performed in a Christian Church, and she answers in the following strain :—

> "Your foot, Almanzor, trode the house of God,
> But a great blindness lay upon your eyelids.
> You found not, true, the merry beam of light
> That dances through an ancient heathen temple,
> And you might miss the week-day easiness
> That nestles in a Moslem's gloomy closet.

Love sought herself a purer, nobler temple
To be her dwelling-place upon the earth.
Within this house a child becomes of age,
A man of age becomes a child again.
Within this house the poor man is made rich,
The rich man is made blessed in poverty.
Within this house the merry is made sad,
The grievèd finds his sorrow lightened here.
   Love once appeared upon this earth,
In likeness of a little weeping child.
Her bed was in the stable's narrow manger,
And yellow straw the pillow to her head,
And sure she shuddered like a cowering doe
Pursued even there by heavy pedantry.
Then Love was sold for silver, was betrayed,
She was reviled and scourged and cruclfied.
Yet at the seven dying groans of Love,
Broke, burst and fell those seven iron castles
Which Satan hung before the gates of heaven.
And when the seven wounds of Love did gape
The seven heavens opened wide once more,
Till sinners and till righteous were drawn in.
It was this Love whom you beheld a corpse
In the mother bosom of that mourning woman.
O do believe me, that in yon cold corpse
Is warmth enough to fire a whole mankind,
That from that blood a fairer flower has sprung
Than bloomed in proud Alraschid's garden-beds.
And from the eyes of yonder mourning woman,
Wondrous, there flows a sweeter oil of roses,
Than any rose of Shiraz ever gave.
You too have share, Almanzor ben Abdullah,
In that eternal body and eternal blood ;—
You too may seal yourself where angels sit
And taste the bread and wine that God has given."

The form is certainly not suited to catch the ear of a modern stage, and is perhaps not really natural ;— Lovers when on the point of being married to men whom they dislike do not perhaps entertain their true loves with such long monologues on the nature of Christianity. But the words and thought are saturated with poetry and truth ;—with the deepest sense of religious sorrow. And there is more in this strain ; but it was written when Heine was young, when he was a Jew: " Christianity was one of his student ideas."

The next piece that I have taken shows a further stage in his thought and language ;—it is from the *Reisebilder*, an explanation of his faith to a pretty maiden of the Harz Mountains. The metre is an old ballad-metre over which he has unlimited command. The ease of his expression defies translation ;—Matthew Arnold has given us it in prose.

"'That your lips are wont to move in
　Prayer I would never say :
From the curl upon your lip, I
　Know that you can never pray.

For that cold and wicked curl
　Makes me shudder once again,
Till your eyes beam pure and holy,
　Silencing my doubt and pain.

For I doubt if you are faithful,
　As is called the faith of most :
Hast not faith in God the Father,
　In the Son and Holy Ghost."

"Child, when I was boy and little
  Babe upon my mother's knee,
I believed on God the Father,
  Kind and mighty ruler He.

He the lovesome earth created,
  And the lovesome man thereon;—
To the sun and moon and stars He
  Foreordainèd how to run.

I grew older and I gainèd
  Larger knowledge, little one,
And I knew that I had reason,
  I believèd on the Son.

Son belovèd: by whose loving
  Love to man has been made known,
But a cross was the reward that
  He receivèd from His own.

Now that I have grown to manhood
  Learning, travel, I can boast,
Swells my heart and from my heart, my
  Faith is on the Holy Ghost.

He has done the greatest wonders,
  Greater He is doing now;—
Broke are tyrants' strongholds, and the
  Yoke 'neath which the captives bow.

The old deathwounds he hath healèd
  And the ancient right renewed:—
Every man by birth is equal,
  All are of a noble blood.

> He has scared the mist of darkness,
>   Creature of an earthly lore ;
> That has grudged us love and pleasure
>   Grinning on us evermore.
>
> Knights a thousand clad in armour
>   Doth the Holy Ghost inspire;
> Chosen to fulfil his bidding
>   He has set their souls on fire.
>
> Now their goodly swords are gleaming,
>   And their lordly banners wave,
> Sweet my child, wouldst thou not love to
>   See a knight so true and brave.
>
> Little one, then look upon me,
>   Look upon me fearlessly,
> For thou seest such a warrior
>   Of the Holy Ghost in me."

This, if read in the original, is an excellent specimen of Heine. Both the thought and the style are at his best, and it is as a lyric poet that his name will survive the attacks of time. His poems are exquisite spite of their naughtiness, for there is a simplicity of naughtiness in them as well as in his prose. He is best known or at least best liked in Germany as the author of the Book of Songs. I am told by one who knows German life intimately that his popularity among the ladies of Germany is greater than even Tennyson's among the same class here.

Heine was filled with the living deadness of the outward world:—a breath of spring rises from his songs, as of primroses and violets and warble of nightingales. He is like the country boy in the fairy tale who had learned the language of the birds and could speak with the flowers face to face: and he too was found worthy to be wedded to the princess of beauty and to be a ruler over men.

Irony, wit and humour ring through his poetry as well as mere prettiness; though surely grace of form is a sufficient apology for existence. But there are deeper tones in Heine than sarcasm or prettiness. He is as bright as the sunset, as peacefully sorrowful as the gathering shadows of night.

As I have said before, he inclines to the horrible;—he does not scruple to introduce a ghost playing the fiddle and maidens dancing among the tombstones;—or old bones knocking against the window pane on a stormy night. It is found most in his earliest work, and is the only approach to vulgarity in Heine's writings. He could never thoroughly master it, for his imagination as well as his intellect suffered from diseases as incurable as was that spine-complaint which rendered him helpless for the last eight years of his life.

Here is a page of the *Reisebilder*, naughty perhaps but lively, and very like Heine the philosopher of pleasure;—

"No doubt the little harp player had noticed that while she was singing and playing I had often looked at the rose in her bosom, and when I put into the tin plate on which she was gathering her fee a piece of money not the smallest in the kingdom, she laughed slyly and asked, in an under tone, if I would like to have her rose?

"Now, I am the politest man in the world, and for the world would never do harm to a rose, even a rose that has lost its sweetness a little. But I thought to myself, even though it smells fresh no longer, and has not quite the savour of virtue as the Rose of Sharon has, I believe, what does it matter to me when I have not got rid of my cold in the head. And it is only we men who are so nice. The butterfly never asks a flower 'Has anybody else kissed you before me,' and the flower never asks 'Have you hovered about another flower.' Besides the night was falling, and at night I said to myself all flowers are grey, the most erring rose as well as the most virtuous parsley. In short, without so long delay, I said to the little harp player, 'Si Signora.'

"Dear reader, think no harm. It was dark and the stars looked down into my heart, bright and pure. My heart was still trembling with the remembrance of my dead Mary. I thought again of that night, when I was standing beside the bed where the beautiful pale form was lying with the gentle, quiet lips. I thought again of the strange look which the old woman cast upon me, who should have watched beside the corpse, but resigned her office to me for a few hours,—I thought again of the violet, standing in a glass on the table with so rare a fragrance, and I shuddered again in doubt whether it was really a breath of wind that had put out the lamp, whether there was not really a third form beside us."

Here is another, containing a little humour not uncombined with pathos. He has been talking of the eagle. "Soon as the sun rises, he (the eagle) feels himself again, flies upwards, and when he is high enough sings to the sun his joy and pain. His fellow creatures, men especially, believe that the eagle cannot sing, and do not know that he only sings when he is beyond their hearing, and that he is too proud to be heard by any one but the sun. And he is right: many a one of his feathered cousins might take it into their heads to review his singing. I have myself heard the voice of such critics. The cock stands upon one leg clucking, 'The songster has no taste;' the turkey gobbles, 'True depth is wanting here;' the pigeon coos, 'He knows nothing of true love;' the goose cackles, 'He is not artistic;' the capon crows, 'His morality is deficient;' the prebendary whispers, 'Alas, he has no religion;' the sparrow whistles, 'He is not productive enough;' landrails, pyots, and owls all are croaking, groaning and hooting;—only the nightingale does not join her voice to these critics: untroubled by the whole world, the red rose is her only thought and her only song; longingly she spreads her wings round the red rose, falls upon the loved thorns and bleeds and sings."

I have not translated any of the amusing passages:—it is worth while learning German to read them fresh from the author's quill.

The next passages that I have translated were written when Heine's mind was at its greatest vigour, I may also say, its greatest rancour: the first year of his residence in Paris. The work they come from is called "The Development of Religion and Philosophy in Germany," and contains at least striking views clothed in most divine language. A good deal of the contents of it will be found in Matthew Arnold's Essay on Pagan and Mediæval religious sentiment.

"Luther was the most German man of his time: all German virtues and vices appear in him in well-defined features. He was a dreamy mystic: he was a man of swift and ready action. His thoughts had hands as well as wings. He was not only the tongue but the sword of his time. He was a cold logical wordsifter: he was an inspired prophet and poet. His day was spent in discussion and dogma, at evening he took down his flute, and his soul melted in melody and worship. He was filled with the most reverential fear of God: he would offer himself up in honour of the Holy Ghost; yet, he knew well what was lovely on this earth, and is author of the famous proverb 'Who loves not woman, wine, and song: lives a fool his life long.' He was a complete and absolute man, in whom spirit and matter dwelt in unity. Let us not blame him if some earthly dross has clung to him from his father's mines. Pure spirits cannot act. The refinement of Erasmus and the gentleness of Melancthon would never have set us so far on our way as the divine brutality of Brother Martin."

"This idea peculiar to Christianity spread incredibly fast over the Romish world: the whole Middle Ages felt it like a fever, and still the cramps are in our own limbs. We are beginning to desire a peace between soul and body, and the fate of Christianity depends only on the need we feel for it. Does it satisfy our wants? For eighteen centuries it was a blessing to mankind: taming the strong and strengthening the tame, and uniting peoples by a common feeling and a common voice. Eternal praise to the symbol of that suffering God, the Saviour with the crown of thorns, the Christ on the Cross dropping blood like a balsam on the gaping sores of men! What symbols are those, and how have they ennobled poetry and art? A Gothic dome is but a note of the same chord: every thing strains upwards: everything changes its substance:—stone sends forth leaf and bough, and becomes an arching tree: the fruits of corn and wine become flesh and blood; man is made into God, and God is a pure spirit."

"This religion cast a veil over the beauty and lovesomeness of nature; men's ears filled with subtilties, were astonished, but horrified by her sweetness."

"In May, 1433, at the time of the council of Basle, a company of spiritual Prelates, Doctors, and Monks of all degrees went to refresh themselves by walking in the copses round the city. They talked and discussed firstfruits and reservations of Thomas Aquinas and Bonaventura: when on a sudden they stopped speaking and stood still. On a lime tree before them was sitting a nightingale singing and sobbing her softest and tenderest melody. The learned body was wonderfully affected, their scholastic hearts began to thaw, and their feelings to awake from a long winter sleep;—they looked at each other astonished and enchanted:—till at last one of them made the wise remark that something must be wrong, the nightingale was probably a devil sent to entice them from their religious conversation by her music, and straightway began '*Adjuro te per eum qui venturus est judicare vivos et mortuos.*' The bird flew away at the words, and they thought they heard the words as she flew, 'Ha ha, ha ha! I am an evil, evil spirit!' But those who had listened to her song fell sick the same day and soon died."

Heine's life was broken and fragmentary:—it did not "congree in a full harmonious close." There is almost only one thing to admire in it, the constancy with which he endured his last sickness. He had never been robust; his body was too weak a temple for a soul so wild and passionate, and only to the wild emotion of his spirit can we trace the early collapse of his bodily powers. The power of his spirit over him was at times uncontrollable. There is a touching story told of him that as he was going through a gallery of statues, he came to a broken Venus, the fragment of some unknown Praxiteles. As he looked at it the form of beauty pierced into his soul; he looked like one amazed, and staggering back to a chair burst into floods of tears,—"Fair world, but thou art ugly still."

Good treatment from friends he could not expect, who had treated all so capriciously and cruelly. His wife was not the best person to minister comfort to a man of genius sick in body and sicker in soul. He loved her as deeply as he loved any one, but it was for her simplicity and childishness only. As is said to be common in Paris among artists and such people, they had lived together several years before they were married. He invited to his marriage feast a great number of his friends who were living in the same way, and called on them all to follow his example, which however it is not recorded that any of them ever did. The daily occupation of his wife was to go out walking or driving on the Boulevards, and on her return tell the sick man what she had seen. She was attached to him, but she was also attached to her pet parrot. "She is the only person I know," says Heine, "who never read a word of my poems." Another time he said to her: "Marie, promise me one thing before I die." "What then?" "That you will marry again." "And why then?" "That one man at least may every day lament my departure."

While he lay helpless and in ceaseless pain at Paris, his old mother was still alive at Hamburg. Her eyesight was failing and she never read in the papers. The only things she did read were her son's letters, written with forced merriment, saying that all was well with him. She died without knowing the truth. How different and yet how similar is the dying scene of William Napier and his wife.

The evening brings all home. In his last sickness Heine began to do what he had never done before, to doubt his own infallibility. It is commonly said that he renounced all his former teaching and became "a Christian and an ordinary man." But this probably is saying too much, though he certainly read the Bible more eagerly than he had for many years, and in the latest preface to the "Development of Religion and Philosophy in Germany," he says that he would not now write the book in the same way. A new light had been shed on his soul, not, as pious people say of him, by his having seen a vision on the way to Damascus;—he would never have heard of Damascus had he not read the noble song where king Solomon compares the nose of his beloved to a tower looking towards that city;—nor had the ass which he had ridden so long opened his mouth at last like the ass of Balaam the son of Beor and told him that after all his pet hobby was but an ass. Yet surely that miracle was but credible and just;—one ass may be allowed to speak like a man when so many men speak every day like asses. No, the change had come over him by his having read a book;—that book from which wisdom has flowed like the water of Pison when it is great, and like the water of Tigris when it overflows in spring; from which reason has flowed like the swollen Euphrates, and like the Jordan in harvest; from which purity has streamed like the light and like the water of Nile in autumn.

We may be allowed to doubt the depth of the change; indeed, in a previous portion of his writings he forearmed himself against such a thing being said of him. "The truth," he says, "shines into the broad bright world, and not into a sick man's narrow stifling chamber. The mind cannot see clearly through a crumbling body." The following story is an intimation of the real case. "I would," he said to his friend Meissner, "I had crutches and could go out." "What would you do?" "I would hobble to church." "What, joking still?" said his friend. "No, I am serious this time; for if I could walk on crutches, I should certainly go to church. If I could walk about fresh and sound and whole, I might prefer a stroll on the Boulevards or a ball at my good Meissner's."

So he grew paler and thinner till he was like a little child, and could be carried about in a nurse's arms. He had been an ungalled hart and had taken his full of play. He had been a stricken deer and had had enough of weeping; and now the end of his weeping is that his world runs away.

> "Death is like the cool midnight
> Life is like the sultry day,
> 'Tis twilight my eyes are heavy
> The long day has tired me quite.
>
> Over my bed there rises a tree,
> There the young nightingale doth sing:
> Of purest love she is singing:
> I hear her through my slumbering."

HORACE

VERY FREELY TRANSLATED

BOOK I. ODE 2.

Jam satis terris, nivis atque dirae, &c.

OF lightning, wind, snow, hail and thunder
We've had enough to rive in sunder
 Stone-steeples and annoy us
With bodings, that the days of Noah
Are coming back again to blow a
 New Deluge to destroy us.

When shoals of herrings, pikes and perches,
On tops of oaks, and elms and larches
    Should high and dry appear:
And swimming o'er Benlomond daily
Whole flocks of crows, and capercailzie
    Be seen, and herds of deer!

Tumbling a torrent foul and frantic,
The Clyde came rushing to th' Atlantic,
    Past Renfrew town, the Cart on,
It swept by Erskine ferry, howling
Against the ships in dock at Bowling,
    And Castle of Dumbarton.

It shook—so monstrous was the swell—
The Monument of Henry Bell!
    The Wall of Antonine
—Had it but stood where erst it stood,—
The hungry Celts on top of flood
    Might float across to dine?

In Yankee-land, it grieves to think on,
That Grant, and Davis, Lee and Lincoln,
    Are cutting throats fraternal,
When they might Canada annex
The soul of Britishers to vex,
Or in Napoleon's spite, old Mex;
    Hold fast in hug paternal!

Whom shall the people choose Dictator
To hang each rebel, rogue and traitor
   Disowns *King-Uncle* Sam?
No Scotchman, Irishman, or German,
Not Grant, nor Sheridan, nor Sherman,
But that true Yankee born, and rare man,
   Our brave old Abraham!

                                        R. B.

HORACE
BOOK I. ODE 9.
Vides ut alta stet nive candidum Soracte, &c.

SEE how Benlomond's swathed in snow:
The frozen streams have ceased to flow;
The groaning woods are bending low
   Beneath their wintry load.
With peats from moss, or coal from mine,
Make grate to glow, make hearth to shine,
And from the cellar's inmost shrine,
   For long four twelve months stowed,

Bring forth the beverage, clear and strong
Was brewed Glenlivet's moors among,
Despite the gaugers' prying throng,
   The genuine barley-bree!
The battling blasts that sweep the plain,
And tear the woods, and toss the main,
Shall soon be laid, and Spring again
   Shall smile on lift and lee.

Bid truce to care, bid truce to sorrow,
Plague not thy pate about the morrow,
But from each day some pleasure borrow
   Ere cankered age do reive it:
And for the sour, tea-bibbing classes,
That ban the cup, and shy the lasses,
Just set them down for oafs, and asses,
   And toss off thy Glenlivet!

R. B.

LAW AND HISTORY.

"Mens et animus et Consilium et Sententia Civitatis posita est in Legibus."

THESE words of Cicero's point to a truth which deserves the contemplation not only of the lawyer but also of the philosopher and the historian. No single fibre of the thread of life can be unwound without disentangling the others. Law interprets History, History interprets Law, Philosophy interprets both. In the following pages we propose to look at this mutual relationship chiefly from its jurisprudential side, and to indicate some of the advantages that legal science and legal practice may derive from the study of History.

We are at issue with two classes of persons, those who, regarding law from a purely empirical point of view, declare the study of legal history to be useless or worse than useless, and those who philosophise on the subject according to mere *a priori* metaphysical notions. The former class tell us that the practitioner would only be hampered and confused by studying the history of law. The existing law, they say, is sufficiently complicated to demand the labour of a life-time and the whole attention of a vigorous intellect, without the addition of a mass of obsolete jurisprudence. But a little consideration will shew us that the real cause of any confusion and difficulty now experienced is the want of a scientific method, and that a scientific method is necessarily to a great extent historical. Indeed the very first requisite of science is *Natural History*, i.e., some means of ascertaining the facts that have to be classified before scientific generalizations can be made, and this is just as true of jurisprudence as of physical science. The study of history is not of course necessary to all lawyers in the same degree. So far as the investigation is for scientific purposes, it is only required that a few should exert themselves in the cause of the many, but it is necessary for all genuine lawyers as a matter of professional training to know something of the history of at least the municipal law, in order that they may [properly understand its principles.

This preliminary historical investigation has been equally neglected by the metaphysicians. They lay claim to search after *truth*. But what is their actual procedure? In one case they reiterate the unscientific theories of their predecessors, but leave them still unconnected with reality, untested by experiment, and therefore as unscientific as before. In the other case, new and divergent theories are started, each claiming to be true, but no criterion is presented whereby this truth can be verified, and all we can do is to sit down and call upon science to come and arbitrate between them.

In short, lawyers have been content with empiricism, philosophers with hypothesis, and the pursuit of jurisprudence as a science has either been neglected through ignorance of its value, or unprogressive for want of a scientific method. Jurisprudence is still in a condition not much better than that of physical science before the days of Kepler and Newton. Until the requisite data were furnished by natural history, science was mere philosophising, and its progress was altogether dependent on accident. Similarly in Jurisprudence, men have been wont either to confine their attention to Positive law as it exists, thus restricting science within narrow and arbitrary limits,—or to reason about a "state of nature" which never existed at all, thus discarding the foundation in fact on which alone science can be constructed.

Before proceeding to point out the necessity for historical researches as a foundation for legal science, we may suggest one or two advantages which the study of the history of law presents to the profession generally. It is by no means necessary, or even desirable, that every lawyer should inflict upon himself a course of minute investigation into the history of law in all or any of its departments, yet, taken in a moderate degree, he should find such studies of great interest in themselves, and extremely valuable as instruments of intellectual culture.

First of all, history throws light on the technical language which the lawyer daily employs. He gains a fuller insight into, and a greater command over, the terms of his subject. They acquire a meaning and an interest in his eyes which they never had before. The principles that underlie legal terminology next share in the illumination. The municipal law does not reveal itself as an arbitrary set of rules concocted by the legislature without regard to circumstances. It is the growth of ages, embodying the ideas and the experience of previous generations as to the relations subsisting between the members of the State and the rights and duties springing out of these relations. It is the wisdom of the past modified by the wisdom of the present. Many particular laws may seem to us to be arbitrary and unsuited to our time, but that is generally because the circumstances by which they were originally warranted no longer exist, or the customs of the people have altered, or the principles upon which the laws depended are no longer recognised as just or expedient. As a general rule we may be sure, that all laws, at least in a free country like our own, have been dictated by some principle of supposed justice or expediency, and intended to meet special circumstances. The principle may still be recognisable, or it may not, and if not our only hope of explanation lies in the study of history. It is impossible therefore to obtain a systematic view of the law as a connected whole, or accurate views of it in detail, without an adequate acquaintance with its history, as well as with the general history of the country from which a knowledge of the special circumstances may be derived.

So far the lawyer's procedure has been analytic. His

attention has been confined to the internal coherency of one system. But the process of comparison is scarcely if at all less valuable, and he ought also to study the Jurisprudence of some other country than his own. For this purpose he can select no better system than the Roman Civil Law, which for comprehensiveness of scope, elaborateness of detail, and internal unity has no equal. Doubtless Roman Law is in great part obsolete and unsuited to the present state of civilisation, but its vitality is by no means altogether extinguished. The principles of Roman Jurisprudence will be found to permeate modern law, especially in Scotland and other countries where it has been one of the chief law sources. But even if it were altogether obsolete, even if it did not form part and parcel of the municipal law, it would still have the advantage of being presented to the student as a finished and entire whole, whose development is well marked, and whose history is well ascertained and complete.

The advantage of comparative Jurisprudence is well seen from the writings of the Roman Jurists. These men possessed in a high degree the power, so valuable to a lawyer, of bringing particular cases within the scope of general principles. This talent results very much from the exercise of the power of comparison which the Roman Jurists had occasion to exercise extensively. As the boundaries of the empire were extended, new systems of law were brought into contact with the old. The Romans, at home or abroad, continued to be governed by the *jus civile*. The provincials continued to live under their own laws. The praetor settled questions between *cives* and *peregrini*, or between *peregrini* of different provinces by laws common to both or by equitable compromise. The *jus gentium*, which originally meant the law common to several nations, was grafted on the Stoical idea of φύσις, and chiefly by means of the Prætorian equity raised by degrees to the level of a *jus naturæ*. By this time the Empire had become universal, and its law cosmopolitan. The highest efforts of the national intellect were directed towards the elucidation of the principles of justice, which ought to regulate the relations of all men. Subjecting these principles to a most elaborate casuistical scrutiny, the Roman lawyers contrived by degrees to give their system something like a scientific unity. The changes wrought on the law from without were chiefly constitutional amendments effected by the military party, the party of progress, who, without regard to the consistency of the law, or any great respect for its antiquity, were chiefly concerned with securing civil privileges, and popularising national institutions, so as to meet the social wants of the times, and calm the dissensions caused by the jarring of class interests. The changes from within were mainly the work of the lawyers, who were engaged in speculating on the principles at the root of the law, in extending the range of these principles, deducing subsidiary rules from them, and working the whole into a harmonious system.

Having thus briefly indicated some of the advantages of historical studies in legal education, we now pass to consider the necessity for more minute investigations as a step towards the formation of a science of Jurisprudence.

It will be proper to begin by explaining what we understand to be the nature and scope of the science of law properly so called. The science is concerned only with *positive* law. Its scope will depend upon the range of facts experimented upon. It has been held to embrace, as a general science, only positive law *as it is*, and as a special science, only the positive law of a particular country as it is. But this distinction between law in force and law that has ceased to be law for the present, though pointing to a boundary which must be observed in practice, is too arbitrary for science, and would be found extremely inconvenient. Its author, Mr. Austin, has practically disregarded it, for his pages are filled with historical explanations. None knew better than he did that the law of his time was inexplicable except through its history. If we must in the science distinguish between law as it is and law as it has been, let us call the departments which treat of them respectively by different names, such as Dogmatical Jurisprudence and Historical Jurisprudence. Supposing we include both within the science, can we say that we have here the whole materials necessary for a general science of law? Perhaps, practically. But law is in a constant state of development and shall we exclude all its possibilities, all that it has the potentiality of becoming? This is the difficulty. It seems to us a sufficient answer to say, that science is progressive, and will progress, but that it cannot progress faster than it can acquire *facts*. It may be very well to say with Kant that Jurisprudence is the science of *Jus*, law as it should be, law as it potentially is,—and we must admit that in the highest department of the science, viz., the central body of principles which should form a basis for legislation, what is wanted is to ascertain the absolute and steadfast characteristics of law, yet, as a matter of practice, we cannot recognise this definition without admitting the unscientific individual theorisings of which we have already made complaint. All the fundamental truths of Law and Morals are to be found in the past or the present. They are hidden under some concrete form, they may be discovered but cannot be invented. New formulae may be found to express them, or widen their application, but their substance is already existing. The process of social development is only a modification of old principles to suit new circumstances. The exegesis of these principles admits no doubt of hypothetical solutions, but however useful hypotheses may be in the search after truth, they must always be confirmed by careful induction, before acquiring any scientific importance. Whatever may be achieved in the way of generalisation will be a product of the science itself, a development of principle, and the boundaries of the science will expand as new generalisations are made. New facts also will come into existence, but they do not exist for us. We cannot look around us from any other point than that on which we stand.

We are of opinion therefore that a science of law has become possible, seeing that all the materials necessary for its construction already exist and are presented to us somewhere in a concrete shape. We have the rational *matter*, we want also the rational *form*. We *know* or may know if we take pains to ascertain; we want also to *understand*. We are not content with the *datum* whether given by the authority of the State, or the interior feeling of the heart. We want to know the truth as science alone can expound it.

The simple disposition of an unbiassed mind is to rest upon what is publicly acknowledged, to accept without question the conventionalities of society, and it is well that this is so. But man is also prone to think, and his sense of freedom, or rather his caprice, prevents him from being satisfied, unless he can think something new or different from what has been thought before. With sufficient force of mind to get this length, but without the scientific spirit or method, theorists start their independent notions and create a confusion which they rather plume themselves upon, and it may easily pass for a sincere earnestness about the matter. But the difficulty is generally of their own making. They cannot see the wood for the trees. Philosophy requires to be corrected by experience, *i.e.* to become science, and unless people can get science they will generally be safer with the conventionalities.

There is no apparent reason, why the science of law should be left entirely to *a priori* speculation, and not aided by observation, or tested by agreement of its principles with historical facts. If nature is admitted to be rational, if the philosopher's stone is to be found within herself, why should it be thought that the spiritual universe has its truth *without* itself, and that every one who chooses may pronounce off hand upon all those questions? But "grave Philosophy's absurdest dream" is that the whole business may be evolved out of consciousness, without recourse to history at all. There are those who profess to depend solely upon intuitions of the mind; they "get their ideas in their sleep." "This," says Hegel, "is the great notion 'of the morbids,' instead of basing science upon the evolution of thought and conception, to base it rather upon immediate apprehension and accidental imaginings, so that the rich articulation of the ethical within itself,—which makes the State, which is the architectonic of its rationality, which, by definite distinction of the spheres of public life and their applications, and by the severity of the measure restraining every pillar, arch and buttress, produces the strength of the whole out of the harmony of the parts,—so that this 'wide arch of the ranged Empire' is to be dissolved into the *slush* of 'Heart,' 'Friendship,' 'Inspiration!'"*

The only possible remedy for this confusion, the only possible escape from the school of dreamers, the only possible way to get science instead of opinion, is to have recourse to history. Science must pass through the Natural History stage. The facts must be collected, not necessarily the whole minutiæ of the history of every country and of every system of law, but all the important facts, all the typical systems, especially of the progressive races. "If," as Mr. Maine says, "we can by means

* Introduction to the *Philosophie des Rechts*, p. 11. The whole Introduction is very racy.

determine the early forms of jural conceptions, they will be invaluable to us. These rudimentary ideas are to the jurist what the primary crusts of the earth are to the geologist. They contain potentially all the forms in which law has subsequently exhibited itself. The haste or the prejudice which has generally refused them all but the most superficial examination must bear the blame of the unsatisfactory condition in which we find the science of Jurisprudence."* Mr. Maine shows admirably by his own treatment of his subject how much knowledge of history elucidates and simplifies the principles of law, and how interesting their study may be made.

A good deal of this preliminary work has been done, and that in a very important direction. The most important remains of Roman Jurisprudence have been restored, and its whole frame-work set up again. The history of Roman Law in the Middle Ages, and its modern phase, have been made clear by the genius and laborious research of Savigny, the great exponent of the historical method. If half the energy which has been spent on the details of Roman Law had been directed to other quarters, we should still have had enough of Roman Law, and a very important contribution to the remainder of the subject. As it is, a large portion, the greater portion, of the whole field is entirely unoccupied. In our own country some important work has been done by such men as, in England, Kemble and Thorpe,—in Scotland, Thomson and Cosmo Innes.

Leaving our investigators in the meantime to pursue

* *Maine's Ancient Law*, Cap. I., p. 3.

their discoveries among the relics of antiquity, and to store up materials for the science, we proceed to explain the general spirit and aim of the historical method, after which we shall glance in conclusion at the procedure of the science when the necessary materials have been gathered together.

History may be treated externally or internally. The former method acquaints us with ancient law as a series of obsolete systems unconnected with each other. The latter regards every system of law as standing in a deep and close relation to the civilisation amid which it arose, as an image of the social and moral ideas of the time and the place. Moreover, it surveys the whole series of legal systems as successive manifestations of one continuous life, as moments in the organic development of positive law.

Construed after this fashion, the science of law will be seen to be intimately connected with the philosophy of history. Their common subject matter is civilisation, the history of the process of human development. Humanity is seen groping its way from darkness to light, beginning with slavery without and within, throwing off by degrees the bondage of external restraint, and freeing itself also from the net-work of inward slavery which its own ignorance originally wove, until at length it recognises the truth in which freedom is consciously realised as the reconciliation of will with law, *omnes legum servi sumus, ut liberi esse possimus.* Civilisation is a whole, of which law, though a significant element, is only one element, and therefore not properly intelligible apart from the others. It is, to use the words of Savigny, "subject to the same movement and development as every other popular tendency, and this very development remains under the same law of inward necessity as in its earlier stages. Law grows with the growth and strengthens with the strength of the people, and finally dies away as the nation loses its nationality."

Ancient law therefore is not to be considered apart from its historical surroundings. It is not possible to understand the forms of ancient life, whether obsolete or extant, without recalling to mind also the mental forms or principles in the light of which they were devised, and through which they were seen. Our own psychological experience will not suffice to explain how these things came into existence. We must carry ourselves back into the past, and penetrate the atmosphere of thought and circumstance amid which they were fostered. We must try to see the roads *before* they were made. Each period is involved in circumstances peculiar to itself, is surrounded by conditions thoroughly idiosyncratic, and therefore neither affords a model for us, nor can its legislation be judged by our standards.

For the application of the historical method our time is ripe. Ancient civilisations were distinguished for their simplicity, modern are characterised by their complication. We have a better chance of being able to express and bring into contrast the various elements of the thought and life of ancient times, now that so many forms of culture have united in one stream. We can look back upon history as a whole, and observe in the successive phases of human development an expanding and progressive law. The life of man as a natural being, has attached to it certain conditions which do return and repeat themselves. The experience of the individual is at the best but a feeble copy of what the race has achieved and endured. He is but one wave in the great tide of human affairs. Yet a science of history, attempting to generalise the laws of a man's life by inductive classification, would only touch the surface and leave unexplained the things that most need explanation. The physical conditions to which he is subject, and the general tendencies of human nature, may be determined with some accuracy; but after all, what has been achieved is the mere statement of a fact, an aggregate of human activity, a formula for the *average* man. No scientific law has been discovered. The *how* or *why* of the matter is unanswered. No rule has been laid down for enabling us to predict the individual's conduct. For such a pretended science the eccentricity of genius and such occurrences as to human knowledge depend on chance, are inexplicable difficulties. No doubt a great man is to a large extent produced by surrounding circumstances. He, too, is no more than a single wave, but he is *the* wave, which at the flood breaks through the narrow strip of sand that had so long confined his fellows, and through the opening which he makes they can all enter in.

But as Aristotle has said, humanity in search of immortality, having failed to find it in the individual finds it in the race. The loss of one is not perceived because he is replaced by another. In nature the seed rots only to generate a second life. So in history we see forms of civilisation passing away, yet living on under new shapes. When a nation dies its estate is distributed among its heirs. They inhabit its palaces. They adopt many of the external conditions of its life. But a new spirit lives within. Progress there is, but not a constant and invariable progression. Progress there is, but not over all the world, not without times of retrogression, real or apparent. The sacred fire does not always blaze, yet when it seems to have gone out the flame shortly reappears fanned by some other hand. " One generation waxes, and another wanes: a little time and all living things are changed: the torch of life is passed from hand to hand." *

Enough has been said, too much perhaps, on this topic. We have been anxious to enforce the inseparable unity of history, to exhibit it at the same time only as a broken unity, in which nature is careful of the type, though careless of the single life, in order to show how inseparable is law from history, and history from law, and philosophy from both. It seems quite clear that without the historical investigation of positive law the science can never progress beyond empiricism, can never establish the foundations of its doctrines in human nature, or trace throughout its extent the links of reason which bind its parts together.

Having thus attempted to express in general terms the manner in which history is regarded by Jurists of the historical school, we have only in conclusion to consider

* Lucretius. *De rer. nat.* II., 73.

shortly what the nature of the further procedure of the science of Jurisprudence should be when the necessary facts have been brought within reach.

In the first place each system of law which has been made the subject of investigation may have an exegesis or philosophy of its own, *i.e.*, a set of rules drawn from the facts ascertained which can be applied to solve particular questions falling within their range. In the next place, a comparative view of the respective systems may be taken in order to show their historical connection with each other, and with the history of the world. Lastly, the absolute characteristics of law may be ascertained and exhibited methodically, as the basis of a complete philosophy of the subject. When an experimental science has been thus formed, its principles will furnish a good foundation for legislation, which is the corresponding practical art. Concerning the art of legislation we would only offer one remark in this place. From the legislator's point of view the conception of law seems to undergo a change. He probably does not himself feel the pressure of necessity. Law seems to be in his hands an active force which he may apply beneficially to modify in some degree the tendencies of society where they are bent in a wrong direction. Reason *is* the universal solvent, but not reason in the abstract. The only reason he can carry into effect is the reason of the governed, or at least he cannot run counter to it, for he must have their consent before they will obey his behests, and their reasoning never differs very far from that of the generation that went before them. The legislator may sometimes be

H

foolish enough to disregard the law of historical development and attempt to establish an ideal state. In vain! Philosophy indeed may seat itself on a hill top, and profess to descry the destination of mankind afar, but poor humanity must nevertheless plod its way step by step over the intervening ground.

W. S. P.

THE RIVER.

He sailed along, along,
Borne down the gently-sliding seaward slope,
Through curving eddies of the river glass:
The sky was grey above, unbarred with blue,
The chilling wind moaned slowly past his ear,
His heart was heavy, and his tongue was dumb,
And the dull river crept along, along.

On either hand stretched undulating knolls,
Covered with faded heather; and between
Lay swampy bottoms, firmed with thickset gale,
Wherefrom there trickled black unmurmuring rills;
Without a plash against the clayey banks,
Deep swollen with rain, and sable-dyed with moss,
Eddied the sullen stream along, along.

On either hand stretched out the boundless plain,
Knee-deep with rank grey grass, with stunted shrubs;
There was no mound, no ridge, no far off blue.

THE RIVER.

The edgeless, mingled clouds drove overhead,
His heart was sad, but sad not utterly.
A list of osiers hemmed the river bank;
Without a plash among their swaying stalks
The stealthy river slid along, along.

The dull grey heaven grew greyer overhead;
Above him towered the ever-during hills;
Their sides were lost in fog, their feet below
Were barren slate and water-eaten schist;
Brown moss, green lichen, fringed the smooth cut slabs,
That trickled bright with drizzlings of the mist;
Without a sob against the upright walls,
The sullen water glode along, along.

The river broadened out, the eddies curled
More slow, in lesser dimples spun the stream:
The clouds were fled away, the heavenly cope
Above him gleamed with blue immortal fire;
More warm the breezes wantoned in his hair,
And rustled all the branches of the trees,
Whose long files stood upon the river banks,
Drinking the golden gladness of the sun.

The foggy dark shut out the heavenly fires;
And all down either shore were lines of quay,
And sheds of merchandise; and there before
Lay ships of every freight, an endless file.
Among their rigging shone the slope-built town,
Bright with ten thousand lurid earthly flames;

He caught the clamour of the town, the quays,
As one who dreaming hears, and yet hears not:
Without a gurgle on the vague black hulls
The oily swellings crept along, along.

    Without an end stretched out the flooded plains;
Dawn blushed not yet: but palely grey above
The heaven looked down on pale grey flats below.
And all the stars, save Lucifer, were sunk,
Drowned in the deluge of the rising light.
There was no shore on any hand to see;
But pollard willow-rows, and island clumps
Of beech, and avenues of ash and elm
Standing above the level on low ridge.
And the cool wind of dawn refreshed his cheek,
Nor raised a ripple on the moveless glass;
He waited for the redness, glad at heart.
Without a murmur, as without a bank,
The undistinguished current flowed along.

AFTER MANY YEARS.

I.

Ah! with what other heart and other hope
    All eager for the strife,
I saw slow stealing up far hill and cope
    The dust and smoke of life.

Then all my spirit with a proud disdain
    Went ever forth in song,
The warm young blood shot tingling through each vein,
    Full, even-pulsed, and strong.
A fierce ambition, like a mighty wind,
    Swept sudden o'er my soul,
I too should mingle in the fight, and find
    The ever longed for goal.

II.

I fought—I conquered, and the years have fled
    With much that made life sweet,
And youth lies buried and fair loves lie shed
    Like spilt wine at my feet.
I hardly care to grasp the world-sought prize,
    Mine after many years,
Nor joy it brings nor sudden glad surprise,
    But pitiful sad tears.
Oh vanished loves! fair faces sorrow-stained!
    And pure regard for truth!
Take, cruel years! what glory I have gained,
    Give back one hour of youth!
I gave up love, with much I now hold best,
    For *this*—how dearly bought!
A passionate yearning after perfect rest,
    Rest and *release from thought*.

THE NATIONALITIES OF SHAKESPEARE.

It is striking to find, when we run over the subjects of Shakespeare's plays, that there is only one comedy, the Merry Wives of Windsor, whose scene lies in contemporary England. The events of all the other plays are supposed to happen either in former ages, or in remote countries, or both. But a distinction is to be drawn between those countries, such as Rome, Greece,* and especially modern Italy, which really had made an impression upon Shakespeare's mind, and whose local colour goes for something, if not in the main construction, at least in the details, of the play; and those which are but convenient and euphonious names for imaginary lands, where the poet's fancy may take freer range. Such are Sicilia, Bohemia with its famous seaport, Vienna in Measure for Measure, Illyria in the Winter's Tale, the forest of As You Like It, and the enchanted island of the Tempest.

It might seem a natural inference from this universal preference of foreign countries, that the diversities of national character would form an important and characteristic feature of the Shakespearian drama. But it needs a very slight acquaintance with Shakespeare to discover that this is not the case. As the scenes of his dramas are ideal, so also are his personages. Their nationality does not as a rule strike us. Falstaff and his companions are English, and of the poet's own day: but when do we think of their being English, rather than Bohemian or

---
* In Midsummer Night's Dream, Timon, and Troilus and Cressida.

Illyrian? The shepherds and shepherdesses of the Winter's Tale, Sir Toby and Sir Andrew in Twelfth Night are just as near to us. Shakespeare was probably never beyond the four seas of Britain, and his visit even to Scotland is a very problematical though possible inference from an entry in the records of the burgh of Aberdeen. He had no immediate acquaintance with any form of character but that of the Englishmen of his own day. His notions of foreign society are gathered from Montaigne (the only book we know to have belonged to Shakespeare), or the novels of Cinthio and Bandello: his notions of ancient life from schoolboy recollections, floating talk, and North's Plutarch. He probably knew something of Latin, certainly nothing of Greek—Scott is a curious parallel;—he was evidently familiar with French, of which he constantly introduces sentences, and even once a whole scene; whether he possessed any Italian beyond a few phrases may remain more doubtful. He paints human nature, not as it appears in any particular country, but in the true ideal manner; giving not the minutely, but the typically true; not the photographic letter, but the scope and spirit, of human action and human life. Hence his choice of distant and unfamiliar scenes as a background to his figures. The names are something: they are points of attachment to the firm earth of reality, and add something to the definiteness of that material instrument by which art must always express itself: but the real importance of Verona or Athens to the poet is that it yields just that distance which "lends enchantment to the view;" that remoteness which gives to a good picture the bloom of unity and perfect composition; which transforms the unpoetical details of to-day into the glorified ideal that is independent of place or time.

Still, though in a minor and subordinate degree, there is a good deal about national character in Shakespeare; and this we now propose to consider, beginning, as is natural, with the poet's own country.

When Shakespeare says anything about the English character, it is generally in the way of half-serious satire. His countrymen's want of pliancy, their awkward manners, their love of novelty and their idle curiosity, their never being able to make enough of a good thing, their moodiness, melancholy, and supposed madness, are none of them spared. "Ay, marry, why was he sent into England?" "Why, because he was mad: he shall recover his wits there; or if he do not, it's no great matter there." "Why?" "'Twill not be seen in him; there the men are as mad as he." "Were I in England now (as once I was) and had but this fish painted, not a holiday fool there but would give a piece of silver: there would this monster make a man; any strange beast there makes a man: when they will not give a doit to relieve a lame beggar, they will lay out ten to see a dead Indian."—"What say you then to Faulconbridge, the young Baron of England." "You know I say nothing to him, for he understands not me, nor I him: he hath neither Latin, French, nor Italian; and you will come into the court and swear that I have a poor pennyworth in the English. He is a proper man's picture. But, alas! who can converse with a dumb show? How oddly he is suited! I think he bought his doublet in Italy, his round hose in France, his bonnet in Germany, and his behaviour everywhere." There is one great exception to these good-natured sarcasms. In the camp of Henry V. in France are assembled men of several different nationalities: and it is obviously one part of Shakespeare's plan to contrast these. The three English soldiers whom he introduces discoursing at some length are drawn with a loving and discriminating hand. They are brave, as becomes "good yeomen, whose limbs were made in England," but fully alive to the black side of things, which they expose with merciless perspicacity; depressed by the thought of to-morrow's battle, but only the more dangerous on that account; reverencing rank, but undismayed by the royal person; very sensible to merit in their king and officers, but setting no bounds to their criticism: cool and reasonable even in the full current of their faultfinding: and admirable proficients in the national art of grumbling. The Frenchmen are made to bear witness to some of these qualities. "That island of England breeds very valiant creatures; their mastiffs are of unmatchable courage, and the men do sympathise with the mastiffs, in robustious and rough coming on, leaving their wits with their wives; and then give them great meals of beef, and iron and steel, and they will eat like wolves, and fight like devils." The Scotchman and the Irishman in the same play, though but slight sketches, are both characteristic. Captain Jamy is determined and cool; a little pedantic, and dearly loves an argument about "first principles:" "a marvellous, valorous gentleman, and of great expedition and knowledge in the ancient wars, upon my particular knowledge of his directions." But Captain Macmorris! "of my nation? what ish my nation? what ish my nation? who talks of my nation ish a villain, and a knave, and a rascal." This style of oratory has not been wholly unknown in subsequent times. Macmorris is hot and impetuous, and very ill pleased with everybody's work but his own: and though Gower calls him "a very valiant gentleman, i' faith," we cannot help having extremely little confidence in him. Shakespeare lived in an age when Ireland was no favourite with his countrymen generally. "I was never so berhymed since Pythagoras' time, that I was an Irish rat, which I can hardly remember." "The howling of Irish wolves against the moon." "Like a kerne of Ireland." "The uncivil kernes of Ireland are in arms." Such phrases seem to indicate a general prejudice. Scotland is spoken of much more respectfully, not without twits at the supposed poverty of the nation. "That very valiant and approved Scot." "Ten thousand bold Scots." "Those same noble Scots." "The noble Scot, Lord Douglas." "Where Scotland?" "I found it by the barrenness, hard in the palm of the hand." "What think you of the Scottish lord, his neighbour?" "That he hath a neighbourly charity in him; for he borrowed a box of the ear of the Englishman, and swore he would pay him again when he was able." This is the bitterest allusion to our dear country in Shakespeare.

Shakespeare seems to have a kindness for the Welsh

character. Twice he has drawn a Welshman at full length, and both times produced a universal favourite. Who does not like Sir Hugh, with his hot temper, his pedantry, his amusing mistakes, his finger in every man's pie, his desperate valour in the field, his readiness to help in any fun that is going ("I will be like a jack-an-apes also, to burn the knight with my taber"), his kind heart, and his inexhaustible good nature? "Let us command to know that of your mouth or of your lips: for divers philosophers hold that the lips is parcel of the mouth." "It is *qui, quae, quod;* if you forget your *quies,* your *quaes,* and your *quods,* you must be preeches." Fluellen has the same general qualities, modified by his profession. He is a man of courage and honour, and an excellent soldier; but he has an exquisite hot temper, which is especially intolerant of any sort of pretender: he is not fond of being corrected, but loves dearly to lay down the law; he is very proud of his birth and of his nation, and of the fact that the king is in a sense his countryman, by having been born at Monmouth; he is a terrible pedant in matters of war, and measures everything by book-knowledge and ancient example. "Look you, the mines is not according to the disciplines of the war; the concavities of it is not sufficient."—"He (Macmorris) is an ass as in the 'orld: I will verify as much in his peard; he has no more directions in the true disciplines of the wars, look you, of the Roman disciplines, than is a puppy-dog." Yet he is not too learned: a soldier is better accommodated than with a too exact memory; and "it is out of his prains what is the name of the other river; but 'tis all one, 'tis alike as my fingers is to my fingers, and there is salmons in both." Nor are his cumbrous disquisitions confined to such matters; he likes to hold forth learnedly upon any subject. " By your patience, ancient Pistol. Fortune is painted plind, with a muffler afore her eyes, to signify to you that Fortune is plind: and she is painted also with a wheel, to signify to you, which is the moral of it, that she is turning, and inconstant, and mutability, and variation : and her foot, look you, is fixed upon a spherical stone, which rolls, and rolls, and rolls;—In good truth, the poet makes a most excellent description of it : Fortune is an excellent moral." And all this time he is keeping Pistol from saying what he wants. To prevent all mistakes as to his character, King Harry is made to sum it up in two familiar lines. "Though it appear a little out of fashion, there is much care and valour in this Welshman." The curious reader may draw a parallel with Sir Dugald Dalgetty and the Baron of Bradwardine, and compute how much of the later portrait is derived from the older.

A like national prejudice to that we have mentioned against the Irish appears in the case of the French. The whole scene in Henry V. (III. 7), which is too long to quote, gives the light in which Shakespeare generally shows the French. He makes them vain, thoughtless, flippant, perpetually bragging, but by no means distinguished for actual achievements. " How say you by the French lord, monsieur Le Bon ?" "God made him, and therefore let him pass for a man. In truth, I know it is a sin to be a mocker. But he ! why, he hath a horse better than the Neapolitan's; a better bad habit of frowning than the Count Palatine: he is every man in no man: if a throstle sing he falls straight a capering; he will fence with his own shadow: if I should marry him I should marry twenty husbands: if he would despise me, I would forgive him; for if he love me to madness I shall never requite him." "In France, among a fickle wavering nation." "O foul revolt of French inconstancy!" "The confident and over-lusty French." "Done like a Frenchman; turn, and turn again!" Yet how little store Shakespeare really sets by such caricatures appears from those plays whose scene is laid in France, Love's Labour's Lost, All's Well that Ends Well, and As You Like It, which are quite free from these acrimonious sallies. Dr. Caius in the Merry Wives is a much more good-natured portrait. The flightiness and vivacity which we are accustomed to associate with the idea of a Frenchman are excellently hit off in the irascible doctor. He comes skipping in—"Vot is you sing? I do not like dese toys: Pray you, go and vetch me in my closet *un boitier verd;* a box, a green-a box; Do intend vat I speak? a green-a box?" "You are John Rugby, and you are Jack Rugby: come, take-a your rapier, and come after my heel to de court?"

Germany and Denmark come in for some sarcasms about melancholy and heavy drinking. Every one remembers the lines;

"And to my mind, though I am native here,
And to the manner born, it is a custom
More honour'd in the breach than the observance.

> This heavy-headed revel, east and west,
> Makes us traduc'd, and tax'd of other nations ;
> They clepe us drunkards, and with swinish phrase
> Soil our addition."

"The county Palatine doth nothing but frown ; as who should say, 'An you will not have me, choose :' he hears merry tales, and smiles not: I fear he will prove the weeping philosopher when he grows old, being so full of unmannerly sadness in his youth." "Therefore, for fear of the worst, I pray thee set a deep glass of Rhenish wine on the contrary casket: for, if the devil be within, and that temptation without, I know he will choose it."

Germany is but seldom mentioned in Shakespeare; but Italy fills a very prominent place, and had evidently a strong hold upon his imagination. Six plays have their scenes laid there, not counting the Winter's Tale and the Tempest. Verona, Mantua, Padua, Venice, Messina, are all actual scenes of plays. We must remember the literary position of Italy at this time. It was in Italy that the revival of letters had begun and had been most vigorously conducted. The literature of France, if we except Charron and Montaigne, had produced little or nothing of firstrate excellence; and that of England, although in its bloom, had no prestige of antiquity. Italy could boast Dante, Boiardo, Tasso, Petrarch, Ariosto, Boccaccio, to say nothing of the minor writers whose translated stories found such favour in England. Even at a much later date, it is to Italy that Milton travels, as to the fountainhead of all things literary. It is Italian that he studies, not French, or German, or even Spanish, and in

Italian that he occasionally writes sonnets. Such considerations may help us to understand why Italy should hold so foremost a place in the public opinions of the Elizabethan period. But with all this inclination to Italy, Shakespeare touches little on Italian character; when he does, he makes it cruel, jealous, dark and saturnine, and given to plots and poisonings. It is very noticeable that his two worst villains, Iago and Iachimo, are both Italians. People of other nations commit all sorts of villanies in his plays: but they do not lay deliberate plots against unoffending persons. Shylock also, though a Jew, is an Italian Jew. And the excess of passion, which is so characteristic of Othello and of Romeo and Juliet, seems to us not fortuitously exhibited upon an Italian scene.

"Tut! a toy!
An old Italian fox is not so kind, my boy."

"What false Italian,
(As poisonous tongued as handed) hath prevail'd
On thy too ready-hearing?"

"Mine Italian brain
Can in your duller Britain operate
Most vilely."

"Ay, so thou dost,
Italian fiend!"

"That drug-damned Italy hath out-crafted him."

Greece has left no direct impress upon Shakespeare's mind. His notion of it is a faint reflection, derived through a Roman medium, and that too the later times of Rome, the time of the *Graeculus esuriens*, when the haughty Roman looked upon the Greeks as a nation of slaves, adventurers, tools, and bad characters generally. This seems to be the drift of Troilus and Cressida, in all respects the most enigmatical of Shakespeare's pieces. In Timon of Athens and the Midsummer Night's Dream, although the scene be laid in Greece, it might nearly as well be laid anywhere else. In Othello there is a curious allusion to the proverbial ἀπάθεια of the Lacedæmonians;

> "O Spartan dog!
> More fell than anguish, hunger, or the sea!"

But the Roman history and the Roman character had evidently powerfully influenced his imagination. He has given three plays to Roman themes: Coriolanus, Julius Cæsar, and Antony and Cleopatra. The lofty and commanding genius of the Romans, and their undaunted deaths, when death was better than life, he had really conceived as national characteristics. Bassanio says of Antonio that he is

> "The dearest friend to me, the kindest man,
> The best condition'd and unwearied spirit
> In doing courtesies; and one in whom
> The ancient Roman honour more appears,
> Than any that draws breath in Italy."

"Let's present him to the deities, like a Roman conqueror."

"Why should I play the Roman fool, and die
On mine own sword?"

"I will imitate the honourable Romans in brevity."

"Are yet two Romans living such as these?
Thou last of all the Romans, fare thee well!
It is impossible that ever Rome
Should breed thy fellow."

"This was the noblest Roman of them all."

"I liv'd, the greatest prince o' the world,
The noblest: and do now not basely die,
Nor cowardly put off my helmet to
My countryman,—a Roman, by a Roman
Valiantly vanquish'd."

"We'll bury him; and then, what's brave, what's noble,
Let's do it after the high Roman fashion,
And make death proud to take us."

"Sufficeth
A Roman with a Roman's heart can suffer."

"Thou art a Roman; be not barbarous."

"I am more an antique Roman than a Dane;
Here's yet some liquor left."

"Rome, thou hast lost the breed of noble bloods!"

"In the most high and palmy state of Rome,
A little ere the mightiest Julius fell."

Cum multis aliis. Surely this perpetual harping on the greatness of Rome points not only to much conning of North's Plutarch, but to the grammar-school education, which, as Mr. Knight well points out, we can scarcely imagine Shakespeare not to have received.

We have now briefly reviewed the allusions of Shakespeare to national character in ancient and modern countries. It will be seen how slight they are, and how little weight the poet lays upon them; it will also be seen how they coincide with popular prejudices; apparently Shakespeare has simply availed himself of these feelings to point his lines with an occasional sarcasm at the expense of a foreign country, or now and then at that of his own.

GLAUCUS.

The poets sang beside the shining sea
The story of the Eubœan fisherman,
How Scylla waked his slumbering heart to love;
And how thro' all the seas, from mouths of Nile
To western shores Ulysses never reached,
He sought to win the bright-tressed Nereïd;
And how he, woo'd by Circe, daughter of the Sun,
Passed days of dalliance in her cursed isle.
At length he broke her wicked lures and fled
To find his love, the pearly-shouldered maid,
Disfigured by the wily witch's curse.
Then his were days of darkness, weary days.
But he grew wise in knowledge of the deeps,
And of the antique lore of Primal Gods,
And of the forces working in the world,
And Beauty the supremest; and at last
The spell was sundered and his love was crowned..

The poet tells the tale of many a life,
The youth with health's full music in his veins
And all the world before him, will be great
And clothe his life in all ideal good.
Strong-hearted, eager-eyed, he seeks the strife
To reach his bright Ideal, but the way
Is long, the struggle arduous, and his hopes
Fall withered one by one upon the dust.
Now, tired, he drains the cup of vain delight,
The false joy dims the brightness of the true,
The sensual triumphs and the man is lost.
Then follow anguish and the salt of tears
And prayers and strivings ere the soul regain
The noble attitude of uprightness.

THE START.

The beetles shimmer in the grass,
    The ants are running here and there,
The dandelion's feathers pass
    In dream-like motion thro' the air.
Bright petals gleam in sun and shade,
    And brightly shines the calm great sea,
A deep full joy pervades the glade,
    A smile serene is on the lea.

The lights and shades are tossed and mingled,
    The soft air wanders in the boughs,
The chemist wild-bee golden-cingled
    Sinks loaded to his treasure-house.

The cosmic robe conceals the heart
    That beats below in sun and shower,
And life with aye-creative art
    Works in the calm of mighty power.

With life astir the buried seed
    Puts forth germ-leaves and feels for day;
The earth and air the fibre feed,
    And in the cell the juices play.
The lily weaves her robe of light,
    The pine trees climb the mountain stern,
And in a hundred summers' might
    The oak wades knee-deep in the fern.

A power is moving everywhere,
    A change is working, death and birth—
A vital essence fills the air,
    An Artist-spirit holds the earth.
God in His wondrous temple spreads
    The flower damask'd altar-cloth:
His finger stamps the million threads,
    He lights the star and paints the moth.

My heart throbs with intelligence:
    The red blood circles in the brain,
A life is given of thought and sense—
    To live and not to live in vain.
The spirit feels the coming throng
    Of days with vague stir touch its chords,
Like poet's heart that shapes a song
    Ere yet the song has taken words.

THE PAUSE.

The pause—the pall—to this I come :
    In vain I seek for peace in strife ;
And vain the heart's long martyrdom,
    It cannot reach the good of life.
The splendour yet is in the day,
    The glory lives in flower and tree
But rayless glooms the onward way
    Where Hope and strong-eyed Faith should be.

How bright the outset, this the end !
    Our life is lived before we think ;
A gallant fleet and bravely manned
    We proudly sail away—to sink ;
Or, all but wrecked, with canvas riven,
    Unhelmed we drift from day to day,
Wind-baffled, thwarted, tempest-driven,
    To seek whatever port we may.

The fresh desire all-winged to soar
    Flew with the eager-striving mind
To reach the laurell'd Fame before
    And leave a guerdon'd path behind.
Then all the way was flushed with light,
    The distance beckoned on and on,
And in the visioned sleep of night
    We dreamed the dream of Solomon.

Then God was with me by my side ;
    His blossoms burst where'er I trod ;

His beauty kept me as a guide—
   I held a garment-hold of God.
The Forces working moulded Form,
   The lower life strove for the higher,
The crocus from its withered corm
   God-crowned arose in golden fire.

Why sought I more? The why and whence
   Have quenched the simple trust of youth,
And cold beneath the knife and lens
   Glitters the heartless barren truth.
In vain the search, the phantasm flies,
   The soul's sweet phantasm vapour-born,
And like a lying prophet dies
   The rainbow radiance of the morn.

CIRCE.

Drink, while it glows, the cup divine!
   Life as a winter bough is bare,
But sprinkled with the generous wine
   Its blooms will warm the midnight air.
Like sunlight thro' each tingling vein
   The joy goes flashing swift along:
The wild thought brightens in the brain,
   And struggles forth in wit and song.

Let loose the glittering coil of hair
   To curl like snakes upon your breast:
The world may toil its little care
   And grovel hell-wards: here we rest.

The fervid sparkle of the wine—
  Life-fire to stir the soul that sips,
Is dark beside these eyes of thine,
  And passion's drink is on thy lips.

Fool I to chase an empty fame,
  And squander all my strength of youth,
And barter life to buy a name—
  The name of wisdom and of truth.
Here, crowned with love and beauty's spoil,
  Our moments brighten more and more.
What matters all the age's toil,
  And what the sage's barren lore!

The grass is rank upon the grave
  Of many youthful hearts we've known,
And soon its green will dance and wave,
  To rot unheeded o'er our own.
A worm is nestled in the clay,
  Sharp-toothed (who cares?) for you and me;
The wild delight is ours to-day,
  The future, death's-head, let it be.

A bumper! sorrows come unsought,
  And witless they who will be ever
Darkening the noon of life with thought,
  And vain Ixion-like endeavour.
Fool, too, Ixion! many a maid
  Would prize thy love in Grecian grove.
But thou would'st skyey heights invade
  To clasp the white-armed queen of Jove.

Far-flashing on their golden seats
    Above the clouds from earth that rise,
The gods enjoy the Olympian meats,
    And quaff the vintage of the skies.
They mellow o'er the kindling bowl,
    And heaven's courts are filled with laughter.
We'll live like them, in no control,
    Or shadow cold of an hereafter.

THE CURSE.

The degradation is complete,
    The serpents in my vitals move;
The earth is heartless at my feet,
    The heavens are adamant above.
The curse is heavy on my soul,
    And round and round where'er I go
Dead hopes affright and deeds unroll
    Their deathlessness in ceaseless woe.

A woe that must be all lived out,
    No pang foregone, no thought of death
To still the tempest and the doubt,
    And ease a coward's puling breath:
A weary length of days to come,
    Wherein this sentient soul must know
The dregs and agony of doom—
    Its dread capacity for woe.

On, my brave horse, across the moor
    Plunge thro' the starless midnight gloom,

Unrest behind, no peace before,
    And all within the fire of doom.
Breaks thro' the night above no light:
    No light breaks to my soul within—
A restless never-ending night
    Of passion, error, pride, and sin.

Miles of the moorland stretch away
    Into the dark; Bayard, well done!
A new world greets the coming day
    But peace returns not with the sun.
Joy flushes forth its short deceits,
    Or sorrow breaks what hearts it can,
And in the vast of nature beats
    No pulse in sympathy with man.

THE ESCAPE.

The calm of eve is in the air,
    The poplar's leaves are scarcely stirred:
Here let us sit, my love, and share
    The joy of yonder singing bird.
Affection's peace is in your face,
    That lovely face I know so well,
That saved me by its tender grace,
    And raised the stricken soul that fell.

You met me sad among the gay,
    Or 'mong the gay the wildest there,
Hiding in vain the heart's decay,
    In laughter masking my despair.

You found me lone among the throng,
    A stranger to the many there,
Your voice came like an angel song,
    And broke the bands of my despair.

O eyes that looked away my pain!
    O voice that lulled it till it slept,
And to my heart like summer rain
    To summer flower in sweetness crept!
Then strengthened life rose purified
    To assert once more its ancient claims,
O'ercome its doubt, o'erthrow its pride,
    And clothe itself in lofty aims.

Ere yet the act became the life,
    And all the soul was gloomed with sin,
The devil's peace to God's high strife
    Preferring, darkening all within—
A human soul, with all its fires
    Radiant from God, and framed to soar
With grossness clogging what aspires,
    And ever, ever sinking lower.

O not in vain the youthful hope
    To sound the depths of love and lore,
To climb creation to the cope,
    And catch the glory on before!
Thro' deathless love with starred brow
    Lit by the clear pure heavenly flame
The soul regains the eternal now
    Beside God's footstool whence it came.

A life we live not lost to learn
　That here indeed we ne'er attain
The ideal life for which we yearn,
　The marriage of the heart and brain.
Day comes: all things not yet are clear,
　We must live out our little span,
Here in the Shadow and the Fear
　Must ever beat the heart of Man.

A. S.

A LECTURE ON DRAMATIC POETRY.

WHAT is the essential distinction of Prose and Poetry? The question has often been asked and often insufficiently answered even by poets. For, it is possible to enjoy or it may be even to write poetry without being able to tell what it is. Nay, perhaps the poet who does his work in a kind of divine unconsciousness of art may be the last person to analyse and define what he is doing. But for us who look at poetry from without, who come to enjoy and to admire, it may be well to understand why we are pleased, and it is the true work of criticism to tell us that, and so to save us from wasting our admiration on unworthy objects.

Let us compare two examples of poetry and prose speaking on the same subject: the fall of the three hundred Spartans at Thermopylæ: we will easily see what is the difference we are analysing. Prose gives us this account. "It is narrated that 300 Spartans fell at Thermopylæ where they fought against 300 myriads of Asiatics." Hear now poetry as it speaks of the same event in the inscription on the tomb of the Three Hundred. "O traveller, go tell the Lacedæmonians, that here we lie in obedience to their laws." How different is the effect on our minds. The former leaves us as cold and unaffected as the obituary in a newspaper: the latter lifts the veil and shows us the secret springs of heroism, that made these Spartans think it good to die. It tells us of the stern discipline of Sparta, and the instant fidelity of her sons; of the courage that asked no question and had no time to admire itself, and saw in the greatest act of the world's heroism nothing but a simple and natural act of obedience from which it would have been a shame to shrink. "O stranger, go tell the Lacedæmonians that we lie here in obedience to their laws."

Poetry, then, does not give us bare abstract ideas on the one hand, nor the simple narration of facts on the other. But it so narrates facts that we can see the ideas through them. It describes the outward world which we call real, but so that the ideal meaning that is in it becomes manifest. What science does for the reason, poetry does for the imagination; it makes the world become transparent, so that our eye, instead of being stopped by the outside of men and things, passes on to the thoughts, the feelings and the desires which they half conceal and half reveal. It takes away the veil from our eyes, so that we see the spiritual presences that are ever with us, and know when we have been entertaining angels unawares. In the Iliad the goddess Athene is made to open the eyes of a hero, so that where he had before seen merely men, he now saw gods fighting in the plains of Troy. Poetry is our goddess Athene, who opens our eyes to see the hidden powers that guide the apparently aimless and uncertain swaying of the battle of life. The cloud hangs thick about us in our daily life, and its trifles are apt to seem mean and vulgar. The crowding cares of every day come and immerse us in unmeaning detail. We can scarce believe that there is a higher purpose or spirit in it all. Then we open our poets, and wherever that divine light of imagination is cast it transforms and makes all things new. The little things of the world seem great and its greatness seems little, for we measure by a new standard. We are transferred to another world, "which is not another," but simply our own as it might always appear to us, if our eyes were always unveiled.

It is, then, the office of poetry to emancipate us from the weight of custom and commonplace that lie upon our lives "heavy as frost and deep almost as death." All poetry does this, but the Drama does it in the most daring and complete manner. It gives us back our life, not altered and transformed as in some other kinds of poetry, but simply transfigured by the light that shows it clearly. In its best form the Drama presents to us not some ideal utterly divorced from life and held up high above its entanglements, not some picture of "passionate perfection," pure partly because of its unreality, in which every discordant feature is eliminated, but a picture such as our actual life presents, of discordance, struggles and imperfection, in which error and success, right and wrong, are mingled in constant antagonism, and the solution only comes to us after a while, when we are able to look back and see faintly that a higher result has been attained. Art never can be quite like life: because in perfect art there must be a "poetical justice;" that is, we must see the harmony realized, which life never perfectly attains, however it may strive to attain it. But dramatic poetry seeks to come as near to life as it may, consistently with remaining art. It seeks to give not a simple strain of music, the utterance of one feeling without complexity or change, but a great masterpiece like those of Beethoven, which admits of many discords and jarring notes if only they be lost and solved at length in the final harmony.

We may illustrate this by comparing dramatic poetry with that kind of poetry which is furthest removed from the Drama—to wit, Lyric Poetry. We have all been conscious at times of dissonances between the world without and the world within us. The outward world remains as it was in spite of our intensest feelings: it does not joy with our joy or sadden with our sorrow. Our own feelings fill us with an absorbing consciousness, till there seems no room for anything else in the wide universe; when we emerge from the close furnace of our own passionate feeling we find that nature is unsympathizing, and the world "wanders its own wise way." The sun shines mockery upon the grief that seems all important to itself: and the storm rages and destroys when all is peace within us. The world does not play chorus to the drama of our souls, but has a drama of its own to play which goes on without regard to us.

This unsympathizing, almost ironical face, which nature puts on toward our passion, our weakness, our eagerness, and our pain, is to us sometimes that which weighs heaviest on us, and makes us feel most alone in the world. The fresh passion in us struggles against it, and would, if it could, make the world speak with it and for it, with its own voice and in its own words—would break through the contradictions of life and make all things subservient to the expression of its own joy and its own sorrow: but this it cannot do. Yet if we cannot bend the world thus into an organ of our wishes, we can *imagine* it to bend. We can idealize and invent a world in which passion shall not be cramped by antagonisms, but shall have its free course of utterance, where the sun shall shine with us, not against us, where nature and man shall be at one : and this world is the world of *lyric poetry*. The imaginary accord of nature and man is the theme of half of our best songs. Mark how the wounded heart takes nature, as it were, into its confidence, and assuming her sympathy finds it a sort of compensation for the wrongs and desertions of man—

> "Blow, blow, thou winter wind,
>   Thou art not so unkind
>   As man's ingratitude,
>   Thy tooth is not so keen,
>   Because thou art not seen,
>   Altho' thy breath be rude.

> Freeze, freeze, thou bitter sky
> That dost not bite so nigh
>   As benefits forgot.
> Though thou the waters warp
> Thy sting is not so sharp
>   As friend remembered not."

Or hear again how the sad voice of despair in Shelley summons all nature's powers of gloom and storm to express it—

> "Wild wind that moanest loud
>   Grief too sad for song,
> Wild wind when sullen cloud
>   Shrieks all the night long.
> Sad storm whose branches stain
>   Deep caves and dreary main
> Wail for the world's wrong."

Or take a still higher echo of the same note from the lament of David over Saul, "Ye mountains of Gilboa, let there be no dew, neither let there be rain upon you any more for ever: for there the shield of the mighty was vilely cast away." With what loud, imperative command does man's sorrow call upon nature to obey it at once and for ever in this great song of Israel! Or to take one final example from Tennyson, in which all nature becomes, as it were, but a voice to recall the image of a lost friend—

> "Thy voice is on the rolling air,
>   I hear thee where the waters run;
> Thou standest in the rising sun,
>   And in the setting thou art fair."

Here we have the genuine lyrical burst of emotion which sweeps all before it, and colours all heaven and earth with its refractions, unfixes the settled frame of things and half-creates and half perceives a world of its own—whose every voice and form is in harmony with the soul. And as lyric poetry suppresses the disharmony of nature and man, so it suppresses most often the disharmony of man with himself. It lives in a world of pure ideals and simple passions, forgetting the constant jarring of one feeling with another, the mingled motives, the half-realized ideals amid which we have to work out our lives. No purest patriot, no Garibaldi or Mazzini ever intensified and refined his life to that purity of heroic passion which is in the battle songs of nations. There is in him a struggle with self and with the conditions of life which is not represented there. No lover or friend ever lived in that continuous strain of emotion which In Memoriam represents to us. He who expects to find lyrical feeling purely embodied in life, might as well expect to find somewhere in this actual world

> "The island valley of Avilion,
> Where falls not hail nor rain nor any dew
> Nor ever wind blows loudly : but it lies
> Deep-meadowed, happy, fair with orchard lawns,
> And bowery billows, crowned with summer sea."

Into how different a sphere does dramatic poetry translate us—no more pure earnest ideals, but a struggle between the ideal and the actual, a contest between the comic and tragic, the lower and higher elements of our nature, is here presented to us. The Drama professes only to elevate us above life in so far as it concentrates its meaning into a brief space, and gives us in five short acts the "brief abstract and chronicle of the time." Much indeed is involved in this ideal concentration of life, but still so far does the resemblance maintain itself between them that the same moral objections which haunt us in relation to the existence and the knowledge of evil in the world, have been brought against its mimic on the stage. How is it right, it has been asked, to present life as it is with the evil as well as with the good in it, the confused struggle of virtue and vice? The ancient Stoics, the modern Puritans, revolt at it, and ask us again and again what profit can there be in the exhibition of evil. Above all, these objections are urged against comedy—or any representations of life into which a humorous element enters. And however we may feel that there is somewhere a falsity in such objections, it is not so easy to answer them. There must be a place in the universe, we feel, if not for Falstaff, then for the mind that created Falstaff— and that mixed good and evil amidst which we have been set as our best moral discipline, may surely be repeated in art without losing its moral effect. We are sometimes tempted to cut the knot and answer such objections with Falstaff's creator. "Dost thou think because thou art virtuous there shall be no more cakes and ale?"

Yet let us search a little deeper, and see for a moment with the objector's eyes, that we may find a better answer for him. How can it be right, he would urge, to create new representations of evil? should not Art rather furnish an ideal type which life may imitate though it may not be able to realize it? how can it be right to admit that humorous tone which is almost essential to the Drama, and which turns the struggle of destiny into a jest? In art as in life the comic side of things seems almost sinful to some minds. In a life full of wonder and mystery, where there is so much to do and so little time to do it, where the shadow of another world is as it were ever falling across our path, how should our frame of mind be ever other than earnest, serious, intense? When the imperfections of our circumstances, the narrow conditions of life and its vulgar wants and cares, are ever uniting with our own weakness to drag us down to a lower level of existence, ought we to allow our eyes to dwell on those things except with the stern gaze of those who watch their foe to see where he will strike? How should we for a moment turn without danger from the earnest attitude of a soldier, to look on life as a mere spectator with that genial humorous, all-tolerant eye which distinguishes above all our great Dramatist? Shakespeare makes no sermonizings over his characters: he is not afraid to recognize evil amid good, or good amid evil. He always awakens our sympathy for the worst of characters by some touch that reminds us that there is a human heart beating even beneath the ribs of death. Lady Macbeth's "Had he not looked my father as he slept I had done it," is a little touch letting us know that we have to do not with a demon but with a woman. Edmund in Lear, as near a perfect villain as any Shakespearian character, is yet pictured to us as finding his last comfort, when defeated and dying, in the thought of the love he has awakened.—"Yet Edmund was beloved." Or think, again, how we are led in the comedies to feel our kindred with even the low rascality of an Autolycus, or the drunken humour of a Sir Toby Belch. All this seems to some minds a confusion of evil and good, a tolerance that weakens the sinews of virtue. How shall we find a moral ground upon which to vindicate our great dramatist for misleading us into sympathy with vulgarity, meanness, even vice?

Some German commentators, like Ulrici, are not content without attempting to prove that the plays of Shakespeare are deliberately arranged with a view to teach us all the main doctrines of the Christian Religion. But it is not the office of the artist to preach, and there is no more "moral" in Shakespeare than is shut in the "blossom of a rose." He shows us life or the concentrated essence of life, and leaves us to find the moral in it if there be any. The moral lies only in this that Shakespeare's representation of the world is true: that the same laws are at work in his plays guiding and ordering the fates of his characters which guide and order the consecution of events in the world. There may be supernatural machinery in some of the plays, but any one who examines can see that it is human passion working out its own destiny, and not the machinery that determines the catastrophe. If, therefore, we ask for the moral of Shakespeare, we seem to be asking for the moral of human life, or a part of that moral. Let us try to show what moral in human life the Drama most prominently developes, and illustrate it by examples from one or two of the plays of Shakespeare.

It is the double nature of man ever in war with itself that the Drama expresses for us. It lifts the veil from that internecine struggle between man's higher and lower nature which is ever going on within and around us. It carries away the mist that hangs over life, and lets us behold for a moment the spiritual powers that are carrying on their warfare beneath it. It reveals to us in other words that deep division and antagonism in our being, which we call by many names, but which preserves the same nature through all. There is the antagonism between the real and the ideal, between the actual aims and uses of life on the one hand, and its spiritual meaning on the other, between the petty enjoyments of to-day and the infinite that seems so near us. Is it not strange and inconsistent that a being with low appetites and desires should yet have duties and aspirations that rise above time and chance, that such creatures as men so often are, should have the mighty destinies of man to fulfil? Every man, it has been said, wavers between his ideal and his caricature, between that possibility to which he is true in his best moments and that to which the circumstances of life and his own weakness tend to drag him down. Within and without us, in the strange warp and woof of things, we see mingled and striving for the mastery the divine and the human, the heavenly and the earthly, ideas and interests, thoughts that are eternal, and passions that are of the hour. Nor can we disentangle the threads that twine so closely together, for as the thinnest leaf has an inside and an outside, so the material and spiritual, the real and ideal side of things are one and inseparable. There is nothing great in man's life which has not its earthly basis, nothing little which does not rise towards the divine. Like two enemies chained together they never cease to struggle, yet never can break loose from each other.

It is this contrast and antagonism which comedy and tragedy alike seize upon. The difference lies in this, that comedy looks at the contrast from beneath, tragedy from above. Tragedy looks first at the higher ideal side of life, and when it sees our spiritual energies matched in unequal battle with time and chance, and limited and thwarted by these on every side, its tone cannot but be earnest and sad. It views the higher nature as a noble prisoner in the grasp of enemies who are beneath him, whom he despises, and yet from whom he cannot free himself. Comedy looks at the same contrast from beneath, and views the higher ideal as a solecism and an inconsistency which mars the completeness and self-satisfaction of the lower life. The tone of true comedy is a kind of humorous half pity, half recognition of the ideal as something that will not fit in with life, but which yet gives a tinge of poetry to it. To comedy man is a noble kind of fool who is to be loved and laughed at more than if he were wise. There is ever present in all high specimens of comedy, a subtle hint of the ideal higher nature of man, contrasting with the sensuous and earthly element of his nature which occupies the foreground of the picture. Without this contrast comedy sinks into farce, ever a low and contemptible kind of art, which can never deserve the name of poetry, because it shows man in his meanness without any hint of his greatness. Take even the most unlikely characters, take Falstaff, and see how the subtle presence of this contrast is what gives zest and meaning to the humour. The whole point of Falstaff's wit is the contrast between his own sensual existence, which recognizes no law but whim, and the earnest side of life. The point and humour of his words lies in continually suggesting a type and ideal of life which is furthest from his own, yet never allowing that ideal to come so far forward in the picture as to put us in an earnest frame of mind. Sometimes he gives to his own occupations the attributes of virtue. "Thieving" is "his vocation," and "it is no shame for a man to labour in his vocation." He has "lost his voice with hollaing and singing of anthems." "A plague on sighing and grief: it blows a man up like a bladder!" Sometimes he speaks of himself as an infant corrupted by others. "Thou hast done much harm upon me, God forgive thee for it. Before I knew thee, Hal, I knew nothing—now, I am, if a man should speak truly, no better than one of the wicked."_ "Thou knowest in the state of innocency Adam fell, and what should poor Jack Falstaff do in these days of villainy." Thus he is always tempting a comparison between his own life and ideas of religion, duty and honour: but his resources of wit are so inexhaustible that he makes these ideas seem to us for the moment mere abstractions, and he lies, steals, and shows the white feather in battle without exciting any moral indignation; yet, we would cut out the very heart of his wit if we took away the subtle contrast of his own occupations with a higher kind of life which he is always suggesting, though only remotely and in glimpses, as it were.

Falstaff is in a sense the heroic of comedy, the highest point to which comedy can go without ceasing to be merely comic. And it can only be maintained by a continual conflict with reality. The comic is a momentary existence like its expression laughter. It is a flash struck from the inconsistencies of life, and passes away as soon as it is born. To make it the substance and main material of life is as unnatural as would be the expression of a countenance distorted by a continual laugh. The Prince must abandon Falstaff when he is called to life's duties, hard as it may seem; and Shakespeare shows that wondrous sense of justice which is ever present to him, in his account of Falstaff's death, one of the most tragic things ever written.

There is a higher kind of comic than this, the humour that looks the truth full in the face. This is the humour that lives in Hamlet, in Jacques in "As You Like It," and in the Fool in "Lear,"—a humour in which the inconsistencies of man's life are not kept in the back-ground but clearly seen; but this humour is near allied to sadness and to tragedy, and easily passes over into it. Look at it on one side, and how absurd are the results of life, many a lost ideal merging into a caricature, many a high purpose bringing forth infinitesimal results. Look at it on the other side, and how sad it is that a great ideal or purpose should be so dwarfed and obscured and defeated by the means it has to use. Hence the peculiarity of the style of great humourists like Carlyle; in them sorrow is ever dissolving into laughter and laughter breaking down in tears. When man "plays his fantastic tricks before high heaven" he makes other men laugh but he "makes the angels weep." The humourist does both,—he laughs with one eye and weeps with the other.

Think of the wonderful pathos and humour of that description in Carlyle's French Revolution, of the morning dawn as it arose upon King Louis flying from Revolutionary France. What a mixture of crowding feelings of awe, pity, contempt and merriment we have in the abrupt rise and fall of the sense?—

"Midnight clangs from all the church steeples; one precious hour has been spent so; most mortals are asleep. The glass-coachman waits, and in what mood? A brother jarvie drives up, enters into conversation; is answered cheerfully in jarvie dialect; the brothers of the whip exchange a pinch of snuff, decline drinking together, and part with good-night. Be the Heavens blest, here at length is the Queen lady in gipsy hat; safe after perils; who has had to enquire her way. She too is admitted; her courier jumps aloft:—and now, O glass-coachman of a thousand—Count Fersen, for the reader sees it is thou —*drive!*"

"And so the royality of France is actually fled. This precious night, the shortest of the year, it flies and drives. . . . And so they rush there, not too impetuously—through the wood of Bondy :—over a Rubicon in their own and France's history. . . Great, though the future is all vague. O Louis, and this all round thee is the great slumbering earth (and overhead the great watchful Heaven) the slumbering wood of Bondy—where long-haired Childeric Donothing was struck through with iron, not unreasonably in a world like ours. Those high-peaked towers are the towers of Rainay, towers of wicked Orleans. All slumbers save the multiplex rustle of our new Berline. Loose skirted scarecrow of an herb-merchant with his ass and early greens toilsomely plodding seems the only creature we meet. But right ahead the great north-east sends up evermore his gray-brindled dawn; from dewy branch, birds here and there with short deep warble salute the coming sun. Stars fade out and galaxies, street lamps of the city of God. The universe, O my brothers, is flinging wide its portals for the Levee of the great High King. Thou, poor King Louis, farest nevertheless as mortals do, towards Orient lands of Hope: and the Tuileries with its levees, and France and the earth itself is but a larger kind of doghutch, occasionally going rabid."

Who shall tell us, to take another example, whether Jacques' great speech "All the world's a stage" is comic or tragic? It lies in the debateable territory, and combines both. It is as he calls it a "humorous sadness," or a "melancholy humour," that touches with a loving, pitying hand the strange inconsistencies of a being half sensual, half divine. The infinite pathos and humour that mingle in Hamlet's meditations in the grave-yard, as he dwells on and plays with the contrast of death and life, has its principal charm for us here. The most horrible details of corruption seem to take on a mist of unreality as we bring them into contact with the life and energy of the soul which once dwelt in what are now only the mortal remains of Yorick. "Where be your gibes now, your gambols, your songs, your flashes of merriment that were wont to set the table in a roar?"

Thus comedy in its deepest form passes into tragedy, humour into melancholy. "Look upon this picture and on that," and you will see that they are the same viewed from opposite sides. For what is tragedy but this same contrast between the ideal and the real, between the infinite passion, the aspiration, the dream and desire of human hearts, and the finite circumstance, the laws of things that hinder its realization? Let us look in conclusion at two of the great tragedies of Shakespeare, at Romeo and Juliet and Hamlet, and we will see how this great contrast varied, yet the same, is the centre of every truly tragic plot.

Romeo and Juliet is the tragedy of pure passion, of passion that does not regard or respect any of the limits or conditions which circumstance sets to it. This utter self-abandonment to passion—be it of revenge, of love or of grief, rules not only the principal characters but all the characters of the play. The humorous Mercutio, the fierce Tybalt, the passionate Juliet, are all alike in this that they follow without restraint the whim of the moment, heedless even if it is carrying them to destruction. The centre of this whirlpool is Romeo, who takes up into himself all the passions of the others, and from the beginning of the play to the end is driven like a ship by gales from all quarters. When we see him first he is already feeding on an imaginary passion, which seems to fill his fiery soul till a genuine love drives it out. Then as the tragedy proceeds, love, revenge, remorse, despair, seize on him, and drive him unreflecting, unhesitating to his doom. In this play we find that true spirit of lyric poetry in which the feeling of the moment makes all nature but its reflection and its voice. Shakespeare has thrown even a dash of extravagance into it, as if to mark that passion had burst its bars, and owned not even the ordinary laws of imagination.

> "But see, what light through yonder window breaks,
> It is the East and Juliet is the sun;
> Arise fair sun and kill yon envious moon
> Who is already sick and pale with grief."

This is the language of passion dead to everything but itself. It translates us into a world from which all reflection and prudence are cast out: where all the characters declare open war on the conditions of life, and regard the laws of nature no more than the laws of Verona. And the inevitable result follows: in the clash of jarring passions with each other and with the world's law there is ruin and shipwreck of these frail vessels of mortality. The friar gives already a presentiment of the issue in the words with which he greets Juliet,—

> "Here comes the Lady: O so light a foot
> Will ne'er wear out the everlasting flint."

And so it is. In the ideal world of lyric poetry pure passion may prevail and give its law to everything: but in the actual world it must wait for thought: else it will soon strike upon the everlasting flint, and beat out its life against it.

In Hamlet we find the same contrast of the real and the ideal from another side. If Romeo and Juliet is the tragedy of passion, this is the tragedy of thought. Hamlet is a civilized man amid a world of savages: a man of thought, ideas and refinement cast amid fierce passions and rude impulses. He rejoices in the play and encounter of wit with his companions, and uses every art to heighten the intellectual capabilities of every situation in which he finds himself. The violence and rudeness of his half barbarous country, "the oppressor's wrong, the proud man's contumely, the law's delay, the insolence of office, and the spurns that patient merit of the unworthy takes," are abhorrent to him. His highly cultivated nature instinctively hates everything that is rude and ferocious, and shrinks from action, because action to be effective in these barbarous surroundings must be arbitrary and violent. Conceive such a sensitive contemplative mind wounded by his father's death, wounded, offended, and scandalized still more by his mother's speedy marriage, revolting against such an act, quite as much on its æsthetic as on its moral side.

> "So excellent a prince that was to this
> Hyperion to a satyr."

He is disgusted with a world—"weary, stale, flat and

unprofitable"—where such things can be done. Then comes the ghost's appearance and its revelation, urging him to instant action—to the counter-murder of his father's murderer. For a while the sudden disclosure rouses the native force in him to vow that he will sweep to his revenge with wings "as swift as meditation, or the thoughts of love;" yet ere this burst is cold, he breaks down into unseemly merriment, and declares that a part has fallen to him which he loathes, and for which he is inadequate—

> "The world is out of joint. O cursed spite,
> That ever I was born to set it right."

Driven between doubts and conflicting scruples, he fears on the one hand to leave his father unavenged, while, on the other, he shrinks from the violent deed which alone can avenge him. There is no *ideal* course open to him, no course but that which cuts the knots of fate which it cannot untie. He looks to the escape of suicide, and rejects it only because it involves that same irrational barbarity of impulse which he hates. Refusing to condescend to any of those practical compromises with fact which action involves, he dreams, speculates, and argues: he becomes fatalistic, and calls it being guided by Providence to be guided by chance. "If it be now, 'tis not to come: if it be not to come, it will be now: if it be not now yet it will come." So he drifts, in his thought becoming grander, in his action more wayward, and his hesitations lead to worse results than the utmost violence. He does a thousand crimes because he could not resolve to quench his scruples to one, and finally falls amid the havoc of all that he loved as well as of all that he hated. In this tragedy we see at the highest point the contrast of the real and ideal, of the weakness and the strength of man. The warp and woof of life are, as it were, severed, and the difficulty of weaving them together in harmony is truly seen. How grand is the conception of man and his possibilities, and yet on what trifles are his destinies hung. "What a piece of work is man, how noble in reason, how infinite in faculty; in form and moving how express and admirable: in action how like an angel, in apprehension how like a god: the beauty of the world, the paragon of animals, and yet what *is* this quintessence of dust."

This is the great contrast which the tragic and comic drama alike bring out for us, the contrast of the mighty hopes and thought of man and the trifling circumstances out of which he has to build his life: and the truth of this contrast is the vindication of the morality of the Drama. It is the contrast that gives dignity both to life and art. Without the contrast of the higher life comedy sinks into the base form of farce: without the contrast of the lower necessities, tragedy becomes a mere cold picture of impossible virtues. And so we find in life that there is a kind of merriment which can never be serious; but this is found only in utterly vulgar and meaningless characters: and on the other hand there is a kind of ascetic virtue that can never relax or unbind, that ignores little things, that never confesses weakness in itself or pardons it in others. All honour to the ascetic character, it is high but not the highest. It is somewhat forced, unnatural, unlovely at the best. It has something unreal in it, something untrue to the nature of man. It tries to be greater than man and thereby it becomes less. For man's glory is not in unvarying, unbending will, nor in a purity that keeps itself apart from all the claims and entanglements of life, but in making these shadowy vapours of our existence the means of expressing a higher meaning. His is not a strength that rises above the possibility of weakness and fall, but it is his littleness that makes him great, his greatness that makes him feel so little.

IMITATION OF THE OLD BALLAD.

THE sun shines fair on Lowther side,
   Where burnies brattle to the sea,
The lambs they bleat, the cloughrets call,
   And the wind waves over moor and lea.
A broad moor lies on Lowther tops,
   Bleak and bare as ye may see;
There's moss and bent and wan water,
   But neither bield of stone nor tree.
High on that moor, where the wind and water shear,
   Is a cairn and cross of broken tree.
Under the mould lies the laird of Troloss,
   Catherine, his wife, and their bairnies three.
Ilka Sabbath morn to Durisdur kirkyard
   There gathers a goodly companye,

The shepherd lads are laughing, the shepherd lasses
    daffing,
Though the bell ring never so dolefully.
But they lie their lane where the winds make their
    mane,
Or ever and again the sun blinks bonnily,
Where out owre the bent the lamb bleats to the ewe,
And curlews pipe their lullaby.

FUGA TEMPORUM.

How rapidly the moments fly
    When pleasure wings with them along;
How slowly creep the seconds by
    When linked with loneliness or wrong.
As if the pleasure-laden hour
    Were of its moments due bereft,
To lengthen out the dreaded power
    Of weary seasons by the theft.
But though the mountain piled on high
    Seems cheated of its proper space,
It catches radiance from the sky,
    And lends the wider plain a grace.
O happy hours that fleet so fast,
    Flying before our sadder years,
'Tis yours to radiate the past,
    And with your sunshine gild our tears.

R. A. S.

PSALM CXXI.

I will lift up mine eyes unto the hills,
  from whence cometh my help.
My help cometh even from the Lord,
  who hath made heaven and earth.
He will not suffer thy foot to be moved,
  and he that keepeth thee will not sleep.
The Lord himself is thy keeper, the Lord
  is thy defence upon thy right hand.
So that the sun shall not burn thee by day,
  neither the moon by night.
The Lord shall preserve thee from all evil,
  yea it is even he that shall keep thy soul.
The Lord shall preserve thy going out and
  thy coming in, from this time forth for evermore.

PSALM CXXVII.

Except the Lord build the house, they labour in vain that build it: except the Lord keep the city, the watchman waketh but in vain. It is vain for you to rise up early, and to sit up late, to eat the bread of sorrows: for so he giveth his beloved in their sleep.

KING HENRY VIII. ACT 3, SC. 4. GRIFFITH.

At last with easy roads he came to Leicester,
Lodged in the abbey: where the reverend abbot,
With all his convent, honourably received him:
To whom he gave these words;—O Father abbot,
An old man, broken with the storms of state,
Is come to lay his weary bones among ye:
Give him a little earth for charity.

Ἀμβλέπω ὠγύγια προτὶ οὔρεα χεῖρας ἀνασχών,
ἔνθεν ἀοσσητὴρ ἦλθε καὶ ἄλλοτ' ἐμοί.
ἄγχι γὰρ ἄμμι πάρεστι πατὴρ ἀνδρῶν τε θεῶν τε,
γῆν ὁ στηρίξας, οὐρανίην τε θόλον.
οὐδ' ὅγ' ἐάσει σὸν πόδ' ὀλισθέμεν, οὐδ' ἠβαιόν·
οὐδέ ποτ' ἂν βρίζοι κεῖνος, ἀρωγὸς ἐών.
αὐτὸς γὰρ δαίμων σέο κήδεται, οὐδὲ μεγαίρει
αἰὲν ἀμύνεσθαι σοὶ παρὰ δεξιτερῇ.
τῷγ' οὔθ' ἡμερίη ἴς σε σφαλεῖ ἠελίοιο,
οὔτε σεληναίη νυκτερινῇσι βολαῖς.
τοῖός σ' ἀσκηθῆ τηρεῖ θεός. οὐδέ τις ἄλλος
σὸν βίον ὀρθώσει πάντ' ἄτερ ἀμπλακίης.
ὄρθριος εἴτ' ἐξεῖσθ', εἴθ' ἑσπέριος πάλιν ἥκεις,
ἐκ θεοῦ ἔρρωσαι νῦν τε καὶ ἐξοπίσω.

Μάτην γάρ, εἰ θέμεθλα μὴ βάλλει θεός,
πονοῦσιν οἱ βάλλοντες· εἴ τε μὴ πόλιν
σώζει θεός, φρουροῦσιν αἱ φρουραὶ μάτην.
καί σοι μάτην ἑῷον ἐξανεστάναι,
νύκτωρ δ' ἀγρυπνεῖν, κἀκ πόνων μεμαγμένα
φαγεῖν ἄλευρα· τῷ γὰρ εὐσεβεῖ θεὸς
εὕδοντι πέμπει δῶρον ἀφθόνῳ χερί.

Τέλος δὲ Δελφοὺς ἵκεθ' ἡσύχοις ὁδοῖς,
θεοῦ προσίκτωρ· ᾗ μιν αἰδοῖος γέρων
φίλως ἐδέξατ' αὐτός, οἵ τε πρόσπολοι·
οἷς ἠγόρευε τοιάδ'· ὦ πάτερ φίλε,
ἥκω γέρων ναυαγὸς ἐν σάλῳ πόλεως,
κάμνοντα δαρὸν γυῖα κοιμήσων ὕπνῳ·
ὑμεῖς δὲ λεπτὴν πρευμενεῖς κόνιν δότε.

OUR ENGLISH PROMETHEUS.

"Midst others of less note, came one frail form,
A phantom among men, companionless
As the last cloud of an expiring storm,
Whose thunder is its knell; he, as I guess,
Had gazed on Nature's naked loveliness,
Actœon-like, and now he fled astray
With feeble steps o'er the world's wilderness,
And his own thoughts, along that rugged way,
Pursued, like raging hounds, their father and their prey.

A pard-like spirit, beautiful and swift,
A love in desolation marked;—a Power
Girt round with weakness;

*   *   Of that crew
He came the last, neglected and apart;
A herd-abandoned deer, struck by the hunter's dart."

Such are the beautiful, sad words in which poor Shelley describes himself, and, taken in conjunction with what we know of his life, they give us the key note to his poetry. Through all those strange, misty, yet wondrously beautiful poems of his, with their sudden alternations of light and gloom, there runs a deep, real, undertone of sadness and despair—

"O world! O life! O time!
On whose last steps I climb,
Trembling at that where I had stood before;
When will return the glory of your prime!
No more—Oh, never more!

> Out of the day and night
> A joy has taken flight :
> Fresh spring, and summer, and winter hoar,
> Move my faint heart with grief, but with delight
> No more—Oh, never more !"

This is the burden of his song—the death's head continually peering out from under the chaplet of roses. It says much for Shelley that with all this infinite sorrow, that never ceased to darken his life, he never became morose. Like Hood—that Mark Tapley of literature—he was essentially an unselfish man, and his poetry, like the "Bridge of Sighs," is saturated with an intense humanity. Roughly speaking, Shelley's poems may be grouped under these four heads,—political, personal, dramatic, and lyric. Under the first of these (which might be more properly named politico-metaphysical) we shall treat of "Queen Mab," and the "Revolt of Islam." The former, if regard be had to the extreme youthfulness of its author, its rhythmical beauty of language, and imaginative splendour, must be ranked among the extraordinary efforts of poetic genius. More than one passage in it (noteably that one descriptive of a virtuous man, and the other in which the peacefulness of night and the horrors of war are contrasted) are unsurpassed by anything in his maturer writings. The following simile is very powerful,—

> "A brighter morn awaits the human day,
> When every transfer of earth's natural gifts
> Shall be a commerce of good words and works ;
> When poverty and wealth, the thirst of fame,
> The fear of infamy, disease, and woe,

> War with its million horrors, and fierce hell,
> Shall live but in the Memory of time,
> *Who, like a penitent libertine, shall start,
> Look back, and shudder at his younger years.*"

So much for the purely literary character of "Queen Mab;" regarded ethically it is beneath contempt. Commerce is called a "venal interchange;" religion is said to "people heaven with slaves;" vegetarianism is preached in eloquent words, and to the eating of flesh is attributed "all evil passions and all vain belief, the germs of misery, death, disease and crime;" chastity, "that virtue of the cheaply virtuous," is "dull and selfish;" and "no fetters of tyrannic law" are needed to "rivet with sensation's softest tie, the kindred sympathies of human souls!" Law and order, commerce and trade, monarchies and rulers, priests, religion and God, are attacked in no measured terms. But the being written of in "Queen Mab," under the name of "God," must be carefully distinguished from God himself. The former was a mere phantom of Shelley's diseased imagination, born of distorted notions concerning the world and religion. The plea of genius and difference of temperament as an excuse for looseness or eccentricity of life and thought, is always dangerous and nearly always unsatisfactory. It is extremely difficult to hit upon the exact point where a man's conduct becomes excusable, and where the excusableness—if we may be allowed the expression—ends, simply because he differs, or appears to differ, from ordinary men by reason of superior intellectual, or deficient moral, development. Yet it would be eminently unfair to Shelley, if, in trying to estimate the character of his life and writings, we were to be deterred by such considerations from giving due weight to his peculiar moral and intellectual nature, and the influence thereon of the special circumstances of his life and education. Shelley was not only a genius, but that of a very peculiar type. His nature, sympathies, upbringing, manners, and whole intellectual and moral being were as unlike those of any other man, or even poet whom we meet in life or read of in History, as can well be imagined.

Out of the false impressions of life and human nature which the unfortunate circumstances of his early education had given him, Shelley gradually and unconsciously evolved a false and one-sided system of Ethics. Left to himself by his parents to grope his way through the mysteries of religion and social life; seeing in schools and teachers but a vast system of tyranny and wrongdoing, the reflex as he thought of the tyranny and wrong of the outside world; taught in a cold, hard fashion that God was the master of all things, the punisher of all evil and the revealer of all good,—Shelley misapprehended the character and objects of providence, and in his unaided efforts to reconcile the existence of evil and eternal punishment with his own ideal of the Divine, his mind lost itself for a time in a hopeless entanglement of doubt, despair, and mis-not un-belief.* He began while at

* Mr. Dallas in his "Gay Science," evidently referring to Shelley *cum aliis* writes as follows. After remarking that "great poetry, if it shows some scepticism of current dogmas, is essentially religious in temper, and, in fact, often creates a religion," he goes on to say,—

College, or shortly before going there, to doubt the existence of a God at all, for belief in a God whose character was of the cold, unfeeling, and revengeful type which rightly or wrongly he supposed to be a tenet of the calvinistic creed, was impossible to a nature whose main characteristics were a passionate love of truth, mercy, and beauty, and a yearning after sympathy and responsive affection. The unfortunate circumstances of his later life, his expulsion from College and his mistress (who also jilted him on theological grounds), the treatment which he received from his kindred, his friendship with Godwin and Godwin's daughter, his runaway marriage, the evil influence of his sister-in-law, and the absence of any true friend possessing poetic sympathies, combined with sound liberal religious views and common sense,

"The names of infidel poets in this very century may be cited on the other side. But if we do not accept their infidelity, neither need we condemn it utterly. There was a hard mechanical theory of the world and its relations to the Deity prevalent in the earlier half of this century. The poets, whom we condemn for their scepticism, saw before them but two types of theology—theology in the cold-blooded school of Paley, reduced to a system of clever contrivances, with springs and pulleys, and most ingenious machinery; theology in the more ardent school of the Wesleys and the Whitfields, reduced to a system in which there was less of love and mercy than of hell and damnation. If thus in the earlier half of the century there flourished among us a mis-shapen theology, a clockmaking theory of the universe, which represented the Almighty as a sempiternal Sam Slick, hard of heart, but of infinite acuteness and softness of sawder, those are not wholly to be blamed who revolted against the creed *because in their zeal they carried the revolt too far.*"—*The Gay Science*, vol. 2, pp. 220-1.

to advise and steady him—all served to confirm these
erroneous impressions of his youth. It can hardly be
maintained that Shelley at any period of his life actually
disbelieved in or denied the existence of a God. What
he did deny was the existence of such a God as the followers of Calvin believed in. Shelley fell into the error of
generalising hastily and from insufficient data. When he
wrote "Queen Mab" he was but a boy, passionate, earnest,
sceptical, and in the first terrible recoil of his young and
sensitive soul from the sins and sorrows of mankind, and
the prevailing theology of the times in which there was
much of hell and little of heaven, he wrote this mad protest against a system and docrine which he considered to
be so fraught with evil. That he recognised the necessity
and even then believed in the existence of an all-powerful
and all-wise being, over-ruling and guiding all things, is
evident from his frequent allusions to the Spirit of
Nature: which term he employed to distinguish his own
idea of the Almighty from the false God of the extreme
Calvinists. That this was so is confirmed by what he
himself writes in his preface to the Revolt of Islam.
"The erroneous and degrading idea which men have
conceived of a supreme Being is spoken against, but not
the supreme Being itself. The belief which some superstitious persons whom I have brought upon the stage
entertain of the Deity as injurious to the character of
his benevolence, is widely different from my own."
Writing even in 1811 he says,—"Before we deny or
believe the existence of any thing, it is necessary that
we should have a tolerably clear idea of what it is. The

word 'God'—a vague word—has been, and will continue to be, the source of numberless errors, until it is erased from the nomenclature of philosophy. Does it not imply the 'soul of the universe, the intelligent and necessarily beneficent, actuating principle?' This it is impossible not to believe in, though I may not be able to adduce proofs, but I think that the leaf of a tree, the meanest insect on which we trample, are, in themselves, arguments more conclusive than any which can be advanced, that some vast intellect animates infinity, and it is the future punishment which I can most readily believe in."

Ten years later (1821) we find him writing these beautiful lines in " Hellas."—

> "A power from the unknown God ;
>   A Promethean conqueror came ;
> Like a triumphal path he trod
>   The thorns of death and shame.
>   A mortal shape to him
>   Was like the vapour dim,
> Which the orient planet animates with light ;
>   Hell, sin, and slavery came
>   Like bloodhounds wild and tame,
> Nor preyed until their Lord had taken flight.
>   The moon of Mahomet
>   Arose, and it shall set :
> While blazoned as on heaven's immortal noon
>   The Cross leads generations on.
>
> Swift as the radiant shapes of sleep
>   From one whose dreams are paradise,
> Fly when the fond wretch wakes to weep,
>   And day peers forth with her blank eyes :

> So fleet, so faint, so fair,
> The powers of earth and air
> Fled from the folding star of Bethlehem:
> Apollo, Pan, and Love,
> And even Olympic Jove,
> Grew weak, *for killing Truth had glared on them.*
> Our hills, and seas, and streams,
> Dispeopled of their dreams,
> Their waters turned to blood, their dew to tears,
> Wailed for the golden years."

Here we have a distinct recognition of the truth of the gospel, though still clouded with much error. Yet even this acknowledgment shows a great advance.

"Queen Mab" is mainly interesting now as representing one of the stages, and that among the first, through which the fiery young soul swept in its blind search after truth. Only a few years after its publication its author disavowed the sentiments contained in it as explicitly as possible: expressing his regret at having published it, and his resolution never to recognise, although he was too honest to disown, it. As to the alleged danger of allowing such a poem to remain in any collected Edition of the poet's works—it is purely imaginary. Necessity (Spirit of Nature), the cold, atheistical Goddess of the young enthusiast, is about as likely to win worshippers as the statues of Apollo and Diana. We cannot sympathise with those indiscriminating moralists who would condemn the poet and his poetry, *en masse*, on account of one or more such poems as "Queen Mab." Shelley was an intensely honest man, and we consider it no disgrace to him that he declared boldly opinions to which a passionate love of truth first led him, and from which the same devotion caused him to depart. If a man is possessed of a great truth (or what he honestly believes to be a great truth), let him out with it. If true, it benefits the world and himself; if false, it finds its level and educes fresh truths by the discussion it provokes. The cause of truth is oftener harmed by timid silence than by honest outspokenness. The great question is not, "Is what this man says true or false?" but, "Is it said honestly?" Does he speak or write from a sincere conviction that his words are those of truth, and will do good, or is he animated by a mean desire for fame or a little brief notoriety? If the man be honest he is bound to speak, whether his thoughts be true or false. To him meantime they are true—time will settle the rest. An eloquent writer referring to Shelley says, "The infinite nature of duty was still dimly present to him; living without God in the world, of God's light he was not utterly bereft. It was this saving principle which led him onwards, by a slow and interrupted, but certain transition, from subjective to objective religious feeling—from his former search for a Deity within the mind, to the sense, although vague and unconfined, of His personal and independent being."

Of the "Revolt of Islam" we shall say little, for while containing many passages and isolated thoughts of surpassing beauty, it is yet, by reason of its metaphysical obscurity, exaggeration, and want of human interest, very unsatisfactory. We have here, as in much of Shelley's poetry, a confused and gorgeous panorama of life and death, right and wrong, genius and liberty, heaven and hell, all blended, or rather huddled, together in a weird dance of words. Shelley is to poetry what Turner is to painting. In some of his most ambitious efforts, what with the profusion of imagery, brilliancy of colour, and oppressive richness of thought, all enveloped in clouds of misty transcendentalism, it is difficult to make sure of anything but the obscurity. Much of this was doubtless owing to the poet's fertility of mind. Shelley was literally crushed beneath a weight of thought, which not unfrequently mastered his power of expression—itself wonderful. His poetry, like his life, was marred by a want of repose. The mind's eye is pained with excess of splendour. His long poems are a continuous riot and fever of ideas, and are full of gaps. Thoughts rushed upon him like an avalanche, crushing the thinker beneath them, and leaving him panting and hopeless of overtaking them. Hence the feverish haste with which he wrote—like one possessed. If at a loss—as continually happened—for a word, he seldom paused to search for one, but, leaving a blank to be filled up at the "some time" that never came, hurried on.

Of his subjective and personal poems "Alastor" and "Prince Athanase" are the most important, as being attempts by the poet to depict his own character and life. The former, to use Shelley's words, is "allegorical of one of the most interesting situations of the human mind." It represents a youth of purity and genius, led forth by an inflamed imagination to study nature. He drinks deep of the fountains of knowledge, and is still insatiate. He is profoundly impressed with the beauty and grandeur of the external world, and so long as it is possible for his desires to point towards objects thus infinite and unmeasured, he is happy. But the time comes when these objects cease to suffice. His mind is seized with a yearning for intercourse with an intelligence similar to itself. He images the Being whom he loves, and clothes his ideal with all beauty and wisdom and virtue. For this his prototype he seeks in vain, and, blasted by disappointment, sinks to an early grave. The poem is in Shelley's best style, and "beautiful exceedingly." In it we have a picture, only too prophetic, of the author himself—the boy-poet thirsting with a divine thirst after immortal truth and beauty, and, after much sorrow and infinite pain, perishing just as his lips are about to kiss the heavenly chalice. "Prince Athanase" is inferior to "Alastor" in artistic beauty, but presents us with a still closer description of the poet, with pointed allusions to his youthful sorrows and domestic afflictions.

Of his dramatic writings it is only necessary to refer to the "Cenci." Shelley's genius was as paradoxical as his character. That the imaginative faculty is inborn, we know; but how the dramatic talent can be acquired intuitively—demanding, as it does, for its development, knowledge of the world, familiarity with the feelings and pursuits of men, and experience of the passions—is less evident. The characters in the "Revolt of Islam" are mere abstractions, lay-figures on which to hang political and metaphysical theories. Their want of individuality made it seem unlikely to readers, otherwise unacquainted with Shelley, that he could be dramatic. That he did, however, possess dramatic talent, and that of all but the highest order, is amply proved by the "Cenci," of which it is difficult to speak in terms of sufficient praise or blame. For masterly delineation of character, powerful breadth of effect, careful discrimination between infinitely varying shades of the same affection, general grasp of subject, severe simplicity of style, and imaginative strength, the "Cenci" is quite unrivalled in modern dramatic literature, and for its equal we must go back to the works of the great dramatist himself. Of its minor beauties the portrayal of the hesitation of the two intending murderers is admirable.

"Your cheeks are pale," says Marzio to his comrade in a terrified whisper.

"It is the white reflection of your own
Which you call pale,"

is the reply. So also the description of the banqueters on hearing Cenci call on them to rejoice with him over the death of his two sons. Several of the guests rise, threateningly, and

"Every one looks in his neighbour's face
To see if others are as white as he."

Just before the Count announces his sons' death, Beatrice is smit with sudden terror at seeing him so joyous and affable, and whispers to her mother in an agony of fear—

"My blood runs cold.
I fear that wretched laughter round his eye
Which wrinkles up the skin even to the hair."

But while admitting the great merits of the drama, we cannot help regretting the choice of subject and method of treatment. The plot is repulsive, turning, as it does, on a nameless and unnatural crime. Horrors are piled on horrors to such a degree that even the character of Beatrice, nobly as it is conceived, affords no relief or contrast to the universal gloom of the tragedy. The story, we are aware, is historically true. Count Cenci, Beatrice, and the other leading characters did actually exist at some remote period in Venetian history. But though historically true, it is æsthetically false. A poet should deal with the grand characteristics of human nature—his personages should be not only true to one chapter of history, but to the general tenor of all history. They should be real, actual representatives, not of exceptions but of classes, and should recommend themselves to the reader's mind as natural embodiments of such intellectual and moral qualities as he himself is acquainted with, or his experience or instinct has prepared him to accept as natural. The poet has no more right to depict the actions and passions of an inhumanly sensual and brutal man than the sculptor has to spend his strength in carving monsters, remarkable only for their ugliness. Beauty refines and educates; deformity repels and disgusts. The dramatist may teach and ennoble by contrasting virtue with vice, but neither the vice nor the virtue must be extreme. Ideally good heroes are insipid; villains of unnatural baseness are repulsive. It may be true (though we take leave to doubt it) that Count Cenci was possessed of so unnatural a hatred towards his two sons as to invite his friends to a feast in joyous celebration of their death, but that is no excuse for Shelley seizing on the circumstance and weaving it into the thread of his story. The legitimate object of the dramatist is to hold up the mirror to nature, and bring its general features into bold relief. When therefore he steps aside to search for exceptional monstrosities, he is untrue to himself and to the art of which he is an exponent. Yet with all these defects the drama is a very noble one. No one beginning to read it, and getting into the fierce vortex of passion and thought, can help reading it through. The awful speed and certainty with which events hurry on to the fatal night in the castle take away one's breath. The reader is like the doomed men in Poe's story of the Mælstrom, who have incautiously allowed themselves to drift into the dangerous current, and are now being hurried with ever-increasing velocity to inevitable death.

So much for Shelley's dramatic powers. The best known of his shorter poems are, "The Cloud," "Arethusa," "Lines written in dejection at Naples," "Adonäis," "The Sensitive Plant," "Mount Blanc," "Among the Euganæan Hills," "Hymn to Liberty," and the "Skylark." He is perhaps most widely and popularly known by the last of these, and may be said—if our readers will pardon the conceit—to have soared to heaven on the wings of a skylark. Each line is rich with melody, and the metre —the four short, tripping lines, ending in the full, long swell of the alexandrine—has a peculiarly fine effect. Like many artists in different departments, Shelley not unfrequently achieved most where he attempted least. It is not after all the longest poems that have the longest lives. A "Scots wha hae" by Burns, a "Song of the Shirt" by Hood, or a "Cry of the Children" by Mrs. Browning—some unpremeditated snatch of song welling up spontaneously in a happy moment from the deep, immortal springs of human nature—has often done as much as even our noblest epics to refine the thoughts, and touch the sympathies of the common people.

There are not many, even of his admirers, who are acquainted with Shelley's prose writings. These are few in number and fragmentary in character, but their purity of style and vigorous fertility of thought sufficiently attest that had Shelley cared he might have ranked alongside our best prose writers. The few Essays of his that remain are singularly pure, noble, and flexible in style, rich in suggestive thought, and abounding in passages of surpassing eloquence. His "Defence of Poetry" alone, though comprising only a few pages, proves the truth of what we have advanced. Not so sweet, or perfect in arrangement or indeed as an artistic whole—it is only a fragment—as Sir Philip Sidney's essay on the same subject, it is yet more vigorous—stronger both in thought and language. We can afford space only for a brief quotation or two,—

"Poetry is indeed something divine. It is at once the centre and circumference of knowledge; it is that which comprehends all science, and that to which all science must be referred. . . A man cannot say, 'I will compose poetry.' The greatest poet even cannot say it; for the mind in creation is as a fading coal, which some invisible influence, like an inconstant wind, awakens to transitory brightness; this power arises from within, like the colour of a flower which fades and changes as it is developed, and the conscious portions of our natures are unprophetic either of its approach or its departure. Could this influence be durable in its original purity and force, it is impossible to predict the greatness of the results; but *when composition begins, inspiration is already on the decline*, and the most glorious poetry that has ever been communicated to the world is probably a feeble shadow of the original conceptions of the poet. I appeal to the greatest poets of the present day, whether it is not an error to assert that the finest passages of poetry are produced by labour and study. . . This instinct and intuition of the poetical faculty is still more observable in the plastic and pictorial arts; a great statue or picture grows under the power of the artist as a child in the mother's womb; and the very mind which directs the hands in formation is incapable of accounting to itself for the origin, the gradations, or the medià of the process.

"Poetry is the record of the best and happiest moments of the best and happiest minds. We are aware of evanescent visitations of thought and feeling sometimes associated with place or person, sometimes regarding our own mind alone, and always arising unforeseen, and departing unbidden, but elevating and delightful beyond all expression: so that even in the desire and regret they leave, there cannot but be pleasure, participating as it does in the nature of its object. It is as it were the interpretation of a diviner nature through our own; but its footsteps are like those of a wind over the sea, which the coming calm erases, and whose traces remain only, as on the wrinkled sand which paves it."

"Poets are not only subject to these experiences as spirits of the most refined organisation, but they can colour all that they combine with the evanescent hues of this ethereal world; a word, a trait in the representation of a scene or a passion, will touch the enchanted chord, and reanimate, in those who have ever experienced these emotions, the sleeping, the cold, the buried image of the past. Poetry thus makes immortal all that is best and most beautiful in the world; it arrests the vanishing apparitions which haunt the interlunations of life, and veiling them, or in language or in form, sends them forth among mankind, bearing sweet news of kindred joy to those with whom their sisters' abide—abide, because there is no portal of expression from the caverns of the spirit which they inhabit into the universe of things. *Poetry redeems from decay the visitations of the divinity in man.*"

"Poetry turns all things to loveliness; it exalts the beauty of that which is most beautiful, and it adds beauty to that which is most deformed; it marries exultation and horror, grief and pleasure, eternity and change; it subdues to union, under its light yoke, all irreconcileable things. It transmutes all that it touches, and every form moving within the radiance of its presence is changed by wondrous sympathy to an incarnation of the spirit which it breathes, and its secret alchemy turns to potable gold the poisonous waters which flow from death through life; it strips the veil of familiarity from the world, and lays bare the naked and sleeping beauty, which is the spirit of its forms. . . . Poetry defeats the curse which binds us to be subjected to the accident of surrounding impressions. And whether it spreads its own figured curtain or withdraws life's dark veil from before the scene of things, it equally creates for us a being within our being. . . . It reproduces the common universe of which we are portions and percipients, and it purges from our inward sight the film of familiarity which obscures from us the wonder of our being."

"Poets are the unacknowledged legislators of the world."

Speaking of his own times he writes—

"We let, '*I dare not* wait upon *I would*, like the poor cat i' the adage.' We want the creative faculty to imagine that which we know; we want the generous impulse to act that which we imagine; we want the poetry of life; our calculations have outrun conception; *we have eaten more than we can digest*. The cultivation of those sciences which have enlarged the limits of the empire of man over the external world, has, for want of poetical faculty, proportionally circumscribed those of the internal world; *and man having enslaved the elements, remains himself a slave.*"

"The true poetry of Rome lived in its institutions; for whatever of beautiful, true, and majestic, they contained, could have sprung only from the faculty which creates the order in which they consist. The life of Camillus, the death of Regulus, &c., &c. . . . These things are not the less poetry *quia carent vate sacro*. They are the episodes of that cyclic poem written by Time upon the memories of men. The Past, like an inspired rhapsodist, fills the theatre of everlasting generations with harmony."

"The imagination is enlarged by a sympathy with pains and passions so mighty, *that they distend in their conception the capacity of that by which they are conceived.*"

"Even in modern times no living poet ever arrived at the fulness of his fame; the jury which sits in judgment upon a poet, belonging as he does to all time, must be composed of his peers: it must be impanelled by Time from the selectest of the wise of many generations."

"A poem is the very image of life expressed in its eternal truth."

Shelley's merits and defects as a writer are soon told. His main excellencies are vivid imagination, rare delicacy of taste, great powers of thought, dramatic talent of a high order and marvellous command of language, all united to a passionate, though ill regulated, love of truth. Shelley is the most poetical of poets. In exquisite sensibility to external influences he is unsurpassed, and he sympathised with nature's ever varying moods as only Wordsworth among his contemporaries could sympathise. Impersonation of natural objects is a leading feature of his poetical diction, as it is, in a less degree, of that of the author of the "Excursion." Natural objects are commonly used to illustrate the phenomena of human life. In Shelley's poetry these phenomena become attributes of the objects themselves. Perhaps the most powerful, certainly the most painful instance of this feature to be found,—we had almost said in the language, is the following from the "Cenci."

> "Two miles on this side of the fort, the road
> Crosses a deep ravine ; 'tis rough and narrow,
> And winds with short turns down the precipice ;
> And in its depths there is a mighty rock,
> Which has, from unimaginable years,
> Sustained itself with terror and with toil
> Over a gulf, and with the agony
> With which it clings seems slowly coming down ;
> Even as a wretched soul hour after hour
> Clings to the mass of life ; yet, clinging, leans ;
> And, leaning, makes more dark the dread abyss
> In which it fears to fall : beneath this crag
> Huge as despair, as if in weariness,
> The melancholy mountain yawns—below,
> You hear but see not an impetuous torrent
> Raging among the caverns, and a bridge
> Crosses the chasm ;"

In thus idealizing the real, and investing the material universe with a soul and voice, Shelley has to a certain extent anticipated the Philosophy of Emerson and Walt Whitman.* Another feature of his poetry is profusion of imagery. An intellectual millionaire, he squanders his riches with splendid prodigality. Here is no stinginess— every one is welcome. He was ever ready to assist his

---

* The following sentences from "A Defence of Poetry" might have been written by Emerson.

"The great secret of morals is love ; or a going out of our own nature, and an identification of ourselves with the beautiful which exists in thought, action, or person, not our own. A man, to be

friends in their literary undertakings, and Trelawney informs us how much Byron was indebted to him. There was nothing of the miser about Shelley poetically or morally. Earth, heaven and hell, the stores of classic learning, the mines of German thought, the repositories of the wit and wisdom of all nations—are ransacked for images. The universe pays tribute to his muse.

We have already referred to his command of language. The most delicate shades of thought are expressed with the nicest precision,—the words fitting into the sense as mist into the crannies of a rock. He only fails where, through very wantonness of strength, or a vain effort to express an infinitely fine abstraction which eludes the most delicate mesh of words, he attempts the impossible. Take the following as examples of delicate expression.

> "There late was one, within whose subtle being,
> As light and wind within some delicate cloud
> That fades amid the blue noon's burning sky,
> Genius and death contended."

Of a lady wasted by grief he writes—

> "Her hands were dim, and thro' their wandering veins
> And weak articulations might be seen
> Day's ruddy light."

greatly good, must imagine intensely and comprehensively; *he must put himself in the place of another and of many others;* the pains and pleasures of his species must become his own."

Take also the line from "Queen Mab,"—

> "Yet every heart contains perfection's germ,"

as well as the passionate deification of nature that characterises his poetry.

Or the following from "Adonäis," where he describes the mourners over the grave of Keats—

"All he had loved, and moulded into thought
From shape, and hue, and odour, and sweet sound,
Lamented Adonäis—Morning sought
Her eastern watch-tower, and her hair unbound,
Wet with the tears which should adorn the ground,
Dimmed the aërial eyes that kindle day ;
Afar the melancholy thunder moaned,
Pale ocean in unquiet slumbers lay,
And the wild winds flew round, sobbing in their dismay."

Shelley's defects as a poet were many, but might almost all be resolved into what after all was the main defect of his life—want of precision. His genius was great but wanted balance. The most poetical of poets he was also the most impulsive of men. His mind recoiled from hard lines and set rules, giving itself wholly up to the whim of the moment. Fancy and a "most sweet disorder" were his taskmistress. The passion of his life was intellectual Beauty.

"Spirit of Beauty!" he cries, "I vowed that I would dedicate my powers to thee and thine!"

His language, generally so apt and musical, is yet often disfigured by harsh collocations, and such unpoetical words as "consentaneous," "hyperequatorial," "uglification," and the like. In the matter of pronunciation he is wilfully perverse, and he too frequently affects the worst faults of the Cockney school. As a thinker, he despised antiquity and swore by whatever was novel. Nothing that was old—nothing that was venerable—was sacred to him; while the most fantastic theory, if it had but novelty to recommend it, was readily adopted. A severe logician, he was yet too impulsive to reason well, and, woman-like, was given to hasty generalisations. We have left ourselves no room to discuss the influence which the French Revolution exercised on Shelley and his brother poets—an influence which inspired Wordsworth to write his sublimest sonnet. Its dawn was to Shelley full of infinite promise of life and liberty—its sudden and terrible collapse powerfully tinged the whole current of his thoughts. Its awful shadow was ever around him, and cowering wistfully in the shade he tuned his lyre to immortal song.

With all his great dramatic talent it is doubtful if he could ever have risen to the first rank of dramatists. His writings and life prove him to have been destitute of humour. He might have given us Hamlet, but Falstaff never: poor Shelley was too terribly in earnest to be witty. His influence on contemporary and succeeding poets can hardly be over-estimated. Keats adored him, and his friend repayed him by composing in his honour the most sublime In Memoriam (excepting perhaps Tennyson's) in the language. Hunt, who loved Keats much, loved Shelley more. Trelawney, the cool unsentimental man of the world, was captivated by the charms of his manner and the modesty of his character. Byron deferred to him alone of all men. Coleridge, after once meeting him, acknowledged the goodness of his heart. A beautiful lady, wealthy and well-connected, renounced her husband and home to follow him round the world, and on his refusing with all tenderness to allow her to accompany him, died of a broken heart; while Medwin, Scott, Hobhouse, Smith, Lamb, and a host of others, unite in praising him. Though for a long time, as he himself once mournfully said, he could count the number of his readers on his fingers, and had to stint himself in bread to pay the printer, there was always a choice band of thinkers who appreciated his poetry. Every second-rate versifier reviled him in public, and stole from him in private, nor is it too much to say that whilst he himself was little indebted to others, all succeeding poets have been largely indebted to him. Bailey and Tennyson have studied him deeply, and in not a few of the Laureate's shorter poems we catch the airy ring of the "Skylark" and the rippling music of the "Cloud." Though not a sensationalist himself, Shelley was the real founder of the sensational school of poetry, one phase of which found its apotheosis in the works of Smith and Dobell—the other and more objectionable side in those of Algernon Charles Swinburne. Shelley's life was inspired by the noblest spirit of humanity. His constant cry was "Liberty." He reminds us of an imprisoned God shrieking for more air. As he himself once said, he had a passion for reforming. His appearance and dress betrayed the democrat. He could brook restraint in nothing—neither in politics nor in dress. His throat was bare, his waistcoat open, his neckcloth loose, and his hat, when he walked the fields, tossed aside. He was whimsically generous, granting one time an annuity of £100, and on another giving £20 towards a subscription to liberate Leigh Hunt, when the giving of it left him without a penny. He was extremely modest and loveable. English people, Trelawney informs us, who had taken up the idea that he was a sort of monster, were instantly captivated by the charms of his manner on meeting him abroad; and Byron, who never loved anybody but himself, loved him. Gilfillan has called him the "immortal youth," and the expression is happy. To the last day of his life Shelley was but a boy. His face—despite the marks that sorrow had set there—never lost its intensely youthful appearance. It seemed as if, like his verse, he never could grow old.

Every man is more or less a bundle of contradictions. Shelley was eminently so. An enigma to his own age, and to none more so than to his friends, he will remain an enigma to all times. So courteous and polished in his manners that authorities in etiquette pronounced him the most perfect gentleman in England, he was yet often sullen, and disagreeable,—breaking the most pressing engagements, and rushing from a crowded drawing-room in shrieks of laughter; shrinking from the sight of everything cruel and unlovely, yet when he took up a newspaper—which was seldom—skipping everything but the paragraph devoted to murders and disasters; of an extremely loveable disposition and tender heart, yet by his thoughtless conduct precipitating the death of the woman he had sworn to protect and love: loving his species, yet kind and forbearing towards individuals; actuated by the sincerest regard for truth and the happiness of his fellows, yet miserable in himself and the cause of misery to others; honourable and honest in all things, yet delighting at times in telling the most improbable stories; these and many other contradictory qualities combine to form one of the strangest characters in History. Absolute impartiality on the part of a biographer is a rare—we might add—an impossible virtue. In criticism above all things it is difficult to preserve the golden mean. It is doubly difficult in the case of Shelley. The author of "Queen Mab" is either praised or blamed, according as men do or do not sympathise with his opinions. To those who, admiring the beauties of his poetry and the many charms of his character, are yet alive to his moral defects, the task of pronouncing judgment upon Shelley is a hard and unpleasant one. No good, however, can result from a perversion or retention of truth, and Shelley has suffered more from the extravagant defences of his admirers than from the exaggerated detraction of his foes. Much that he wrote and did amiss may be excused on various grounds. He was not the first poet whose views on matrimony were the reverse of orthodox, for Milton a century previous had advocated, with all the eloquence of an interested party, the advantages of polygamy, and shown up the inconveniences which often result from a too binding social tie. Many of his errors must be pardoned on the ground of peculiarities of training and character, and indeed his faults were more of the intellect than of the heart; but we cannot honestly acquit him of blame in his conduct towards his first wife. His relations assert that they possess proofs of his innocence in this matter, but until

these are published we must be excused laying at any-
rate the larger share of blame on the husband. We do
not find fault with him for holding what are generally
considered to be loose opinions on social subjects, and
especially on that of marriage, believing as we do that
he held them honestly; but after allowing him every
indulgence we cannot help characterising his conduct to
Harriet Westbrooke as thoughtless and unfeeling. That
her tragic death affected him powerfully there is little
doubt. A spirit of unrest and settled melancholy took
possession of him, and not until the blue waters of the
Spezzian gulf closed over him did the unhappy poet find
that peace for which during life he had yearned. It is an
ungracious task, however, to cast stones at one at whom
so many have been cast, and after acknowledging the
witchery of the song to revile the singer. Let us rather
call to mind the many charms of his character—his
unaffected modesty—the warmth and impulsive generosity
of his nature—his child-like simplicity and intense unsel-
fishness—the splendour of his genius—his zeal for truth,
and the terrible sorrows that marred and wasted his young
life, and judge leniently one who, if he sinned grievously
at times, was greatly sinned against. Had Shelley
survived a few years longer, we doubt not he would have
redeemed the follies of his youth, and it is a matter of
profound regret not to us only, but to all coming ages,
that just as a prospect of brighter days dawned upon
him, and his apprehension of matters, social and spiritual,
had become more clear and promised to become more
settled, he should have perished so suddenly, with all

the crude error of much that he had said and written unrecanted, and the brilliant promise of his maturer intellect unfulfilled.

J. F.

LET'S LOVE WHILE LOVE WE MAY.

THE year is fast a-dying
   The while we laugh and sing,
And Time is swiftly flying
   With Summer on its wing.
The flowers wade deep in dew, love,
   Spring doth not last for aye,
While yet these hearts beat true, love,
   Let's love while love we may.

As we, my girl, grow older
   This face will lose its charm,
Divided hearts grow colder,
   While wedded hearts keep warm.
These locks will soon be grey, girl,
   These roses pale and die,
The Gods abide for aye, girl,
   So do not you and I.

But give, sweet heart, the keeping
   Of thy young self to me,
And the years we'll set a-sleeping,
   And the world we'll let a-be.

I do not plead in vain, love,
    You will not say me nay—
Ho! let the Seasons wane, love,
    And love while love we may.

AUTUMN.

I LOVE the Season when the corn-fields bright
    Are reaped and gathered in.
I love the Season when the low sun's light
    Is sifted pale and thin.
When the clear atmosphere is purely bright,
    The turbid heats gone by;
When winds are cool, and the thin curl-clouds white
    Hang deep within the sky.
The labouring circle of the year is done,
    And rest is come for all;
The weary winds have well-nigh ceased to run,
    The last red leaves to fall.
And when the gentle day is gently sped,
    The Moon comes out on high,
Full, silvery, round, a queen in the Sun's stead
    Within the tranquil sky.
And heaven and earth beneath her glances glow
    With magic misty light,
She floats in blue, with Jupiter below,
    The planet most of might.

And meditation lifts her grave bold eye,
And with suspended breath
Thinks almost to have found in musings high
The keys of life and death.

SPINOZA.

THE MAN AND HIS SYSTEM.

"THE most monstrous scheme imaginable, and the most diametrically opposed to the clearest notions of the mind —which has been fully overthrown even by the weakest of its adversaries." Such is the judgment of Bayle, quoted with approval by a modern authority, regarding a system which, more nearly than any other, is the true centre of modern thought. For Spinoza seems to stand midway between Plato and Hegel in the development of human thought. His notion of "Substance" is more elastic and more subtle than Plato's "Idea," less vague, if less comprehensive than Hegel's "Absolute." Disciplined by his strict logic, the Modern can explore with a more discerning and appreciative view the depths of Greek speculation, and braced by his pure clear thought he can rise freer to view the heights of German Metaphysics. Spinoza may not answer our questions fully, but he teaches us to put them clearly.

The incidents of his life are not numerous but they are noteworthy, as proving, better than most, how closely the man's life is connected with the thinker's doctrine—how empty a thing philosophy is, if separated from the experiences it formulates.

Baruch or Benedict de Spinoza was born in Amsterdam in November, 1632. He was the son of a Portuguese Jew, who gave him a liberal education. At an early age he was entrusted to the hands of the Rabbis of his Synagogue, by whom he was instructed in the Talmud and other text books of Jewish orthodoxy, with such explanations as had hitherto sufficed for the requirements of their pupils. Spinoza's questions, however, trenched on ground they had never found it necessary to investigate; and, like many teachers, more disposed to support the dignity of their office by stopping questions than to glorify it by answering them, the rabbis merely shook their heads and wondered how he might turn out. It is little wonder that the honest, earnest-souled Spinoza got disgusted with these retailers of borrowed phrases, who had no food for his hungry soul save the dry husks of empty formula, which seemed to satisfy themselves. But to the orthodox Jews it was no excuse for absenting himself from ordinances pronounced by the authorities to be proper for all, that Spinoza found them to himself personally profitless; when therefore arguments, entreaties, and even bribes had been tried in vain to induce him to conform, in act, to what he felt in his heart to be worthless and a sham, he was solemnly excommunicated with all the direful ceremonies proper to that rite. Spinoza did not, however, wither under the terrible denunciation, though all the pomp of Jewish ritual had contributed to its terrors, but calmly betook himself to the performance of daily duty for the provision of daily bread in the service of Frances Van den Ende, a learned physician who kept a school for the better class of young Dutchmen. Not only did he live, he dared to love, and the daughter of his master smiled not unkindly on his suit. And now, if fate had not interfered, Spinoza might in all human probability have become a comfortable and respectable burgher, with no great need to satisfy, and no sharp spur to urge him on to grapple with the mystery of life, and wring from thought an answer to his misery. Amsterdam would have possessed an able schoolmaster and an accomplished mathematician, but the world might have lost the clearest statement of human doubts, and the most perfect demonstration of all that logic can do for these, that it has been given to this or any age to see. If Spinoza had had his way it seems probable that fireside duties would have satisfied his heart; for human ambition had no place in his simple nature, and, content with cherishing his wife and guiding his children to their Father in Heaven in the wholesome comfort of a happy home, he would never have felt the burning misery which consumed his own soul, that it might illuminate the world. But things had been otherwise ordered, and his betrothed, tempted by the dazzle of a richer match, forgot her promise to the poor teacher, and became the bride of a Hamburgh merchant.

An outcast from his home, friendless, alone, his big heart bursting with its sense of wrong, with none near to hear his plaint or to speak soft words to soothe his torture, Spinoza retired to privacy and quiet to grind lenses for his daily food, and to settle as he best could the turmoil of thoughts and necessities which raged in his breast. Nor yet did he become a morbid sceptic or a moping misanthrope, for we learn that though for the most part he avoided society he was ever gentle and courteous to those who were brought into contact with him, and loved in the intervals of his leisure to gather little children around him, to amuse them with pleasant stories, or to touch their young hearts with a sense of the solemnity of life as he admonished them to love one another and reverence their parents, or spoke to them of their Father in Heaven, to whom they might some day go, if they were good and faithful. One staggers at the mystery of life as he ponders the strange spectacle of a man so utterly cut off from all the joys of his fellows from no fault of his, but seemingly only that he might be the better fitted to do his appointed work, in the reward of which all the world was to share. Yet such is the way we find in every age the world's great workers fitted for their task, for "fate manages its great thinkers as men do singing birds; you overhang the cage of the singer and make it dark, till at length he has caught the tunes you play to him and can sing them rightly." "What indeed is pain to a true man but as that of piercing the ears is to a maiden, and God hangs jewels in the wounds."

And not only was he thus prepared for his work; just look at the conditions under which he had to do it. Other philosophers have discussed their theories with admiring friends, and been cheered by their sympathy and benefitted by their hints, and most have in their hearts a hope that the conquest of truth may one day be theirs, and that after years may reverence their name while they benefit by their teaching. Though in their studies they may often feel the exhaustion of overstrained effort and taste the despondency of baffled speculation, yet in their class-rooms—surrounded by the eager faces of anxious listeners as they see truths strike home and it may be doubts dispelled—if they endure the toil of battle they at least taste the joys of victory, and in the admiration of their immediate circle have forecast of the day when the world will write their names in the record of its worthy workers. But no such adventitious aids helped Spinoza on his task; no such hope cheered him on his way. Alone in his garret he fought his dark fight. For him kinsmen had only jeers and hate, and the outside world at best a half-contemptuous wonder, and life offered him no hope except if possibly he might find peace. Like Jacob of old he wrestled for the blessing, not for himself but for posterity, through the long dark night alone, and when morning broke it was time for him to die.

When we read in his own works the rules he lays down for his noble simple life, and in the story of his life learn how he despised all things that men call good, and resolutely put them from him lest they should divert him from his great task, we feel that here indeed is the true chivalry of thought. A higher ideal is this than Spenser's Red Cross Knight who left the court of Gloriana to track the dragon to his lair, and deliver the people from the monster's ravages. For his was a deed which all could appreciate and would reward, but the thinker must take up his task in silence and alone—must go out into the desert whither perhaps he himself knows not with no landmark on the earth no loadstar in the Heaven. If he fails there is but pity from others and despair within himself. If he wins he has peace only when perhaps too exhausted to enjoy it.

> "By pain of heart now checked and now impelled,
> His intellectual power through words and things
> Goes sounding on—a dim and perilous way."

The thinker's reward is all the world's, but not for the men he knows just now and loves—only the far-off hope that some day posterity may come to understand. To "do and suffer" seem almost syllables of the same word for the work of great men, and the why we may not ask. Only it seems to be the way of Heaven that its witnesses for truth should give their testimony to the world for the most part on the rack.

Nor is it useless, in approaching the study of our author's system, to review the circumstances of his life, and attempt to realize the conditions under which he did his work. For in the study of his writings it seems to us quite necessary that we should realize as much as possible the totality of his life, so that we may be able to see clearly the bearings of his doctrine as he himself saw them. No man can be justly criticised from without, and the more original and strong the thinker is, the more insufficient does such criticism appear. He, it seems to us, is in the best position to understand a doctrine who can take most nearly the stand-point whence his teacher has worked, and test the results not by measuring how this method conforms to another's rules or how this conclusion tallys with the dicta of other teachers, but who, assuming the man's own position, can try how it was possible with his method and conclusions to form the circle of a real human experience. This gives a moral sympathy, not merely a logical one. It is this sympathy alone which can quicken the dry bones of a system into the breathing beauty of a real life. Thus only can we read in books the essential characteristics of the *man*. All other reading gives us merely the accidents which betray the *writer's* dialect. In all philosophy, which is more than mere mechanical talk, the attainment of this position is the first necessity of the critic.

About few have so divergent and so extreme opinions been pronounced. Some have denounced him as an impious cynic—a blasphemous Atheist. Those who knew him most intimately and understood him best call him "*Benedict of Blessed Memory*," the "*God-intoxicated Thinker*." We may have to qualify this admiration of his philosophy, but we certainly hope to show that the abuse is as absurd as it is untrue. In studying Spinoza's system we think we can detect three distinct stages in its development. The first includes the "Principia Philosophiæ" and "Cogitata Metaphysica." The second the "Treatise de Emendatione Intellectus" and the "Ethica;" and the third his "Treatise de Deo et Homine." The "Tractatus Politicus," the Tractatus Theologico Politicus" and the letters are valuable, as elucidatory of the application of the system of which these are the body. It has been too much the habit of English critics to confine their attention to the Ethica. Neglecting the Emendatio Intellectus in which he rises to the axioms of the Ethics, they abuse these last as gratuitous assumptions. And taking his conclusions apart from the application Spinoza makes of them, they criticise these not as he meant them, but as they understand them. Spinoza seems to have anticipated this hasty and unfair criticism of his system when he says of it, "*Nam res illa non ex parte sed tota aut nihil ejus innotescere debebit*" (no partial knowledge of this will do, one must know it as a whole, or he will know nothing about it).

In the Principia and its appendix we seem to trace more clearly the steps by which he reached the standpoint whence he proceeded to reason out his theory of human knowledge, and dogmatize on the circumstances and duties of human life, and in the third we think we see hints of what might have been a further declaration of his views, if fate had not decreed that his work for human thought was done, and called him hence in the prime of his days. He died at the age of 45.

It is worth noticing that Spinoza himself seems to have been conscious of this process of development in his thought; for, when in 1673, about four years before his death, Dr. Fabritius, by the Elector Palatine's orders, wrote to him from the University of Heidelberg, inviting him to remove thither and fill the chair of philosophy in that University, "*cum amplissima philosophandi libertate,*" but annexing to this offer the expression of a hope that he might be able in his speculations to avoid collision with the existing states of belief, Spinoza replied that he did not see clearly within what limits his philosophy might be contained, and therefore declined the invitation.

Spinoza's object in philosophizing is purely ethical. He tells us that he found himself miserable, yearning for a good he had not, and so he determined to search whether there was not something which was a true good and of itself communicable, and by which his mind might be affected without regard to all other things, nay something which found and mastered, he would possess uninterrupted and perfect joy for ever. He had looked round on other men's work and conditions, and seen that they fretted themselves in a vain struggle after pleasure, riches, and honour—that most missed their mark, and the few successful ones gained their end only to discover that all these things were vanity. And so he felt that it was terribly necessary he should seek some relief, and should go out on the search by some other way than those around him had taken, though it might be uncertain as yet whither that road might lead him.* He notices that no strife, sorrow, envy, fear, hate, or any other passion excites men's minds except with reference to something that they love—that the objects of their love are transient and perishable—that where there is rivalry for the

* "Veluti," to give his own words, "aeger laetali morbo laborans qui ubi mortem certam providet ni adhibeatur remedium illud ipsum quamvis incertum summis viribus cogitur quaerere; nempe in eo tota ejus spes est sita."

possession of the object strife arises—if it perishes sorrow is excited—if it is possessed by another envy is felt—where nothing is loved there is no disquiet of the mind. Hence he concludes that all happiness or unhappiness depends on the quality of the thing loved, *i.e.*, that change in the object, experienced or apprehended, alone produces the commotion in the mind, which is misery. The infinite and eternal, *i.e.*, the changeless alone can furnish the mind with pure joy and is itself unmixed with bitter. We may here notice what we shall have occasion to dwell on more fully, that Spinoza tacitly assumes the entire passiveness of the subject; given a changeless object, the subject must be calm—preparing us for the further assumption he immediately makes—given a calm subject the object must be changeless, *i.e.*, *eterna veritas*. Further, we remark the negative character of his philosophy. It is joy to be free from sorrow *(expers tristitiae)* as in thinking it is perfect method to refrain from irrelevancies *(cohibere ab inutilibus);* so too it is perfect wisdom to be free from inadequate notions. Peace is all he desires to attain. The eternal verity is that about which he cannot distress himself with perplexing imaginations. In philosophy he seeks for a medicine to relieve pain which will cure himself and may cure his fellows similarly affected. He does not profess to explain everything; it is sufficient for him to show that a human life may be ordered in contentment without examining such questions. Indeed, he has an utter contempt for those who are subtle in suggesting doubts. If one can order his life in peace ignorant of these he is constantly asserting how useless it is to trouble oneself with them. So in his works we are ever coming across impatient reference to questions started where the doubt goes no deeper than the lips *(ubi scilicet verbis quamvis animus non dubitat)*. It is true doubt alone which, till settled, makes the path of duty dark and the life forlorn, which he will deal with, and so he will have nothing to say to those who care more how things are called than what they are *(qui de nominibus non vero de rebus sunt soliciti)*, or whom he describes as *(nodum passim in scirpo quaerentes)* seeking a knot in every reed. Those therefore who look on philosophy as a food to give strength for duty, not merely as a balm for pain—who seek from it light to guide for future work as well as relief from present perplexity—who think that no doubt is possible to the human breast which man may not answer with patience and with time—who believe that disquiet is a symptom that circumstances may be improved, not merely as Spinoza would say that resignation must be acquired—may expect to find many things different from their own thought advanced by Spinoza. If we are right, it will save much grappling with apparent discrepancies to keep this in view. It is common we know to figure the "relentless logician," "the impious Atheist," charging in the full panoply of intellectual armour at all the opinions men hold dear and sacred. But when we turn to hear his own statement of his case, not to pick out phrases to carp at but honestly endeavouring to understand how this intellectual Titan succeeded in making his lot tolerable, we understand the weary wistful gaze that meets us in his portrait, and seem to hear the teaching of an earnest, noble man, who had found life a weary, weary march, and fain would tell his fellows how he had found peace, and had come to see that all things were indeed very good. His was the courage not of insensibility but of duty. He saw the truth clearly so far as it was given him to see it, and within his circle advanced to his conclusions unwaveringly, and yet he shrank when men called him an Atheist.

An instructive proof of the influence which the end the philosopher proposes to himself has on his system, is found in a comparison between this system of Spinoza and the almost contemporaneous method of Bacon. Both felt dissatisfied with the methods they found around them—both sought a remedy for error in purging the intellect from the phantoms of the imagination—both sought to effect this purpose by attaining particular knowledge instead of vague generality—both started from the same point but each took a different way. Back to back as it were the great type of German speculation and the great type of English Empiricism went out, each his opposite way to find the secret he sought. The one looked up from nature to find its source, the other down to nature to trace its working; the simplicity of Bacon was the last possible analysis of each thing, that of Spinoza the last attainable synthesis of the whole; Bacon neglected what united his particles; Spinoza took no note of what was united by his substance—and this naturally from their respective objects. Bacon sought substance as a power to work with, Spinoza sought it merely as a cause wherein to rest. Each was the complement of the other, for each dealt with but half of the question. Man wants at once light to see duty and power to do it.

Remembering, then, Spinoza's attitude and purpose, we come to consider this new method by which he proposed to relieve the misery which he himself felt and saw others suffering. He says he found, when he applied himself to serious thought, that the passions which disturbed him were quelled—that he was enabled to look on all circumstances as indifferent. At first this state was difficult of attainment, but practice made it easier. And so the purpose of his institute is to show the mode in which he attained this state of tranquility which he calls "*summum bonum.*" He thinks it necessary for men to acquire some knowledge of their own nature to give them facility in reaching this state.

He finds, his thought proceeds through four stages, in the highest of which he obtains the perfect peace he craves. The ideas in these four stages are referable respectively to hearing alone, pure empiricism *(vaga experientia)*, belief *(fides* or *opinio)*, and lastly clear knowledge the highest of all. He illustrates these stages by reference to the rule of three. When one hears the operation described he may remember it, but properly speaking his knowledge is as yet mere hearsay. This knowledge is *ex auditu*. Next, when he applies his knowledge to an actual operation, and finds that what he has heard produces the promised result, he is satisfied that the rule is correct, but not on sufficient grounds, for he makes the experience of one particular the rule of all. Thirdly, when having compared many particulars, he discovers a rule, he has "the cause of the proportionality of numbers," and a rule which he sees never could have deceived and never will. This third kind of knowledge exists when the being of a thing is inferred from something else *(essentia rei ex alia re concluditur)*. The object viewed in this way is still *(extra intellectum)* known only logically. This knowledge enables us to speak the marks of a thing; there is a higher still in which we know its nature. In these third and fourth stages Spinoza marks the difference so often missed between what we cannot doubt and what we know. In the third stage, though we cannot doubt the thing is so, we have such a notion of it only as a blind man has of form. In the fourth stage, things are seen *(sub specie eternitatis)* above the conditions which limit our logic. Thus, when from God's works we conclude the existence of Deity—from His acts of kindness, His love, our knowledge is in the third stage. There is manifestly, however, a higher stage than this. Thus, the knowledge a son has of his mother's love is something infinitely wider and deeper than any synthesis of her several acts of kindness. So, too, he who *knows* God is not dependent for his faith on the logical consistency of theories or on the historical connection of evidences documentary or otherwise. Such an one can trust God's love in absence of any special favour, nay in spite of suffering which the general idea of mankind would call harsh. He won't risk his belief in God's existence on a discussion about the date of any book.*

* See further "Tractatus Theologico Politicus," cap. xii. § 32, and "Letters" 21-29.

Such, then, is the fourth stage when there is union between the thinker and his object—when we see it and know it by immediate intuition *(intuitu facientes nullam operationem)*. Nothing is, then, between the thinker and the light. No change can take place in the matter of his thought, for it is *"eterna veritas;"* nor in the thinking subject, for this is the highest perfection to which man can attain *(summa ad quam homo pervenire potest perfectio)*. One who remains in the first two stages of mental experience cannot, properly speaking, be said to think at all. He is merely in a waking dream, and so long as he continues in this state there is no possibility of his improvement. The third stage is useful, not because in it we can see truth, but because it tends to purge our mental eyesight. The fourth is the intellectual state from which man surveys truth and is at rest.

In order to understand fully this scale of knowledge, we must examine in order the experiences of each stage. Thus only will Spinoza undertake to teach us. He will not talk, he says, of colour to the blind. His institute is intended for those only whose intellect and desires are the same as his own. "And if anyone is inclined to reject these things as false, it will be worth while to examine first the order in which he proves them, and then such an one will go away satisfied that he has attained the truth." Indeed, the gist of his system is his psychology.

The man who first attempts to think, Spinoza says, feels within him confused ideas which he perceives to be imperfect *(mutilatas quasi et truncatas)*. These confused or inadequate notions occasion perplexity and pain, and at the same time there is a tendency to unify these impressions. Hence he concludes, as all painful things are non-natural, it is our nature to form adequate notions, and that inadequate notions must arise because we are part of some thinking entity of which some thoughts in whole and some in part only make up our mental experience. He finds further, that while these notions are perplexing they are made up of separable elements, and so his first work is to unravel them, that the parts may be examined separately—that some of these parts can be straightened out from cause to effect, and when this concatenation has been perfected, *i.e.*, when the observed effect has been referred to its proximate cause, and that again to its next cause, until we come to a cause which is "*causa sui*," of which we cannot ask a cause, we cannot doubt of the truth of the impression. We must commence, then, by defining each observed effect, and the result of definition is, that the mind looks in a single straight line from the observed effect to the uncaused cause which suggests no question. The method is to reject everything in the chain which is changeable, or could be supposed to be otherwise than what it is. The proof that this definition is complete is when the will, which previously had the power to reject or admit in every intermediate stage of the definition, finds this power of rejection cease, and the impression is looked upon as necessary and single. So far, then, as this particular idea is concerned the mind has a *certain* truth—a *direct* ray from the light of the world has struck on the mind. But there are more ideas than one discovered in mental analysis, and there is an impulse in the mental life not only upwards from cause to effect as regards single ideas, but also sideways to unite these. A single idea, if it existed alone, would be perfect when distinct, but that the light of the mind may be *clear*, ideas must have commerce—must be related to each other. Each observed impression is next to be treated in the same way by definition, and everything is to be looked at particularly, not abstractly. The result of thus examining everything particularly, will be, that all our ideas will be referred to a cause beyond which there is no impulse to ask for a further cause : the impulse in our minds to unify its impressions will then be satisfied. The proof that the process is complete is, when the will has lost its power of rejection and the imagination its power of feigning. Our notions, then, are distinct when this process of definition has been completed, that is, when without any interruption we look from the effect to the last cause : they are clear when all our ideas are perfectly connected so as to form a harmonious whole. Then we are free from doubt and have certainty, for doubt can arise only when about the same matter two or more ideas are present both or all of which cannot be true. Of these one comes direct to us from the fountain of light, and is therefore capable of being referred straight back to that fountain, the others are fictions of the imagination. But let the intellect once assert its power to arrange in due order, and the imagination loses its power to distract, for it has power to act only where the intellect is not brought to bear. Over and over again Spinoza compares the man under erroneous impressions to a dreamer who sleeps with his eyes open. Imagination, the root of all error, has power to distract, only because men will not open their intellectual eyes and look. Spinoza has no definition for imagination; for, with him it is only the cause of impressions he finds to be fleeting. These are fictions merely because they do not stand examination.

Though Spinoza is constantly censuring those who confound material processes with mental laws, he seems himself to have been misled by a false analogy with reference to reflection. By the intellect *(intellectus)* alone, says he, have we knowledge of things. This lies encircled and bounded by its conditions; for it is a "mode." It is a mirror constructed to receive the light that comes from above, "a gem to copy Heaven engraven." The result of man's own operation can only be to blur and cloud this mirror, and his work can only be to remove these stains, to polish his intellect that it may lie exposed in all its finite breadth to the face of Heaven. When, therefore, the rays of truth strike straight down from the fountain of light—when, in rigid sequence, our thought goes straight up to its source, we have a firsthand intuition which must be true. When no blot on the surface of this mirror divides the reflected rays, the subject, *i.e.* the reflecting intellect, is in the most perfect state and is at peace. The work of the wise man is therefore not to seek what is *truth* but to remove whatever is *delusion*, which cannot be infinite as it is the work of a finite mind. If there were no imagining there would be no error. If no error there would be no consciousness, for conscious thought is but the effort to throw off those obstructions which we ourselves have made. There are many things the intellect cannot discuss, *e.g.*, the nature of God and the nature of the thing that reflects. All it can do is to arrange within its limits the sum and relations of the given ideas. Man's work is simply to arrange and connect. His only instrument is logic; for the only change possible in the given experiences is that they may be ordered aright. Neither their sum nor their nature can in any way be altered. Spinoza's idea is that both the quantity and possible relation of each thing is fixed. When, therefore, he speaks of Will and Order it is only, in deference to our habits of thought, to mark the evaporation of error from our mind—the stages by which the properties of our intellect become known to us. But it is only in our consciousness that change is. The light that shines on us—the external cause of our knowledge, and the subjective capacity of the intellect to receive this knowledge are always the same. Our life is not a becoming but a revelation of what is and always has been. Remembrance and forgetfulness are mere symptoms of this imagination. The man whose knowledge is complete cannot remember, for that would imply that something has been which is not. Now, all true ideas are in their essence eternal, and whereas we before saw in part confusedly, now in this fourth stage our knowledge includes all the fragments, and we look at them as an ordered whole. Truth is the knowledge of God, and with Him there is no past or future; for He is the "I am."

Such, then, is a general, though necessarily a sketchy view of the psychological system of Spinoza; for no description that abridges can fail to weaken the cleardrawn statement of our author. To do full justice to him he would require to be quoted *in extenso*. Let us endeavour, however, before proceeding to his conclusions, to fix clearly in our minds the points that bound the extremes of his system. Strict limitation of the field possible to thought, then, is its essential characteristic. He finds that all mental experience may be divided into necessary, impossible, and doubtful, *i.e.*, contingent ideas. These necessary ideas he finds are fixed. It does not depend on his will, whether he will believe them or not, and each idea which he applies his intellect to *(deliberans serio)* becomes in its turn fixed. Hence, he argues, the reason of this must be because the cause of this idea is itself fixed; for, as he says, it would be absurd to suppose that his own will, supposing him to have such a thing, could bind itself. Thus, finding there is a limit to each experience, he concludes that if he could reach this limit, once for all, he would have peace, for then, having ascertained the boundary that limits all experience, he would thereafter have no power to vary, and so possibility of change would be over since all thought would then come to him straight and clear from the fountain of nature. This would be the most perfect existence of which he was capable, since his intellect, to embrace it, must be clear of all the fictions his imagination had woven. Having once cleared this limit, he finds that he has a power easily to detect the falsity of all notions, for all thoughts he can refer back to it are fixed; all others, he concludes, must be false. He finds his mind now acting necessarily and easily. The figments with which imagination had interrupted his view are now gone, and his circle of existence is clear. "*Res cogitans*" on the one hand, and "*res extensa*" on the other, hedge him in, and so long as these are clear all doubt is removed. Each experience is ordered from effect to cause, and all are in union with each other. The thinking thing that had formerly reflected only in part is become a whole, and the man is at peace. We have said his system is a logic, but it is an effort to apply logic once for all and have done with it. Man's thought at any time is referring a thing unknown to a larger circle already known, or assumed for the purpose of the investigation to be sufficiently known. It is evident, then, if one could explore a circle wide enough to include all possible experience, doubt and error would then cease; for doubt is merely the want of a proper conception under which to class a given experience, and falsity is merely affirming something of another thing not contained in the conception we have formed of it. This perfect idea, which will include every other idea, he finds in the idea of God. Having attained this idea he is then in a position to describe the media through which it is reached, and the nature of things in their relation to Him. Note now the limit of his enquiry. He finds himself surrounded by mutilated imperfect ideas, in consequence of which his thoughts are wandering and his sensation unresting— when he finds his experiences limited around him and united about him, doubt is removed. Imagination has now no scope to harrass. He sees no possibility of change—he feels no impulse to move. He has attained intellectual peace, and so he concludes he is in possession of eternal truth. Given the peace, he won't discuss the method of obtaining it. However we obtain this idea of Being, the proof that it is true is that it removes doubt. This is the fullest revelation of Deity of which the individual is capable—to speak technically, the potentiality of the subject is then exhausted. This experience cannot be analysed. It is "unutterable glory," which in Spinoza's mouth is not a mere phrase of stupid wonder. What is called the finite and the Infinite is thus properly but the speakable and the unspeakable—the communicable and the purely personal. This last cannot be rendered into words, for words are but symbols of time-experiences, and this experience is *ex hypothesi* above time.

When we ask Spinoza, What then is this truth? he replies, "Can you tell me what whiteness is apart from a white thing?" Truth is a mere subjective state. It is a mere figure of rhetoric to say that things are true or otherwise. If we answer, man wants assurance as well as rest. Peace is disturbed by change, apprehended as well as felt—the possession of eternal truth, granting it to be eternal, may prevent change in thought; but how are we relieved from apprehension of change unless we know that this truth is eternal? Spinoza's reply is ready. "Your question is absurd—you know and you want to know that you know. You want an idea of this idea and would not you be in as much need of an idea of that idea, and so on *ad infinitum*. One cannot prove by reason that he is able to reason otherwise than by reasoning well. We want no proof of truth save truth itself." Thus he reasons in a circle, what we cannot reason about is infinite, and what is infinite, we cannot reason about. His express definition of intellect is that it is a spiritual automaton with a given finite sphere within which it can move, and his only attempt is that within that sphere it may move clearly. Beyond that circle he won't go, and within the circle he does not care for discussion. It is sufficient for him that imagination can now no longer disturb, and mental confusion is ended. "It is sufficient for him," he says, "to see things as they are, or, what is the same thing, that all doubt be removed from his mind." If we ask him, what then is this imagination? His answer is, "It is anything you please, only something different from the intellect by which the soul is caused to suffer." If one objects, is there then no difference between imagination paralysed and truth mastered? He answers at once, "If there had been no imagination there would be no thinking. Truth is given us, and all ignorance is mere privation. It is but our error that separates us from God." It is too evident, he thinks it little matters whether he settles questions or gets rid of them. He wants not to master doubts, but to get beyond them, and his mathematics told him that $\frac{1}{0}=$ infinity, and so he concluded that it is all the same, so far as mere peace was concerned, whether he had scaled the Heaven, and learned infinite truth, or whether a single truth was divided by no doubt.* If we press him further, What is this Ego which of its own power causes imagination, which suffers perplexity and which feels ease when this imagination is done away with—if it can do nothing WHY should it know or suffer anything? Would it not be better to cease the worry of life and be done with it, and if men believed in this kind of nature would it not be the natural way? Then, again, does not the existence of error imply imperfection in nature, for, granting for a moment that this imagination disappears, that it merely is strong when the intellect is not aroused, yet we still have an intellect, created capable of being deceived? To these he replies, he does not know: it is one of the conditions of the creature. Philosophers do not ask what God might have done, but what has he done, and this is the highest knowledge possible to us. To ask such things is beyond our province, and is no more reasonable than to ask why a circle has not the properties of a sphere. Our province is in *Time*, which begins and ends with our conscious thought. This mystery of suffering he will not meddle with. All he knows is that God does not change, and no created thing has the power to destroy itself, of which his only explanation is, that it arises from the nature of the creature.

We have thus been endeavouring to show, not so much that this system is sound, as that there is a point of view

---

* This is not merely an inference from the tendency of Spinoza's reasoning. His express words are "si tantum unica sit idea in animo sive ea sit vero, sive falsa nulla dabitur dubitatio neque etiam certitudo sed tantum talis sensatio."

from which it is intelligible. It is a shallow criticism which thinks to uproot the work of an earnest thinker's life by merely labelling the system Pantheism, or its author Atheist. We see, then, that Spinoza in the first place sought peace. Now—waiving for a moment the question whether that system deserves the name of philosophy at all, which seeks peace by trying to prove that the deep questions which stir the minds of thinking men are impertinent and impossible—we ask first, does Spinoza's experience prove that peace can be obtained by his method, and, if so, what sort of assurance does the system give that the peace so obtained will endure? He commences the examination of thought when already affected by doubt: he watches it through its various stages until he sees a perfect thought formed, in which there seems no scope for further development: the thought thus formed satisfies his soul, and so he exclaims this is "*eterna veritas.*" It is perfect, for enjoyed it gives comfort and strength. So far good, but what does it prove? I observe a seed of corn already in the ground decomposing under the influence of the weather and the soil. I watch it under the process of disintegration, sprouting, growing, developing into a perfect seed-corn like to the first: it is my harvest and he who has had his sowing time and summer may in the autumn eat of the fruit. But is therefore the work of the husbandman over? The cycle of the seasons soon comes round, and the perfect fruit of last year must rot and die before another season's growth gives a new harvest-crop, and wider plains grow white for the sickle, while larger bands gather in the grain. Verily, if it die not it abideth alone. And so when Spinoza finds the mysterious germ of thought already working and sprouting in irregular fashion amid the varied experience of the world, though he see it develope into a perfect fruit, is this therefore the last harvest of the world? Spinoza assumes that there is a given measure of truth *(data idea)* to which all mental experiences possible to man may be referred. Plainly stated, his assumption is that there is a fixed limited knowledge possible to man with a fixed capacity of knowing. Man's work is therefore done when the proportion between the knowing thing and the things to be known is exact. Both these are already fixed within us and around us, and our work merely is to arrange these *debito ordine.* If any one holds that the province of man's reason is indeed a proportioning of knowledge, but a proportion of which the terms are infinite—that knowledge proceeds not with a fixed limit of clearness and a finite possibility of distinctness, but that the contents of our thought multiply as its sphere widens, he will differ in many points from Spinoza. Because we have got rid for a moment of the divisions of the imagination, which, he says, is a shadow of our finite selves, it does not follow that there will be no more shadows. Spinoza feels free from this shadow when he sees *sub specie eternitatis,* but had he never noticed that at noon-day the light of Heaven seems to pause and man casts no shadow before him or behind. But if he watch, the sun that has arisen will begin to set. Thus the theory which bounds the quiet faith—the certain truth of this generation, is but the starting point of criticism for the next. If there were no faith, man's life would fret itself away in scepticism; if there were no doubt, it would stagnate into superstition. Certainty is but the pause in man's search after truth. Thought sometimes rests in faith, but only to gather strength; for faith is the sleep of thought, while dogma is its death.

Spinoza illustrates his doctrine of the conditioned knowledge of God, possible to a creature, by a comparison of this thought with our notion of the equality of the angles of a triangle to two right angles; for so long as our notion of neither varies we work from the one back to the other, and *vice versa*. His notion seems to be, that as we commence mathematical thought by assuming certain things as true, and so shut out doubt by limiting discussion, our possible idea of God—the highest existence—has been bounded in the same way, and we have only to learn the definition that has been given us, to include all possible human problems. This necessitates the frequent use of the argument *ad impossibile*, to which none can assent who believe that "the thoughts of men are widened with the process of the suns." His direction is, "destroy your imagination, restrain impertinent inquiries, and, within the circle of the conditioned, you can draw a conclusion which will satisfy you." This may be a neat enough operation, but it is the problem the creature sets for itself, not the one it finds set for it. What is the use of this conclusion drawn by man—a thought of God that may suggest no doubts now—unless we are assured that the God we know now is the same as we shall meet when time has ceased to be. Every wider comprehension of the creature's experiences is a nearer apprehension of the Creator's character. Fuller revelation of the light is not all man's need; he needs to be trained that he may be able to bear it.

The attainment of rest—the banishment of disquiet, is Spinoza's test of Truth. Is rest then unconsciousness? Is ceasing to feel pain ceasing to know anything? His clear light of truth will, Spinoza assures us, show us humanity in absorbed repose, encircled by the watchful rest of Omnipotence. But is this the sleep He giveth His beloved, or the death where the wicked cease from troubling? To this he does not wish to answer. To understand the state we must share it. It may be the gate of the morning, but it is marvellously like the doors of the shadow of death. However, there is no craning with Spinoza. "You are creatures," he says. "I will show you what you are, things being as they are. I won't discuss what you might be, were things different. I will show you how you may have rest. I don't care to discuss why you have been troubled." Whatever conclusions may follow, he draws them, and with him there is at least no doubt whither his conclusions, if accepted, must lead us. He says we are spiritual automata, and God as we know Him is "Substance." He won't juggle with big phrases about the Conditioned and Absolute, which mean either nothing, or exactly what he says more plainly. It is a curious intellectual phenomenon, how men of intense logical acumen and fiery hearts, seem often awanting in metaphysical breadth, and the patience that can wait for light, and hope for it even against hope.

Such a nature ever craves for some major premiss which may include all possible experience, and so Spinoza finds rest in substance, and Newman finds it in the apostolical authority of Rome. To enable these men to have peace within themselves, there were needed either greater breadth of comprehension, or less capacity for intellectual dissection. The first, increased, led Hegel to "absolute identity," the second, diminished, allows the author of the "Limits of Religious Thought" to be the champion of those orthodox persons who abhor Spinoza far too much ever to have read his works, and love their church far too well to have any sympathy with a weary brother, seeking for the light outside its pale.

Since, with Spinoza, true thought commences only when we have risen above the conditions of time, or rather to the verge of time-limits, and thus obtained that knowledge of God which he calls the hinge of his whole doctrine—we have been forced to take him up at the beginning and mark the steps of his departure from the sphere of ordinary consciousness. It seemed utterly impossible to make out of his conclusions a connected system at all applicable to a human experience, without tracing him through the ascending stages. His logic is so down-right, his conclusions so startling, and his demonstrations so neat, one is apt to forget that this "Substantia" is the God whom we worship, and this Mode the thinking "I," who reads and writes. If we could think of God only as A and man as B, it would seem quite certain that B cannot be. But having followed him thus carefully, we are in a position to turn back and examine, what essential element of experience has been missed in constructing this formula of life.

It is necessary to look at his system from the standpoint of God revealed. If we steadily regard this idea, we see at least how his thought worked in proving that God is all, and beside him there is none else—his idea of substance being accepted man *cannot* be. It is a very different matter to take the position of the Mode and conclude that man *is* not. All finite thought, then, as he says, is concerned with Substance, Attributes and Modes. What, then, is this idea of Substance? It is that which is in itself, and by itself, is conceived,—that is, such a thing as does not require the idea of another thing from which it *may* be *formed*. His idea of definition is nothing but an extension of view, until each thing which presents in its nature any motion, that does not begin in itself, may be referred to something else from which that motion came, and that again to some higher (*i.e.*, wider) nature, until motion (*i.e.*, time) ceases and we reach the uncaused cause which moves all things, and by itself is unmoved. This *Substance*, then, is merely the "*causa sui*," the thought which, when reached, includes all our possible thought. But we have to deal with it not as it is; "for it is high, we cannot attain unto it," but merely as the absolute limit of all effects observed by us. In it we live and move, but it reveals itself to us only as the extreme poles or extreme hemispheres of our knowledge, beyond neither of which anything is known, and without both of which nothing is experienced. Every thought includes the idea of something thinking and the idea

of something thought: so *res cogitans* and *res extensa* limit our widest thought, and both are present in our narrowest. These two, then, are the *Attributes* of substance which we have got when all experiences have been reduced to two. We can get rid of everything in thought, but these and the common notion we must accept; to unite them is Substance. By attribute he understands that which the Intellect perceives about Substance. The *Mode* again is an affection of Substance, is that which is in another, by which that other is perceived. It is best described by negatives. It is that which, observed, does not contain within itself the cause of all its appearances —which one cannot ponder without being directed beyond to something which is more than it, and without which it would not be what it is, or as Spinoza says, "without which we could not think it at all as existing."*
Take, for example, a tree—it has colour from the sun, nutriment from the soil, sap from the rain, particular inclination from the wind; all these and a thousand other things discover themselves on an accurate examination, if any of which were different the tree would not be exactly what it is. To define the tree exhaustively we would need to know the cause of each of these elements which determine it to be what it is, and we have further to account for all of these joining their several influences to form the particular tree. The tree is a Mode. That, then, is a Mode wherein we observe effects which lead us

* In connection with this the viii. cap. of the 1st book of the Ethics should be carefully read. It is, however, too suggestive of discussion to be more than referred to here.

beyond itself in search of the causes of these effects. Substance, with its two attributes, is the existence which is the sufficient cause of all these modes. Substance, be it observed, is not God, for the finite cannot, and does not, comprehend the Infinite. It is, however, the only idea of God possible in the essential limitation of man's Religious thought—the unity by which God has revealed Himself as the self-existent cause of the effects observable by man. Spinoza expressly says, "Although God is not without these attributes, He is not by them. God is them all, but they all are not God."

Spinoza is no Pantheist in the vulgar acceptation of the term. The same twist which makes the term applicable to him would make it applicable to St. Paul. He will measure the idea of God, but only because he concludes that God's *revealed* nature may be measured according to the "measure of a man." Substance is an unfortunate word Absolute Existence would perhaps convey the meaning of our author better, and would clash less with the prejudices of those who care more for the sound of a name than for the true human idea expressed by it. This does no violence to the etymological meaning of Substantia (that which stands under), and better expresses the meaning; for it means with Spinoza only the common ground on which the mutual relation of observed phenomena may be rendered intelligible. Spinoza finds, then, the idea of God as a Being perfect, complete, self-contained, One in knowledge and existence. This existence is necessarily single and alone, for, suppose two such, they either know of each other or they do not.

If they do not, their knowledge is limited. If they do, we have the cause of thought in one outside of itself which is contrary to the idea of substance. Such an existence is also unchangeable, and this can be proved in more ways than one. If it change there must be a cause of change either outside of or within itself. If outside we again violate our hypothesis. If within, the change makes it either more perfect or less perfect. If less perfect, besides the absurdity of a perfect-imperfect we have a cause tending to its own destruction which is absurd; if more perfect, we have a time when it was not perfect, which also is absurd. Spinoza insists that we assume at the outset,—

1st. Whatever we can clearly and distinctly understand to belong to the nature of a thing, that we can truly affirm about it.

2nd. What we cannot reconcile in thought cannot exist in reality for us.

These are the two notions with which he works out his whole problem. It does bring the question to an issue, but his instrument is a two-edged weapon. The knowledge of God being assumed as necessary, all the rest is cleared away as inconsistent therewith. God the existence necessitates that man should be the mode, because the one substance being assumed the other is impossible. But suppose we should assume that the "Ego" is. What then? The question is fairly stated, and Spinoza chooses to assume that God is and so his conclusion is wrought out. It is true that time-experience gives a duality, but thought can deal only with a unity; therefore one of these must be rejected as a delusion; because, he argues, if the attempted unification of thought be not due to a real unity of existence, we must suppose the mind capable of creation, and then nothing objective need be supposed to be true. In this way the 1st Book of the "Ethics," and the Treatise "De Deo," which is a more full exposition of the same idea, proceeds ringing changes on the same assumption in an endless begging of the question.

The idea, then, of God *ens et unicum*—the Eternal "I am"—is the notion by which all phenomena are to be tried. In this universe nothing is contingent; everything is so, that it cannot be more perfect. Will, then, is a chimera, for its thought implies power to do; but in this universe all things are done. What, then, is man? He is a mode. But what is a mode? It is not Substance, for God is Substance, and, as we have seen, there can not be two Substances. The whole object of this training of the intellect is to enable it to see, that nothing is contingent, that all things are necessary. Nothing is good or evil, and this for two reasons: first, the idea of good implies reference to some end which it may further, but there is no end in nature; therefore good and useful are meaningless terms; second, good or useful predicated of anything implies reference to some other thing of the same kind, supposed to be better or worse, but as each thing is in its own place the best possible, since God has made it; this assumed general notion of good or evil is a delusion. To the intellect viewing each thing "particularly," class-notions have disappeared, and so comparison is impossible. If we object, you show us what we should not desire, but we do desire even against our judgment. This, he says, is only imagination: intellect and will are the same thing, and will striving after what it has not is merely the symptom of inadequate notions. If we object, further, that this proposes to us the attainment of an alleged good, but posits as the condition of obtaining it that we lose the capacity of enjoying it. His answer is ready, "Happiness is not the reward of virtue, but virtue itself." If we further object, suppose nothing changes around us or within us, there is at least the clearing up of our ideas: although the subject be fixed and the object, yet the relation at least changes, and as God knows all things He must know this change in our relation, or if you will, the sensation of the mode: is not this a change in His experience? We are rebuked for ascribing imagination to God; for imagination is but a capacity in a creature of conceiving just now, a thing in a way different from that in which he may conceive it afterwards. Only a being who changes can imagine, and God has said "I change not." These things, says Spinoza, are beyond us, for the thought of God is inconceivable to man. The brief summary of this philosophy is, that if we look constantly at Heaven we will not notice the things of earth. If man's life were only contemplation, this might do, but if it be anything more it as manifestly fails. Spinoza, however, does not hesitate. Life is "*perseverare in suo*," and to understand, is man's highest life. Some men have wider and some narrower spheres of life, but, when the adequate experience has been reached, each is beyond the influence of time, and can look straight at the essence of eternity—that unity where no division is. Other thinkers, pondering man and the phenomena of time, have described God as the infinite, the independent, the undetermined, and for this Spinoza censures them, it may be justly, for dealing in negatives. Does it much mend the matter, that he turns his view to God alone, and tells us that man is a mode and a mode is not substance? He tells us truth is what we cannot contradict, and he gives us truth by affirming nothing! Service or duty in a creature is of course by this system inconceivable; for there is nothing given outside of God, by which anything may begin to act. Our highest happiness is indeed, accordingly, to obey God; but our obedience is not to do anything, but to recognize that all that God has done is good. His Ethical system is but an application of the doctrine of the all-pervading, all-absorbing, existence of God, and the nothingness of man. He does not offer to increase man's joy by guiding him to action, but he will quell his sorrow by lulling him into unconcern. He will calm men with "an oblivious melody,"

> "Which whoso hears must needs forget
> All pleasure and all pain, all hate and love,
> Which he had known before that hour of rest,
> And would forget thus vainly to deplore
> Ills which if ills can find no cure from him."

We bring him the scroll of the universe to decipher, and he tells us that these phenomena are symbols. This but settles one question to raise another, if he does not teach us how to construe these symbols. The notion of

"Substance" is a grand one, inferring the common nature and the possibility of union of man with man, but it is small comfort to tell us that there is a way, if he cannot tell us what it is, or who shall walk therein. Spinoza does not explain the finite by the infinite, he destroys the finite. Man wants to see through time-symbols. Spinoza urges him to look over them; for, observe, he does not profess to enable us to see that man *is* not, his argument is, granted this notion of substance, man *cannot* be. He does not explain our perplexities, he invites to a position where we won't see them. Professedly he does not deal with man as he is; if, as he says, we have attained the stage of seeing *sub specie eternitatis*, doubt is destroyed, and we have no questions to solve—until it be destroyed we cannot understand the question. Not human power but human impotence is his theme. Man asks the philosopher how he may do well; and Spinoza answers he can do nothing. He asks what he must love, and the answer is he need love nothing, not even God; for how can man love a God of whom he may not think—not even that he is good. But, alas, nothing is the one thing man cannot do. He feels he must move, and wants to know how as well as where. But Spinoza does not care to discuss such questions. In life he hears no martial music that speaks of a good fight to be fought, of a victory to be won, for to his ears the secret of the world sings but a dirge of which the burden ever is—

"That all our conquest in the fight of life
Is knowledge that 'tis nothing and contempt,
For hollow shows that once we chased and worshipped."

This system deals with man not as an embodied intellect, but as pure intelligence, as it is assumed he has been before the Spirit was clothed, or will be after the Time-vesture is cast aside : it deals with but half the problem of life, and we know not if it be the higher half. Ethics must deal with time for man's duty, though it may deal with Eternity for his comfort, but it is the Eternity of rest which we may attain not the Eternity of unconsciousness whence we issued. We want to know of our work and our destiny. This system turns man back to ponder his origin and his necessity. Spinoza says rightly that the intellect, as he views it, cannot deal with unity. But it is this mystery of union which philosophy believes, it may come some day to understand; for to describe man's life by merely tracing the working of his logic-faculty, is as if one should depict a landscape by pencilling the outlines of the clouds. It is this union,—life, love, sympathy, Substance, call it what you will, the something that makes the family more than a congeries of individuals—gives the State other bonds than fear of a common foe—of which we want to understand the laws. Is it peace to show the human unit that there is a God about whom he must not think—to point him to a hope of which he may not tell, though thousands are perishing around through sheer despair? It is not peace for himself alone, but truth for man which the true philosopher desires. Philosophy to a true man is no Jacob's ladder by which the solitary thinker may climb above the conditions of time, and gaze in lonely bliss into the unutterable glory, but it is the way of truth which, as a pioneer of human thought, he builds now that after ages may enter in. Faith may possibly comfort ourselves, but we need truth if we are to comfort others. Man's life is action as well as thought, and the rest he seeks is not from work neglected but through work well done—not that in the stillness of a forgotten world he may hear the music of the angels, but that, man having finished the work that was given him to do, the discords of time, ordered and arranged in perfect harmony, may ascend from earth in a new song of praise to swell the chorus before the throne.

The interest of Spinoza's system centres in his assumptions and his method. His whole philosophy is but a rigid application of his doctrine of the Conditioned nature of thought and the consequent qualitative separation of belief and knowledge. On the ground he has taken, on the argument he has submitted, any system of the Conditioned must stand or fall. His peculiar virtue is, that he has stated his doctrine clearly and drawn *all* the conclusions fairly. If with pain, but without hesitation, we conclude that his work has but pushed an error to its crisis—that he is a beacon rather than a guide, let us at least be above the littleness of depreciating his work, merely because of the higher power of our age. The experience of two hundred years has widened the view of philosophical criticism, no wonder if its power be more mature: and let us remember, too, that Spinoza was a Jew, and knew the New Testament only as a thinker. To him God was the "I am," to us from childhood his name has been "Love." We have lisped the sacred words at our mother's knee, and drunk in their spirit insensibly in the atmosphere of a Christian home. The familiarity of its phrase blinds us to half the speculative difficulty of its doctrine, and practically we had realized its power in the life, long before we could state its contradiction in thought. Spinoza had to imagine the experience as well as to grapple with the thought. Which of us who presume to judge him, could have done as much in like circumstances? Who shall dare to say how much of our truth results from his error? He had but two talents, did he not make of them other two?

From the study of this man's system we turn away convinced that man's nature is something broader than intellect, his work something higher than logic, his destiny something grander than any human formula has yet compassed, and believing that wherever human wrong makes grief, there is something human work can do, wherever doubt causes pain, there is some answer possible to human thought, we learn to possess our souls in patience, and wait for the hope of the Saints—the New Jerusalem, whose walls they shall call salvation and its gates praise, whose officers shall be peace and its exactors righteousness, wherein all the people shall be righteous, and where God shall be unto us an everlasting light, and the days of our mourning shall be ended.

C. R. M'C.

THE APPLE-TREE.

A GENTLE host indeed was mine
   With whom I lodged but now:
A golden apple was his sign,
   That hung upon a bough.

It was the jolly apple-tree
   With whom I put me up:
Of sweetest food and freshest juice
   He made me free to sup.

And frank and fast to his green house
   Came many a feathered guest;
They skipped, and sipped, and made good cheer,
   And sang their very best.

I found upon the soft green lea
   A place for pleasant sleep:
My host himself he sheltered me
   Within his shadow deep.

And when I asked him for the bill,
   He merely shook his head.
A blessing on him, from the crown
   Down to the rooty bed.

ON SOME CHARACTERISTICS OF SCOTT'S POETRY.

WE do not mean to treat of Scott's poetry generally; it has been often criticised, and never better than in the admirable Essay prefixed to Mr. Palgrave's edition of the Poems. We wish to draw attention to some qualities of his verse which have been less remarked; and those who may think little of our criticism will, we hope, thank us for bringing some fine passages together.

It has been said, that the best kind of criticism is that which does not descant and reason, but simply indicates its own feeling; "That is my favourite; commend me to this." Art has no exemption, any more than anything else, from being submitted to the universal solvent of reason; and there must be a theory of art possible, though we know not where to look for it at present. But if the saying we have quoted could ever be true, it might seem to be so in the case of those forms of art that appeal to the indefinite powers of imagination. Music does this to the highest extent; the charm of the best music would be gone, if it could be quite definitely expressed. Poetry has something of the same kind in some varieties of the lyric. There are lyrics that are as plain and straightforward, and yet of the first class of excellence; Carey's "Sally in our Alley," which Mr. Palgrave gives in his "Golden Treasury," may serve for an example. But we are thinking of those lyrics, or scraps of lyrics, whose charm resides in their indefiniteness, in their only hinting and suggesting. Perhaps the most inimitable specimen of this extant is Coleridge's "Kubla Khan," which is a congeries of fragments, a dream in short, as it professes to be.

> "And 'mid this tumult Kubla heard from far
> Ancestral voices prophesying war!"

> "Weave a circle round him thrice,
> And close your eyes in holy dread,
> For he on honey-dew hath fed,
> And drunk the milk of Paradise."

Shelley also is full of this; and in few places does he show more of it than in the lines which Mr. Palgrave, we cannot imagine why, has omitted from the "Euganean Hills" in the "Golden Treasury:"

> "On the brink of a northern sea,
> Which tempests shake eternally,
> As once the wretch there lay to sleep,
> Lies a solitary heap,
> One white skull and seven dry bones,
> On the margin of the stones,
> Where a few gray rushes stand,
> Boundaries of the sea and land:
> * * *
> Those unburied bones around
> There is many a mournful sound;
> There is no lament for him,
> Like a sunless vapour, dim,
> Who once clothed with life and thought
> What now moves and murmurs not."

Perhaps the charm of this kind of writing resides in its air of infinity. Nothing appeals more strongly to our feeling of the beautiful and lofty than anything that suggests infinity; and it is not easy to see how art can be infinite except by being indefinite, by suggesting mystery. This is the secret of Turner. Whatever we understand of nature, there is always infinitely more behind, which we do not understand. This aspiration, though by no means the greatest or even a large part of poetry, is perhaps its most peculiar and characteristic part; just as the invisible perfume of a rose really is the essence of the palpable rose.

In this quality Scott was by no means deficient. Yet in him it exhibits itself characteristically. There is nothing of the Celtic elegance and fancy which Mr. Matthew Arnold has so delicately indicated in his "Lectures upon the study of Celtic Literature." Scott is grave and restrained, with nothing of the Celtic impulse and airiness; and this corresponds with the strength and breadth which are the chief characteristics of his works. There is no better test of perfect strength than the way in which an author handles pathos; let us show then, by a pathetic extract, what we mean by Scott's strength. We take the last stanza of the "Maid of Neidpath:"—

> "He came—he pass'd—a heedless gaze,
>   As o'er some stranger glancing;
> Her welcome, spoke in faltering phrase,
>   Lost in his courser's prancing—
> The castle arch, whose hollow tone
>   Returns each whisper spoken,
> Could scarcely catch the feeble moan,
>   Which told her heart was broken."

This is pathos of the deepest order—pathos so deep and repressed that to a careless eye it might seem coldness; the pathos of Homer.—"And Hector stood far off from the baleful battle, and changed the armours; his own he gave to the warlike Trojans to fetch to holy Ilium, and the immortal armour he put on, the armour of Pelide Achilles, which the gods of heaven gave to his father dear; and he gave it to his son; for he was old: but the son grew not old in the armour of the father."

Perhaps the most characteristic example in Scott of the impalpable kind of poetry we have attempted to describe, is Lucy Ashton's song in the "Bride of Lammermoor." In this and other pieces, if we cannot persuade the reader to see exactly what we see, we must fall back, not upon any false brocard of "*De gustibus*" but upon the remarks with which we started, that the theory of these subjects is imperfect; and for those who do not feel sympathetically, we can do no more :—

> "Look thou not on beauty's charming,
> Sit thou still when kings are arming,
> Taste not when the wine-cup glistens,
> Speak not when the people listens,
> Stop thine ear against the singer,
> From the red gold keep thy finger,
> Vacant heart, and hand, and eye,
> Easy live and quiet die."

Another exquisite specimen is the song of Louise in the "Fair Maid of Perth :"—

> "Yes, thou may'st sigh,
> And look once more at all around,
> At stream and bank, and sky and ground,
> Thy life its final course has found,
> And thou must die.
>
> Yes, lay thee down,
> And while thy struggling pulses flutter,
> Bid the grey monk his soul-mass mutter,
> And the deep bell its death-tone utter—
> Thy life is gone.
>
> Be not afraid!
> 'Tis but a pang, and then a thrill;
> A fever fit, and then a chill;
> And then an end of human ill,
> For thou art dead."

The notion of the dying man looking around him for the last time is a favourite one with Scott, and harmonises well with his love of external nature. Every one remembers the lines in the "Lady of the Lake:"—

> "Each looked to sun, and stream, and plain,
> As what he ne'er might see again."

We think there is a similar passage in some of the novels, but cannot find it at the moment.

One of the mottoes at the end of "St. Ronan's Well" is in a similar key:—

> "Here come we to our close—for that which follows
> Is but the tale of dull, unvaried misery.
> Steep crags and head-long linns may court the pencil
> Like sudden traps, dark plots, and strange adventures;
> But who would paint the dull and fog-wrapt moor,
> In its long tract of sterile desolation?"

Although it does not bear a very close resemblance to any of our citations from Scott, we cannot resist the pleasure of giving a beautiful passage from an author, who evidently had the rhythm of Scott running in her head, and which is an excellent example of the kind of poetry we have been speaking of;

> "Ierne, round our sheltered hall
> November's gusts unheeded call;—
> And in the red fire's cheerful glow,
> I think of deep glens, clothed with snow;
> I dream of moor, and misty hill,
> Where evening closes dark and chill;
> For lone, among the mountains cold,
> Lie those whom I have loved of old."

These lines are from Ellis Bell. The poetry of Scott had evidently produced a great effect upon all the Brontës; he is often alluded to in Currer Bell's novels. This will not seem wonderful to any one who has visited the upper valleys of Yorkshire, with their bare hills, their dismal stone walls and stone villages, their endless slopes, up which you trudge through heather and gale to come at last to grey stone cliffs, standing up sharp like a cock's comb upon the top of the ridge. This kind of scenery, with its keen refreshing air, is like and yet unlike the pastoral scenery dear to Scott, and must have been yet more like before the abundant woods, which now everywhere cover in the Tweed, the Teviot, the Yarrow, and all the rivers of the South, had been planted.

There is a very fine motto in the "Monastery:" Scott never wrote better than in these fragments. His instinctive and unconscious genius—these are not words of the highest praise—succeeded best when it had no particular goal before it.

> "Yes, life hath left him—every busy thought,
> Each fiery passion, every strong affection,
> All sense of outward ill and inward sorrow,
> Are fled at once from the pale trunk before me;
> And I have given that which spoke and moved,
> Thought, acted, suffer'd, as a living man,
> To be a ghastly form of bloody clay,
> Soon the foul food for reptiles."

An appropriate sequel to this is furnished by the verses put into the mouth of Claud Halcro as an ancient fragment.

> "And you shall deal the funeral dole;
> Ay, deal it, mother mine;
> To weary body and to heavy soul,
> The white bread and the wine.
>
> And you shall deal my horses of pride;
> Ay, deal them, mother mine.
> And you shall deal my lands so wide,
> And deal my castles nine.
>
> But deal not vengeance for the deed,
> And deal not for the crime;
> The body to its place, and the soul to heaven's grace,
> And the rest in God's own time."

The learned tell us that there are no pure and unmixed notes in nature; that every musical sound is made up, not only of the fundamental tone, but of an infinite number of overnotes or harmonics. So we seem to hear, in these simple lines, a great deal more than the obvious meaning. There is not merely a sort of essence and concentration of all Scott's dreams and fancies about the bygone ages; but a sense that all human exertion, and success, and result, though it may be the only end possible to man, is in itself something vain and useless; that the fate of natural sequence hangs over all; and yet that love, and mercy, and forgiveness, are the best of all man's possessions, and the salt of life. Nothing can be more melancholy than Scott's key-note; it is perpetually turning up in all his works; and yet it is fully consistent with the frankest cheerfulness and the broad and sunny atmosphere which overspreads all his writings. The tone of the Iliad is very similar. The Achæans are resolute and merry: but war is a dismal business; and such a life, the poet evidently thinks, is, as Goethe put it, no better than a hell enacted upon earth. Homer is always talking of "miserable mortals," "the woeful war," "the unhappy fray." What does Zeus say to the horses of Achilles? "Oh unhappy, why did we give you to king Peleus, to a mortal man? but ye are without old age and immortal. Was it that ye might have trouble among miserable men? for among all things that breathe and go upon earth there is nought wretcheder than man."

Compare the following in the "Abbot":—

> "Youth! thou wear'st to manhood now,
> Darker lip and darker brow,
> Statelier steps, more pensive mien,
> In thy face and gait are seen;

> Thou must now brook midnight watches,
> Take thy food and sport by snatches!
> For the gambol and the jest,
> Thou wert wont to love the best,
> Graver follies must thou follow,
> But as senseless, false, and hollow."

Any one who has read "Castle Dangerous" will confess that Scott in this story, although himself, is very inferior to his former self; but the power of producing such poetical bursts as we have been quoting had not diminished as the power of writing consecutive prose had. One of the finest things in all his writings is the motto to Chapter XI., where an armed knight appears for a moment to Aymer de Valence, and instantly vanishes:

> "Where is he? Hath the deep earth swallowed him?
> Or hath he melted like some airy phantom
> That shuns the approach of morn and the young sun?
> Or hath he wrapt him in Cimmerian darkness,
> And passed beyond the circuit of the sight
> With things of the night's shadows?"

FROM HEINE.

> BONNY fisherman's daughter,
>   Row your boat a land;
> Come hither and sit beside me,
>   We'll prattle hand in hand.

Lay your head on my heart, child,
  Why should you fear for me:
When every day so fearlessly,
  You trust the angry sea.

My heart is like the sea, child,
  In storm, and ebb, and flow!
And many a pearl lies hidden
  Far in its depths below.

WILLIAM WORDSWORTH.

WE can divide writers, just as we can divide men, into two great classes, not indeed always distinguished by the same names, but very generally recognized, under whatever disguise of appellation. Materialist and Idealist are perhaps the names that will suggest most readily the distinctive features we wish to emphasize. The idealist is the man of faith and hope, who looks to possibilities rather than to actualities, who reminds men of their powers and not of their achievements, who assumes the best till the worst is proved. The materialist (as we may call him) will have nothing but facts; he walks not by faith, but by sight; he says "that which has been shall be;" as a philosopher, he rejoices in analysis and the gathering of the results of the past, while the other half-philosophizes and half-prophesies; as a statesman, his faith is in the effects to be produced by working on the self-interests, the passions, the prejudices of men, and since he takes no account of generous impulse or conviction of the right in his calculations of men's action, he fails to awaken them, and thus seems justified in his estimate. We have spoken of *faith* as a characteristic of the idealist, but will not on that account be misunderstood as indicating a division at all coincident with the theological one into believer and sceptic. Plato is the great prototype of the idealist, the one man who has best succeeded in *preaching*, while truly and deeply philosophizing; with keen insight into *what is*, and yet that thorough geniality and anticipative type of mind that fits him for perceiving *what is* in the light of what *might* and *should be*, enabling him to cast aside the letter that killeth for the spirit that giveth life. Such or such like is the idealist on the ethical side; but an intellectual cast is not less necessary to the conception, and not less distinctive of it than the other. The idealist loves the particular only in and for the general; his very faith and hope spring from his hold in universals, and find in that the guarantee of their permanence. He does not follow in the wake of his brother-man, or even wait for his company on the journey, but boldly takes his path alone to the well-head of truth on the heights of Reason and Faith, returning with copious draughts for his thirsty fellow-men, who have been seeking in vain to allay their noble thirst with the water of hearsay, all too plenteous, but unsatisfying. We shall not now, we think, find much difficulty in assenting to the proposition that all the master spirits of the world, from whom come its life-giving impulses, are more or less of idealists. And yet when we call Wordsworth an idealist we imply something more than mere community with this class: that he strikes us as peculiarly and preeminently idealistic, so that we choose this category rather than any other to describe him; a man not unworthy of being placed alongside of Plato himself, and Plato's nineteenth century disciple, Emerson. We would not indeed think for a moment of comparing either Wordsworth or Emerson with Plato for reach of thought, or encyclopædic erudition, or analytic ingenuity; but we mean that they three together represent a fervid believing cast of mind, altogether free from any tinge of dogmatism, rare enough in all the centuries that separate the two latter from the former. Emerson is classed in theological parlance with the sceptics of the day, but such distinctions as that do not affect the believingness of which we speak; a man indeed who accepts all the dogma which Emerson rejects, may belong to—nay, will be helped by his dogma to gain a place in the same high brotherhood: but if we judge a man as we find him, and not from *a priori* conceptions of the results of particular beliefs or non-beliefs, we shall not fail to admire a soul that can retain its buoyancy without the pabulum which is indispensable to most; we shall even feel that the help which is in him is all the more human as coming to men irrespectively of their theological diversities: and this applies in great measure to Wordsworth also. Although we believe him to have been a reverent worshipper of a personal God, yet his spirit is so largely that of an Intuitionist, and a reader in the book of Nature rather than that of dogmatic theology, that he has been mistaken for a Pantheist. In particular that noble passage in the lines on Tintern Abbey, where he speaks of

> "The motion and the spirit that impels
> All thinking things, all objects of all thought,"

has been wrested to support such a conclusion. So then Wordsworth took his stand behind all the wranglings of the schools, and from a deeply-devout, nature-nurtured mind and heart, preached peace and love, contentment and self-knowledge, reverence and hope, to all mankind.

The entire burst of poetry that took the world by surprise at the end of last century and the beginning of this, has more or less the ideal character as a reaction against the systematized formalism and finality that had been, for a long time previous, but a thin covering for wide-spread scepticism or apathy; but within the new movement itself there were degrees, and Wordsworth's idealism (if we except that of Coleridge) was the most absolute and permanent: it had the widest foundations, and therefore was less assailable than any of the others by special failures or defections of the time. Byron need not detain us long on this score : partly owing to the ill-usage of society, partly to his own restless vanity, he fell into a complaining faithless mood, which limits the most of his writings: so that his moralizing is mainly occupied with admiration of himself under the guise of various Mephistophelean gentlemen with gigantic powers and great capacities of tenderness, who see through the hollowness of all human knowledge and virtue, and in their Titanic scorn will not even deign to respect themselves; —and his philanthropy is reduced to the task, somewhat thankless, one would suppose, of endeavouring to gain for these headless, heartless multitudes the privilege of self-government. We do not say that there was not a better Byron behind all this, but as he did not allow himself to appear in his writings, but only in his enterprizes, with *him* we have nothing to do. Then passing by Moore and Campbell, Southey and Crabbe, as men of less mark, we come to Shelley. Now Shelley's philanthropy was most undoubted: indeed it consumed him; and to this hour, it must be confessed, it kindles a warmer glow of responsive feeling than Wordsworth's; but if there was more heat, there was also less light. Shelley was a sad visionary, and, in truth, as far as "Revolts of Islam" and "Queen Mabs" go, the terrible development of the French Revolution was the *"reductio ad absurdum"* of them, all except the mere setting of glowing imagination and burning love. So, as John Keats was rather a φιλοκαλος than a φιλανθρωπος, we are relegated to the serene granitic faith of Wordsworth in his kind, stimulated undoubtedly, but not determined by, or dependent on, the movement in France.

"When events
Brought less encouragement, and unto these
The immediate proof of principles no more
Could be entrusted, while the events themselves,
Worn out in greatness, stripped of novelty,
Less occupied the mind. . . . evidence
Safer, of universal application, such
As could not be impeached, was sought elsewhere."

Wordsworth's faith in, and love for, mankind were like the feelings with which he regarded the everlasting hills and smiling meres of his beloved lake-land: although mists or darkness might hide the one from view, or fierce mountain-gusts lash the other into fury, he could yet remember the sunset-glories of the hills, the calm beauty of the sleeping lake, and believed that the mists would lift and the storms lull, disclosing once more the native features of the scene unchanged. So, with regard to man, his confidence was in those feelings which are "essential and eternal in the heart," which every man brings with him as his portion from the far land for the ennobling of this poor life of earth, and which, if he continues faithful to them, never desert him during all the journey, and at the end usher him, not cheerless or despairing, into the unknown beyond, which is their home and God's. To rouse these where dormant, to cherish them where active, to summon the benignant influences of natural scenery, terrible or tender, to their aid against the corroding power of society, and pleasure or business, this was the work to which Wordsworth, with rare consistency and energy of purpose, and not a little self-gratulation, devoted his life. And therefore it is that we claim for him, as we have done, the highest place amongst the idealists of that fresh world. Byron and Shelley had more fire, more immediacy,—took a stronger hold, as we see without astonishment, on the time; Scott, like some of the lesser names of the day, was engrossed by the particular and the picturesque; Wordsworth is more of a κτῆμα εισαει. But we must not leave the subject without saying that

Wordsworth, on the social and political side, was as ardent a Reformer, as strong a believer in progress, as even Shelley himself. *Possibly* he had less feeling, *certainly* he had more patience, on this side: he did not put his faith in nostrums or expect nations to be born in a day. Perhaps, after all, this is merely saying that he reached his maturity, while Shelley was cut off in the wrestling-time when opinion and character were being forged under the blows of diverse experience and conflicting circumstance. We know, at any rate, that he too had his throes of heart-sickness;—this at least the Revolution cost all sympathetic onlookers—and was temporarily shaken in faith.

> "Demanding formal *proof*
> And seeking it in every thing, I lost
> All feeling of conviction, and in fine,
> Sick, wearied out with contrarieties,
> Yielded up moral questions in despair."

At length repose returned:

> "Nature's self
> By all varieties of human love,
> Assisted, led me back through opening day
> To those *sweet counsels between head and heart*
> Whence grew that genuine knowledge, fraught with peace,
> Which through the later sinkings of this cause
> Hath still upheld me, and upholds me now
> In the catastrophe."

Thus was the poet restored, through the kindly mediation of the woods and lakes, the streams and hills, to that patient faith in the future and sympathy with the past of the race, which he so finely expresses when he says

> "There is
> One great society alone on earth,
> The noble living and the noble dead."

Having thus exposed, as we think, the key-stone of Wordsworth's soul-arch, we may proceed, as far as our space and powers permit, to delineate its curve, and note the more prominent features of the masonry, observing at once its strong and its weak points. And first of all we may speak of his knowledge and love of nature. Wordsworth was not of the opinion of Plato's master, as reported by Plato, "The rocks and the trees will teach me nothing, but men will." On the contrary, such was his vivid conception of "silent Nature's breathing life," that he might have adopted as his own, and applied to Nature with special emphasis, the affirmative of Socrates' negative "$\theta\epsilon\lambda\epsilon\iota\ \mu\epsilon\ \delta\iota\delta\alpha\sigma\kappa\epsilon\iota\nu$."

> "One impulse from a vernal wood
> May teach us more of man,
> Of moral evil and of good,
> Than all that sages can."

But quotations from Wordsworth to illustrate this point might be multiplied to weariness. From his very childhood, infancy almost, up to extreme old age, Nature was his constant playmate, teacher, reprover, solace, philosopher, friend. What colloquies they two would hold on some lone hill-side or silent lake, speaking to each other things unutterable in the language of men, but whose very echo is sweet to us listeners, sending us to woo in our turn his large-hearted mistress: how they would gaze into the depths of each other's eyes, telling each other all their secrets, joyous or sorrowful, and finding sympathy! And sometimes, too, the mortal lover would come, weary with toil, or heart-sick with hope deferred or disappointed, or stained from travel among the abodes of men, unworthy for the time of such high converse: yet falling on the bosom of his divine mistress, seeing her beauteous face, and hearing the pulses of her great heart, he would return strengthened, heartened anew for the struggle with evil, his noble passion, meanwhile, burning at his heart with redoubled glow. Never, surely, did man love Nature with a love so intense, so absorbing as Wordsworth's; at all events, never did man succeed so well in tracing on dull paper with dull ink and pen, the living characters of a passion that wins its way straight to the heart of every reader, with the least sensibility to natural beauty, the least rudiment of love for rocks, and streams, and mountains.

The question may perhaps occur at this point,—Why was not this feature, so pronounced and so distinctive of Wordsworth, placed in the forefront instead of the one, chosen for that position, which we have named his Idealism? In answering this question, we will at the same time be advancing the argument a stage. Nature was Wordsworth's slave even while she was his mistress. He was well aware that it is the sovereign soul that puts all these deep meanings into nature before it draws them out again,—that adds

> "The light that never was on land or sea,
> The consecration, and the poet's dream."

His own progressive intimacy with Nature, the deeper communion that ever followed an expanded thought and new experience (finely sketched in the lines in "Tintern Abbey," and which forms the staple of the "Prelude") would of itself have taught him this. At first she was his playmate, echoing his shouts of boyish glee, and bearing his iron-bound feet merrily along her frozen waters; at times too, speaking in awful tones to the spirit-half of the boyish nature, "the soul that riseth with us, our life's star:" then as he grew older, and the "animal movements" had lost their keen zest, opening his eye to beauty, and stealing into his heart to be loved for her own sake: anon, as the philanthropic fever with its "*Homo sum, nihil humani a me alienum,*" fired his blood, taking new concrete senses, and delivering hopeful prophecies: insinuating all the while God, immortality, infinitude. There is no analysing this sort of thing: no Kant shall ever write its kritik, and yet it carries with it its own credentials of validity, never questioned by him who experiences it, never understood by him who does not. It is only vouchsafed to the man who is worthy of it: we must keep the eye clear and watchful, the heart pure, the soul attent. Men laugh at it in common hours as moonshine: it is the very daylight of the spirit to him who enjoys it. We call it imagination, and attribute to it highest truth.

It will be understood now, if not before, why it is that we have subordinated Wordsworth's love of Nature to what we have called his Idealism. Nature is but the mirror, as it were, in which the soul sees her own lineaments—or say it is the stimulus that summons into consciousness what was potential merely and latent. No ancient poet ever looked on Nature with the deep eye of Wordsworth: there is nothing at all approaching it in all ancient literature. Lucretius, perhaps, comes nearest to it, but in him it is rather implied than overt. It was needful that Plato should write, it was needful that Christ should live and teach, before these unsuspected depths and untrodden heights could be revealed to tempt the explorer's foot; and if ever they become a pathway for common men, trodden with joy in the intervals of toil and care, Wordsworth will be gratefully remembered as the most intrepid pioneer along the difficult track.

And Wordsworth was not less distinguished by *minutely accurate observation* than by *imaginative contemplation* of Nature. As the latter determined the tone and spirit of his poetry, so he was indebted to the former for the minor graces of happy simile, or pregnant metaphor, or nice description. We would fain quote a passage from the opening of the "Prelude," where he describes a solitary row on the lake by moonlight—a representative passage, typical of many others hardly less fine, where he depicts for us natural scenes, traced in lines of fire on his memory by some solemn experience of awe or transport. This class of passages represents the keen perception of which we are speaking in its finest form, as the adjunct and minister of a half-passive receptive contemplation. But we can only afford to give one or two examples, chosen from the "Prelude," of its use in simile. Thus he speaks of children as being

"Mad at their sports *like withered leaves in winds.*"

Moonlight upon water he describes as

"Changing oft its form
Like an uneasy snake."

In the following the moon forms the other term of the comparison. He is speaking of a theatrical scene—

"Some beauteous dame
Advanced in radiance through a deep recess
Of thick-entangled forest, *like the moon
Opening the clouds.*"

Viewing Wordsworth under these two aspects as an idealist and as a lover of Nature, we think we have almost exhausted his claims upon our admiration and gratitude as a poet and a teacher of mankind. But there are certain defects and weaknesses incident to his peculiar training and habits, and others which follow directly from the original bent of his genius, without some notice of which no account of the poet would be complete. The office of a poetical critic, especially of a critic who deals with a somewhat distant past, and is thus at liberty to choose his subject, under no compulsion to lash contemporary incompetence or immorality, is primarily sympathetic and appreciative; he should be the finger-post or guide-book to a garden of sweets. But when this office has been fulfilled, a further duty remains of calmly estimating this author, with a view to assigning him his place in the muster-roll of fame, and to this a recognition of his defects is as necessary as a recognition of his merits, of his blemishes as of his beauties. On this new ground we immediately encounter the great literary Rhadamanthus of that period—Lord Jeffrey,—and all our admiration of Wordsworth does not prevent our substantially admitting some of the main charges brought against him by the great critic. These may be very briefly summarized as follows:—1st, Unintelligible mysticism; 2ndly, Rudeness of plot and construction; 3rdly, Absence or triviality of incident; 4thly, Perverse preference for scenes and characters of low life, even when incongruous with the sentiment and diction of the piece; 5thly, Mawkish sentimentality, and general tendency to prosing.

We are strongly struck by the want of *content* in Wordsworth. He is full of *forms* which want filling up, he takes refuge constantly in the freedom and joy of the universal from the bondage and contradiction of the particular. He craves repose; to be

> "As a statue, solid set,
> And moulded in colossal calm."

He cannot endure, much less grasp or unify, the noisy

life of cities, the pageantry of conquerers or courts, the joys and fears, the hopes and pursuits of crowding, hurrying men impelled along their intricate paths of life by ambition and love, avarice and lust of pleasure, and all the elements of a complex civilization acting on the original human constitution. Such sights appal and dismay him, and he hastens back to converse anew with Nature and the simple life of the hills. When we come to compare him with such poets as Byron or Sir Walter Scott, or even with Tennyson, we realize how great a defect this was. Contrast the infinite light and shade, the human passions and sins and exploits that enliven Byron's page, or the complex situations and thrilling plots of Sir Walter, or the society-painting so frequent in Tennyson, with the ill-dramatised, ill-connected, tedious disquisitions of the "Excursion," and our poet appears to great disadvantage. It may be yielded at once that he had no notion of a plot, very little, if any, perception of individual character, and no sympathy with it if complicated by social culture, a perpetual tendency to stagnate and moralize and sentimentalize when he should have been proceeding vigorously with the action of the piece, a singular incapacity for choosing incidents either interesting or affecting in themselves, and a concomitant tendency to label his incidents with reasons very often valid only in application to himself, why we should be moved by them,—in a word, absence of dramatic or narrative power as opposed to contemplative and imaginative. "The moving accident was not his trade." It is affecting to read, near the opening of the "Prelude," his lament over lost time, and his eager resolve to treat some great subject, and win for himself a niche beside the authors of "Paradise Lost" and the "Fairy Queen," knowing as we do that he will never attempt any weighty theme, historic or legendary, or if he does, will fail. He can write such gems of simple beauty as "Hart-leap-well," or "Stepping Westward," or the "Highland Girl;" he can sow the long desert of an "Excursion" with frequent oases of true poetry; he can epitomize himself, and distil his whole power of rhythm, language, imagination, kindness, philosophy, religion, into a transcendent "Ode on the Intimations of Immortality;" he can even win for himself no mean place amongst the singers of sustained song by an account of the growth of his powers, a soul-biography: but rear the great structure to which this was meant to be but a porch he cannot, and the "Prelude" remains the crown and master-piece of his genius.

It will be evident from these remarks how far we sympathize with Jeffrey's criticism of our poet. When the reaction set in in favour of Wordsworth, Jeffrey's credit as a critic fell as that of Wordsworth as a poet rose, and he seldom now-a-days has full justice done to his good sense and acuteness *in re* Wordsworth. Yet we would not be understood as endorsing his estimate as a whole. We admit the presence of many of the faults he alleges, but recognize merits that far outweigh them, to which Jeffrey was either wilfully or inevitably unfair. In particular, we suspect that his practical life and forensic habits had so warped him into admiration for the eventful in poetry, and so weakened his appreciation of the ideal and imaginative, that some of Wordsworth's most exquisite graces were lost upon him.

This *mysticism*, with which he is never weary of taunting our poet, is pretty much, we suspect, what has been already commemorated as Wordsworth's highest gift—imagination. There is no poet who makes more claim on a sympathetic spirit, an initial εὔνοια; and no poet who, in the end, rewards such a spirit more liberally. He writes so directly from the heart, with so little afterthought or calculation of effect, so little guarding of the flank in anticipation of the critic's onslaught, that he falls an easy prey to one who comes to him with the design of finding faults. Then, too, he has a strain of the self-willed and even the perverse in him, and will press the application of his principles beyond all legitimate bounds, carrying them into travesty with a serious air, that men may be convinced he means all that he says. At this point, too, he is very vulnerable. But we must not forget that even this exaggerated exhibition of literary simplicity has been of incalculable service to the cause of poetry in England. It was no feeble protest, no slight recoil that was needed to deliver English literature from the rule of an exclusive oligarchy of classical forms, sanctioned by old tradition and the authority of great names; and this is what Wordsworth, more perhaps than any poet of that day, helped to achieve for us, successfully asserting for poetry the whole range of nature and thought, under no limitations but those of beauty and fitness.

But that which we would chiefly set over against the faults in Wordsworth is his majestic *personality*. Here, indeed, in Carlylese phraseology, was a "man," and a "veracious" one; no "gig-man" or "phantom." When we have the happiness of being face to face with a man who is all in every line he writes, who does not address us from behind a series of masks, who never strains for scenic effect, or makes grimaces for our amusement, to whom his art is a true end in itself, so that *life* and *poetic effort* are to him synonymous, *then* we can forgive occasional raptures which leave us behind, inartificialities, occasional tediousness; then we can welcome even Egotism's self as the assurance of the true human flesh and blood behind.

The latest developments of our poetry have been in some measure a reaction against Wordsworth's contemplative Idealism and Nature-worship. Tennyson holds much that is Wordsworthian in fusion with very diverse elements, but is remote from the Wordsworthian spirit, and has nothing of the Wordsworthian intensity. Browning has more of the same noble cast, but his study is Man, as Wordsworth's was Nature: and Swinburne is at the opposite pole of poetry; where the death in life of sensuous passion takes the place of the life of reason and imagination, where the universal is sacrificed to the particular. But this fact, and the feverish, money-making spirit of the day, only furnish us with all the stronger reasons for reverting to the study and the love of William Wordsworth, as the man we need to deliver us from our besetting sins.

F. J. G.

SPRING SONGS.

I. FOREBODING OF SPRING.

O BREATHINGS soft and low!
To me ye bring
The songs of Spring,
And soon will the violets blow.

II. THE FAITH OF SPRING.

The gentle airs are abroad at play,
They are sighing and stirring night and day,
   They are busy on every side.
O fresh new sound, O fragrance rare!
Now, wretched soul, put by thy care;
   To all, to all, must change betide.

The world grows every day more green,
We know not what may yet be seen,
   There is blossom on every side.
Green is the farthest, deepest dale:
Now, wretched heart, forget thy bale:
   To all, to all, must change betide.

III. THE REST OF SPRING.

O lay me not in the gloomy clay,
Below the fair green earth away!
I fain, when I shall die,
Among the deepest grass would lie.

In grass and flowers I lie to-day,
And a flute pipes sweet from far away,
And pure and bright on high
The dazzling clouds of Spring go by.

IV. THE HOLIDAY OF SPRING.

Sweet and golden day of Spring!
   Heart so sprightly gay!
If ever I have sped in song,
   Shall I not to-day?

Yet why should I fall to work,
   Work, on such a day?
A high and holy tide is Spring:
   Let me rest and pray!

V. THE PRAISE OF SPRING.

Sprouting green and violets rare,
Warbling lark and blackbird's lay,
Sunny showers and genial air!

If in words like these I sing,
Needs there any greater thing
In thine honour, April day?

VI. CONSOLATION OF SPRING.

Why, heart, in days like these despair,
When the very briars roses bear?

VII. THE FUTURE SPRING.

Sweet suns of gentle April
  In every twelvemonth shine;
That brightest, mightiest April,
  Take heart! shall yet be thine:
It waits for thee, appointed
  At ending of thy way,
Thou here on earth forebodest,
  And yonder breaks the day.

VIII. THE REVIEWER'S SPRING SONG.

Spring is come, we shall be told:
  I am glad, I must allow,
  One can go a walking now,
And not simply catch a cold.

Swallows coming back I see:
  What a pretty time they've been!
  Do put on a little green,
If you love me, my dear tree!

Yes, I feel a little glad:
  I can bear to hear the lark:
  Philomel is near the mark:
And the sun shines not so bad.

No one need be wondering
  If they see me country-bound,
  Going out to take a round,
In my pocket Thomson's Spring.

From Uhland.

THE CENTAUR.

FROM THE FRENCH OF MAURICE DE GUERIN.

[The aged centaur Macareus gives some account of his life to Melampus, who seeks to know wisdom and the origin of things].

I HAD my birth within the caves of these mountains. Like the river of this valley, whose original drops trickle from the weeping rock in some profound grotto, the first instant of my life fell into the darkness of our remote habitation without disturbing its silence. When our mothers are near the time of their delivery, they withdraw to these caverns, and in the wildest recesses, amid the thickest darkness, they bring forth, without uttering a cry, an offspring as uncomplaining as themselves. In the strength of their powerful milk we surmount without feebleness or doubtful struggle the first difficulties of life; and yet we issue from our caves later than you do from your cradles: for it is held among us, that the first beginnings of existence should be kept secluded and veiled, as days pervaded by the presence of the gods. I grew to almost my full stature in the darkness where I was born. The extremity of my dwelling was so deeply sunken in the thickness of the mountain, that I should not have known on what side the entrance lay, had not sometimes a truant wind, straying down the opening, dashed the stillness with freshness and sudden agitations. And sometimes, also, my mother would come back encompassed by the fragrance of the valleys, or dripping from the waters she frequented. When she returned thus, telling me nothing of the valleys or the rivers, but followed by their emanations, my spirit was disquieted, and I wandered restlessly about in my obscurity. What, I said to myself, can these outside places be, to which my mother hurries, and by what powerful influence is she drawn thither so frequently? or what feelings are to be felt there so conflicting, that every day she returns with a different emotion? For she would come back, now inspirited by a deep joy, and now sad and trailing and like one wounded. The joy that she brought back with her was announced even at a distance by something in her gait, and beamed from her looks. I felt it through all my bosom: but her dejection took a greatly firmer hold upon me, and enticed much farther the speculations of my adventurous thoughts. In these moments my strength made me uneasy; I recognised a power that could not remain in solitude, and betaking myself, now to swing my arms, now to accelerate my gallop through the spacious darkness of the cavern, I strove to discover from the blows I launched upon the empty air, and from the passion of my course, the proper object towards which my arms should stretch and my feet bear me. . . . Since then I have locked my arms about the bust of centaurs, and the bodies of heroes, and the trunk of oaks: my hands have handled the rocks, the waters, the innumerable plants, and the most subtile impressions of the air; for I lift them in the blind and tranquil night to surprise the breaths of wind, and draw from thence a sign by which to guess my way: my feet, see, O Melampus, how they are worn! And yet, frozen as I am in this extremity of age, there are days when, in the full sunlight, upon the mountain tops, I repeat these courses of my youth within the cavern, and with the same purpose, whirling my arms and calling out all the remains of my fleetness.

Such disquietudes were succeeded by long cessations of every uneasy emotion. At such times there was no feeling throughout my whole being except that of growth and of the degrees of crescent life within me. Having lost the desire of excitement, and retired into an absolute repose, I tasted unalloyed the benefaction of the gods that filled my breast. Tranquillity and darkness are the powers that call forth the hidden sweetness of the consciousness of life. O darknesses that possess the caverns of these mountains, I owe to your silent care the hidden education that has so strongly nurtured me; under your keeping I have tasted life pure, and such as it came to me from the bosom of the gods! When I descended from your asylum into the light of day, I staggered instead of paying my salutation; for the light took possession of me with violence, intoxicating me like some deadly liquor suddenly diffused within my bosom, and I felt that my being, till then so strong and so simple, tottered and collapsed, as if it were about to be scattered upon the winds.

O Melampus, who seekest to know the life of the centaurs, by what conduct of the gods hast thou been guided to me, the oldest and the saddest of them all? I have long ceased to live any part of their life. I quit no more this mountain summit where old age has imprisoned me, nor do I use the points of my arrows, except to disengage tenacious plants from the soil; the tranquil lakes know me still, but the rivers have forgotten me. I will tell thee something of my youth: but these recollections, issuing from a weakened memory, ooze slowly forth, like the tide of a sluggish libation that trickles from a shattered vase. It was not hard to express my early years, because they were calm and perfect: the solitary and simple life whereof I drank was easy to remember and to relate. Would not a god, if he were asked for the history of his changeless life, sum it up in one word, O Melampus?

My youth was habitually rapid and full of stir. I lived by motion, and knew no limit to my steps. In the pride of my free strength, I stretched my wanderings on every side into these wildernesses. One day, as I passed along a valley where centaurs seldom resort, I discovered a man following the course of the river upon the opposite bank. He was the first who had met my eyes, and I despised him. "See at the very most," I said, "the half of myself! How short are his steps and how awkward his gait! His looks seem sadly to measure the extent of space. Doubtless he is a centaur overthrown by the gods, whom they have reduced thus to drag himself along."

I often refreshed myself, when the day was over, in some river-bed. While one half of myself, hidden in the water, was in motion to sustain me, the other half remained at rest, and my breast and idle arms rose far above the surface. Then would I forget myself in the midst of the waves, yielding to the invitation of their current, which bore me far away, and led the rude guest past all the beauties of the shores. How often, overtaken by the night, have I floated with the stream under the spreading darkness, which carried even to the recesses of the valleys the nocturnal influence of the gods! My turbulent life was soothed, till there remained only a faint perception of existence diffused equally throughout my being, like the beams of the goddess of the night upon the waters in which I swam. Melampus, my old age regrets the rivers; placid for the most part and monotonous, they pursue their destiny with more tranquillity than the centaurs, and with a more beneficent wisdom than that of men. When I issued from their bosom, I was followed by their gifts, which accompanied me for whole days, and only died away gradually, like expiring perfumes.

A blind and violent waywardness was the director of my steps. In the midst of the most impetuous career, I would suddenly break off my gallop, as if I had found an abyss before my feet, or as if a god had met me face to face. The sudden pause allowed me to feel how my life was moved by these ebullitions. In former days I have cut in the forests boughs which as I ran I lifted above my head: the swiftness of my course suspended the quivering of the leaves, which only gave out a gentle rustling; but at the least stoppage the wind again began to agitate the branch, and the train of murmurs began anew. Thus my life, upon the sudden interruption of my impetuous progress across these valleys, tingled through all my frame. I felt it run boiling along in fiery pulses, kindled by the courses I had so impetuously run. My stimulated flanks struggled against these waves, which pressed upon them from within, and tasted in these commotions the pleasure which is known only to the shores of the sea, that of containing, without losing a drop, a life inflamed and risen to its culmination. Yet still, my head bent towards the wind that brought me coolness, I would consider the summits of the mountains, which a few moments had removed into the distance, the trees along the banks and the waters of the rivers, the latter borne on in a tardy stream, the former rooted in the ground, and moving only by their leaves, the patient slaves of the airy currents that make them wail. "I alone," I said, "have free motion, and at my pleasure I transport life from one end to the other of these valleys. I am happier than the torrents which fall from the mountains never to rise again. The rolling sound of my stride is more beautiful than the groanings of the woods or the babble of the waters; this ringing announces the wandering centaur, who prescribes his own course." Thus, while my agitated flanks were filled with the intoxication of the course, my soul was still more deeply filled with its pride, and turning round my head, I stopped for a time to contemplate my steaming limbs.

Youth is like verdant forests shaken by the wind; it tosses to and fro on every side the rich gifts of life, and some deep murmur perpetually reigns within its foliage. Living as carelessly as the rivers, breathing Cybele incessantly, whether in the bed of the valleys, or on the summit of the mountains, I bounded everywhere like a blind and disimprisoned life. But when night, fraught with the tranquillity of the gods, found me on the slope of the hills, she led me to the mouth of caverns, and soothed me as she soothes the billows of the sea, allowing to survive only gentle undulations which kept away sleep without marring my repose. Couched on the threshold of my retreat, my flanks hidden within the cave and my head under the open sky, I watched the spectacle of the darkness. Then the foreign life which had penetrated me during the day was detached from me drop by drop, returning to the peaceful bosom of Cybele, as after the shower those fragments of the rain that have been caught by the leaves fall away, and join the waters once more. They say that during the darkness the sea-gods leave their deep palaces, and, sitting down upon some promontory, stretch their looks far across the ocean. Even so I watched through the night, having beneath my feet an expanse of life that resembled the lulled sea. Restored to full and distinct existence, it seemed to me as if I had been just born, and that some deep waters, in whose bosom I had been conceived, had newly left me on the mountain top, like a dolphin forgotten upon the shallows by the waves of Amphitrite.

My looks ran freely along until they gained the most distant points. Like shores perpetually wet, the line of the western mountains continued to be steeped in gleams which the darkness had not effaced. Yonder could still be seen, in pale clear spaces, some pure and naked summits. Yonder I saw descend now the god Pan, always alone, now the band of the secret divinities; or some nymph of the mountains would pass by, intoxicated by the night. Sometimes the eagles of Mount Olympus traversed the height of heaven and vanished among the distant constellations or under the inspired forests. The spirit of the gods, passing into motion, suddenly disturbed the tranquillity of the ancient oaks.

Thou seekest after wisdom, O Melampus! which is the knowledge of the will of the gods, and thou wanderest among the nations like one whom the Destinies have led astray. Not far from hence there is a stone, which, touched, gives out a sound like the breaking strings of an instrument, and men tell that Apollo, who was driving his flock through these wildernesses, having set his lyre upon this stone, left this melody behind. O Melampus! the wandering gods have set down their lyre upon the stones; but none—none has forgotten it there. Sometimes, when I was watching all the night in caverns, I have fancied that I was about to surprise the dreams of the sleeping Cybele, and that the mother of the gods, betrayed by her visions, would yield up some of her secrets; but I have never recognised more than sounds that died away among the airs of night, or words as inarticulate as the gurgling of the rivers.

"O Macareus!" said to me one day the great Chiròn, upon whose old age I attended, "we are both centaurs of the mountains; but how opposite are our habits of life! Thou seest, all the occupation of my days consists in the seeking for plants; and thou, thou art like those mortals who have picked up on the waters, or in the woods, and carried to their lips, some stray fragments of reed broken by the god Pan. Thenceforward these mortals, having inhaled from the relics of the god a spirit of wildness, or having perhaps caught the infection of some secret madness, enter into the wildernesses, plunge into the woods, follow the courses of the waters, lose themselves in the mountains, disquieted and driven on by an unknown purpose. The mares beloved of the winds in the farthest Scythia are not more wild than thou, nor, more dejected at evening, when the north wind has passed away. Thou seekest to know the gods, O Macareus, and whence are sprung men, animals, and the beginnings of the universal fire? But ancient Ocean, the father of all things, retains these secrets within himself, and the nymphs who surround him weave as they sing an everlasting dance before him, to drown what might escape from lips half-opened in slumber. The mortals who moved the gods by their virtue have received from their hands lyres to delight the nations, or new seeds to make them rich, but nothing from their inexorable mouth.

"In my youth, Apollo filled me with the love of plants, and taught me how to rob their veins of beneficent juices. Since then, I have faithfully remained in the vast habitation of these mountains, restless indeed, but ever turning aside to seek for simples, and making known the virtues I discover. Dost thou see from hence the naked summit of Mount Olta? Alcides stripped it to build his funeral pile. O Macareus! the demigods, children of the gods, stretch out the lion's hide above their piles, and are consumed upon the summits of the mountains! the poisons of the earth infect the blood derived from the immortals! And we, centaurs begotten by an audacious mortal upon a cloud that bore the semblance of a goddess, what help should we expect from Jove, whose bolt has stricken the founder of our race? The vulture of the gods tears for ever at the entrails of the workman who moulded the first man. O Macareus! men and centaurs recognize as the authors of their being those who have stolen the privileges of the immortals; and perhaps all that moves, except the gods, is but a theft that has been made from them, but a petty scrap of their nature borne far away, like the flying seed, by the almighty breath of fate. The story runs that Aegeus, father of Theseus, concealed beneath a massy rock, upon the brink of the sea, memorials and tokens whereby his son might one day discover his birth. The jealous gods have some where buried the proofs of the descent of things: but to the brink of what ocean have they rolled the stone that covers them, O Macareus?"

Such was the wisdom to which the great Chiron led me. Arrived at extreme old age, the centaur harboured in his soul the most lofty thoughts. His still vigorous bust had scarce at all sunk down upon his flanks, above which it rose with a slight inclination, like an oak vexed by the winds, and the strength of his step was scarcely impaired by marring years. One would have said that he still retained some residue of the immortality long ago conferred upon him by Apollo, but which he had restored to the giver.

As for me, O Melampus! I decline into old age, calm as the setting of the constellations. I have still courage enough to reach the top of these rocks, where I linger, whether contemplating the wild and restless clouds, or watching as they rise from the horizon the rainy Hyades, the Pleiads, or the great Orion; but I feel that I am rapidly dwindling and melting away like a snowflake floating upon the water, and that presently I shall go hence, to be blended with the rivers which flow through the spacious bosom of the earth.

AMOR VINCIT.

Poor?—nay, not poor—the joy of worlds is mine:
The beauty and the wealth of land and sea,
The splendour of the darkness, and the shine,
    Are all for me.

The ever-shifting glory of the sky,
The pale wan moon with all her starry train,
Deep rivers making glad great fields of rye
    And golden grain.

Spring, with her singing birds and glad green leaves,
Soft Summer, strewing rosebuds at my feet,
Hoar Autumn garnering his last ripe sheaves
    With odours sweet.

The music of the woodland, and the joy
In all things fair and goodly and divine,
Dim forms and fancies cherished when a boy—
    All these are mine.

The wealth of all the ages that have fled,
The hope of all the ages yet to come,
Immortal memories of the mighty Dead,
    For ever dumb.

Songs, that have charmed the ages in their flight,
Fair faces, that have made all men their slaves,
Legends of nameless heroes, that make bright
    Forgotten graves.

Wealth of great minds, treasures of antique lore,
With weight whereof the wearied ages groan,
The birthright of the centuries—yea more—
    Are all mine own.

Yea more—sweet girl!—in those dear eyes of thine
I read a love that makes all these seem small,
Oh! heart that beats in unison with mine,
    More thou than all!

For love made smooth the roughest steep I trod,
And love made sweet what else were sour indeed,
And love went ever with me like a God
    In hour of need.

ÆSTHETICS.

IN the following pages we propose to contribute a few suggestions which may be of use in enabling our readers to form a clearer, a more comprehensive, and, as we think, a more correct view than that to which they may have been hitherto accustomed, of the science of Æsthetics and its bearings on several closely allied subjects of thought.

The term "Æsthetics" is etymologically applicable to every perceptive process; but in practice it is employed only in speaking of such perceptions* as are attended with emotions of pleasure or pain. The term would not be inappropriate as a comprehensive designation of the philosophical investigations into the wide field of the phenomena presented by our pleasurable and painful emotions. For the present, however, we propose to restrict its application by considering it as "the science whose object is the analysis of the phenomena and logical exposition of the principles connected with our emotions of pleasure or pain, so far as these are called into action through the medium of ideas, images, or impressions, presented to the intellect." By this we mean to exclude from the consideration of Æsthetics gratifications arising from purely physical causes, *e.g.* the satisfaction of appetite, etc.; though these not only belong to the science of Æsthetics in its more extended sense, but are capable, as we shall show, of being indirectly made the subjects of

* The Greek term has been thought to denote preeminently an appreciative and discriminating perception.

Æsthetical investigation, even in the more restricted application of the term; and we may have occasion to refer to them for illustration. Candour compels us to add that much greater limitation than has been above proposed would be requisite in order to circumscribe the science within the bounds ordinarily assigned to it. The words "images" and "impressions" have been employed, the former to bring the effects produced by natural scenery, painting, and sculpture, the latter to bring those produced by music as well as a variety of gratifications of a character too vague and indefinite to be appropriately described by the word "ideas," into the region of our proposed survey.

The object of the above definition is to draw a clear line of demarcation between processes of intellect and processes of feeling; between the cognitive and the sensitive elements; between the mental and the sentimental departments of philosophy. Æsthetics is thus regarded as the metaphysics of feeling, in contradistinction alike to the metaphysics of intellect and the metaphysics of will. But as the botanist finds it no easy matter to frame an adequate definition of a plant which shall not include zoophytes, while the zoologist experiences no less difficulty in so defining an animal as not to bring these peculiar organizations within the domain of his science, so there is one emotion which does not necessarily partake of the nature of either pleasure or pain, but which, notwithstanding, unless examined by Æsthetical investigators, is likely to elude analysis altogether—we refer to surprise. This emotion falls, therefore, to be added to the emotions of pleasure and pain already specified in the definition.

To appreciate properly the place of Æsthetics in relation to the other two branches of metaphysical science above referred to, let us glance for a moment at those elements in the human constitution which are not merely physical. We may be content to accept the Kantian classification of the human faculties into the Cognitions; the Feelings; and the Conations, or efforts of the will. That within us which reflects, knows, remembers, expects; perceives; compares; believes, doubts, disbelieves; and reasons; is recognized as intellect. That within us which is conscious of pleasure and pain (derived, we at present assume, from impressions communicated to the intellect), —that which feels, desires, loves, dislikes, is apprehended as belonging to the sensitive nature. The mind is that which thinks and knows. The soul is that which feels and loves. There is, however, besides these, a faculty of volition in virtue of which we are enabled to make efforts either in accordance with, or in opposition to, individual inducements presented to us. In every scheme of free-will it is impossible for the nature of these voluntary efforts, and of the faculty concerned in their production, to be too carefully distinguished from the desires, as in those cases in which the direction of the volition is coincident with that of the desire, the two are only too liable to be confounded: a result entailing all the disadvantages in relation to practical morality which are attendant on the acceptance of the scheme of necessity. We have, then, as three main divisions of the human constitution, the intellect, the feelings (in a special sense the soul), and the will. The metaphysics of intellect has for ages engaged the attention of philosophers. The metaphysics of feeling constitutes the science of Æsthetics. The metaphysics of the conations has hitherto been treated of chiefly by writers on moral philosophy, whose stand-point enables them to take up the subject only in its relation to human obligation, with which it is professedly the business of moral philosophy to deal. If, however, the territory of the metaphysics of the will has been but partially and incidentally explored, the sister-province of Æsthetics or the metaphysics of feeling has received nothing like the share of attention to which its importance entitles it; and from its vastly greater extent, its numerous ramifications, and the constant pressure on every one of problems demanding at least a *practical* acquaintance with it for their solution, it is difficult to overrate the disadvantage arising from this cause not merely to the students of speculative philosophy, but to all who desire, by assiduous, mental, and psychical culture to qualify themselves more efficiently to discharge the duties, appreciate the enjoyments, and face the calamities of life.

The science of Æsthetics should begin with an investigation into the nature of pleasure, pain, desire, aversion, and emotion in general: should proceed to enunciate the fundamental laws (so far as these have yet been discovered) which regulate all processes of feeling; and should not conclude without a detailed and systematic catalogue of the various sensibilities to pleasure and pain, which together constitute the large part of our immaterial nature to which we cannot apply the terms "intellect" or "will." One or two observations may be hazarded on each of these topics.

I. Pleasure and pain are terms exceedingly difficult to define, except in their mutual correlation, like heat and cold, light and darkness. The Hamiltonian theory of pleasure and pain, hastily dictated at the close of the metaphysical lectures, is, perhaps, among the least satisfactory contributions to philosophy put forth by one of the most eminent speculative metaphysicians that Scotland has yet produced. "Pleasure," says Sir William, "is a reflex of the spontaneous and unimpeded exertion of a power of whose energy we are conscious." "The more perfect, the more pleasurable the energy; the more imperfect, the more painful."

We meet this with the question, "When a child tastes sugar, what is the power or energy of whose spontaneous and unimpeded exertion the pleasurable sensation is asserted to be a reflex?"

If there were such an energy, we should expect it to gain facility by exercise, and in the pleasure which is alleged to ensue we should expect to observe an augmentation proportional to the facility acquired; but does a piece of sugar taste at all sweeter at the hundredth time than at the first? Hamilton, it will be suggested, may have been thinking of pleasure arising from other than physical sources. But even of such pleasures it is only a small number that can be accounted for on the Hamiltonian theory; and the fact seems to be that the increased facility gained by exercise rather removes the dissatisfaction incident to the encountering of impediments than conduces to the production of positive enjoyment. The terms "desire" and "pleasure" may, to a certain extent, be regarded as correlative: "pleasure" being that which is the object of "desire," and "desire" being that whose gratification (only the word gratification conveys too much) constitutes "pleasure." This observation is not, however, free from exception; for, to revert to the illustration above specified, it is obvious that the child, previous to his becoming acquainted with the sensation produced by the application of saccharine substances to his tongue and palate, could not be conscious of desire for that particular form of pleasure. Still, when once the acquaintance has been formed, the child is found to desire the continuance or repetition of the sensation,—a result which could not be brought about by his mere experience of what we call sweetness, were there not previously inherent in his nature a principle, in virtue of which the presentation of any particular form of pleasure caused its continuance or repetition to be desired. Of course the presentation of any particular form of pain would, in virtue of the same principle, cause its continuance to be disliked, and (unless in consequence of the action of the will in connection with counter-considerations) to be resisted. Pain can be chosen; it cannot be desired. Pleasure can be refused; it cannot be disliked. Pleasure which could be disliked would not be pleasure; pain which could be desired would not be pain.* Desire,

* It will be understood that we speak here of pleasure and pain as regarded in themselves, not in their consequences.

as manifested towards persons, assumes the higher form of affection; we are said to love those persons in whose society we find pleasure. It is questionable whether the purely benevolent affections, as pity, are, strictly speaking, personal; inasmuch as though we desire the relief and amelioration of the sufferer's condition, we can hardly be said to love *him*. But we must pass on to

II. The general laws. A good practical abstract of the more important of these will be found in the late Professor Fleming's useful manual of Moral Philosophy. We shall at present only indicate one or two of them. In comparison with cognitions, feelings are less easily and for the most part less distinctly retained in memory, and are less readily recalled, than the results of intellectual processes; the reminiscence is also in general fugitive and delitescent. While, moreover, the frequent repetition of an idea impresses it on the mind with greater firmness, the equally frequent repetition of a sensation tends to neutralize and deaden its effect, whether for pleasure or pain. The popular proverb "Familiarity breeds contempt" is an expression of one aspect of this Æsthetical law; and there are many tastes and habits which are entirely factitious in their nature and artificial in their origin; having been at first either indifferent to us or positively distasteful, but to which, having once adopted them from some extrinsic inducement, we have become inured, reconciled, and in process of time even attached.

III. There should be a detailed and systematic catalogue of the various sources of pleasure. What and how many are the avenues through which it has been divinely provided that pleasure may flow to the human constitution? This is a psychological investigation, and is usually supposed to be the business of moral philosophy. That science, however, has properly to do with rights and duties; and is concerned with emotions only incidentally, and in their relation, direct or indirect, to the sense of obligation. Turn we to the moral philosophers, and what do we find? A brief list of three appetites, one or two tendencies resembling appetites, and some half dozen desires, which are supposed to constitute in conjunction a tolerable outline of the human heart. This meagre sketch is not wholly useless; but it gives little more idea of what it is intended to depict than a skeleton of which one-third had perished would convey of the living animal. We must go to the poets and novelists, not to the philosophers. Let a staff of fifty *littérateurs* be organized under the direction of some experienced guide; let these men be set to work upon the analysis of such writers (to confine ourselves to modern names) as Lessing and Goethe among the Germans; Molière, Rousseau, and Victor Hugo, among the French; Boccaccio, Goldoni (the Molière of Italy), and Alfieri, among the authors of the sunny south; Shakespeare, Milton, Goldsmith, Thackeray, Tennyson, in our own country; and the late Nathaniel Hawthorne in America; let a dozen authors be selected for every one that we have specified; let the analysis be conducted rigidly on the Baconian system; each investigator pausing at every striking portraiture of motive, passion, character, in the narrative, and indicating in his register the particular desire or sensibility exemplified in each instance; let the results be collected, arranged, and classified; the groups so obtained re-classified under higher and more comprehensive divisions; and we shall be furnished with a map of human nature in its various workings such as the world has not yet seen, which would be of extraordinary value as an instrument of education, enabling the student of character to attain in comparatively a short period what at present requires often the labour of a life-time. For affording instruction as to practical life, too, such a chart would be of great importance. Few will deny that, other things being equal, the course of conduct which is attended with the largest amount of happiness, is the wisest to pursue; although in forming a comparative estimate it is necessary to weigh the pleasures as well as to count them, and to take into consideration the quality as well as the quantity of the gratifications compared. The importance of the above-suggested catalogue, as supplying copious materials for instituting such a comparison, is too obvious to be more than indicated.

But, it may be said, "Is not this to employ the term Æsthetics in its more comprehensive sense? How can the physical gratifications of mere appetite rank as subjects of mental philosophy? *They* do not reach the soul through the medium of the intellect." There is some force in these suggestions. It is certain that the practical application to human action of the proposed catalogue belongs to the extended science of Æsthetics. And the "physical gratifications of mere appetite," which we have spoken of as included in the catalogue, do not, in themselves, reach the soul through the medium of the intellect. But they may be described so as to produce a sympathetic impression on the soul by means of ideas conveyed in language addressed to the intellect; and this consideration suffices to justify their examination by the Æsthetical investigator. Who is there, for example, that does not enjoy a Barmecide repast in the perusal of Keats' exquisite lines :—

> "While he from forth the closet brought full store
> Of candied apple, quince, and plum, and gourd,
> With jellies soother than the creamy curd,
> And lucent syrups tinct with cinnamon."

Intense enjoyment, too, is afforded by Mr. Ruskin's magnificent descriptions, in "Modern Painters," of sky-scenery, Turner's pictures, and the Alpine sun-sets: though in these the impressions of physical beauty are communicated to the soul through the medium of language. We have said enough to meet the objection.

Having endeavoured to illustrate the relation sustained by Æsthetics to other branches of metaphysical science—in particular to the metaphysics of intellect, to the metaphysics of will, and to the subject of ethics or moral philosophy,—we propose briefly to examine its relation to the science of Rhetoric, of which, as an instrument for literary purposes, it is the complement.

As the primary object of Logic is formal truth, so that

of Rhetoric is formal beauty, in language.* Given any two propositions, the logician will examine whether they are connected, and if so whether they are consistent with each other; also, whether any new proposition can be evolved from their combination. Or he may regard each separately as the conclusion of a former argument whose reasoning he proceeds to criticize, pronouncing it valid or the reverse in accordance with the canons of his science. The rhetorician's task is different. Given any thought it is his business to express it in the best possible *form*, or else to elicit from it, by rhetorical processes, one or more other thoughts which will sustain a symmetrical relation to it, or tend to enhance its literary effect. The function of Æsthetics, on the other hand, is to supply the best possible *matter*, *i.e.* in a literary point of view the most interesting. The distinction may be illustrated by a reference to the art of naval architecture. The practical shipbuilder has two problems presented to him for solution. He has, first, to select the best timber, iron, etc., within his reach; and having done so, he has, next, to put the materials at his disposal into the best possible form, that is, the form best calculated to secure the purposes of safety, speed, and commodiousness. The former process illustrates the application of Æsthetics to literary purposes; the latter, that of Rhetoric. The systematic catalogue of the

* The application of the term "Rhetoric" is too often restricted to the art of persuading, *i.e.* of employing arguments to induce one's hearers to adopt some particular course of conduct. The subject of the propriety or otherwise of this restriction we cannot here discuss.

sources of interest which we have already suggested would prove an invaluable repertory to the literary artist; and indeed it is very much in proportion as the genius of individual men has enabled them to gain, it may be instinctively, something more or less equivalent to a practical acquaintance with the catalogue in question, that success has rewarded their exertions. In their case the knowledge, as we have hinted, may have been acquired instinctively. But an intelligent and systematic acquaintance with a subject is, *cæteris paribus*, unquestionably preferable to a merely instinctive one; the man who speaks a language with full knowledge of its grammatical structure, possessing obviously great advantages over one equal to him in other respects but destitute of that special knowledge. And as we have before stated, the effect of such a catalogue would be to facilitate and accelerate human progress by enabling individuals to gain the familiar acquaintance with human nature which it takes them at present ten or twenty years to acquire, within a much shorter period. To teach men to parse not words, but actions; to qualify them to live with a knowledge of the grammatical structure of *life*, and not in the profound ignorance of it or the but partial enlightenment regarding it in which too many of us still linger—this would be no unworthy object of philosophic ambition.

Another illustration of the difficulty of framing definitions which shall leave no boundary-land in dispute between the conflicting claims of bordering sciences, is furnished by the question whether the pleasure arising from Wit ought to be considered as due to the matter or to the form of the thought. If the former it would fall to be treated under Æsthetics; if the latter, under Rhetoric. By wit we here intend to denote the all but identification of two (or more) different ideas with a single term or phrase, irrespective of the particular method *(paronomasia amphibolia,* etc.), by which the identification is effected. The mere accident of a term or phrase being employed in such a way as that the two ideas, apart from any consideration of their nature, are simultaneously suggested to the mind in such close mutual relation as to be almost identified is scarcely sufficient to warrant us in treating wit as, in a strictly logical sense, a *formal* process. On the other hand, in any specific instance it is not anything in the particular term employed or in the particular ideas which are identified with it, that gives rise to the pleasurable emotion; it is the mere fact that two conceptions, different in themselves, are closely associated with each other and simultaneously suggested to the mind by a single term. The enjoyment of wit is, therefore, not so obviously a subject falling within the province of Æsthetics, as is, for example, the pleasure derived from humour, or from the contemplation of images of ideal beauty; while, on the other hand, it is not so exclusively formal in its character as to allow the rhetorician to feel quite at liberty to treat it as on the same level with the other distinctly formal processes of his art. Fortunately, however, the problem is one more curious than useful; and its solution can, perhaps, be best effected by relegating the examination of wit to the investigators of both sciences, so that the subject may receive all the light that can be cast upon it from the two independent fields of research.

The gratification which we derive from literature is of one or other of two kinds, according as the interest with which it inspires us is serious or mirthful. The seriously interesting manifests itself in the forms of the sublime, the beautiful, and the pathetic; between which, especially between the two latter of which, it is not easy to draw any satisfactory line of demarcation. In comparing the sublime or beautiful, with the comically interesting or ludicrous, if each be taken at its zenith the superiority of the former is at once apparent, though there are individual *jeux d'esprit* which rank higher as works of art than individual compositions in the serious style. On the other hand, we can afford to laugh twenty times for once that we earnestly admire; and hence, both in real life and in the higher walks of fiction, we find that the occasions for the exercise of the sensibility to the ludicrous preponderate in number over our opportunities of deep and serious enjoyment—a circumstance which, so far from detracting from the value and dignity of the loftier style, rather enhances both. We may add that most of the sources of pleasure comprised in the systematic list formerly indicated, may be employed by the literary artist, so as to produce an effect, either of a serious or of a ludicrous nature.

It remains only for us, in conclusion, to express our wish that the treatment of this important theme had fallen into more competent hands than those which have for years been almost exclusively occupied with very different matters. Nevertheless we are not without the hope that our efforts, such as they are, may be of service in aiding those of our readers whose interest in the subject has induced them to peruse the foregoing pages, to form a more definite, comprehensive, and satisfactory conception than they have hitherto done, of the nature, relations, and value, of the science of Æsthetics.

LOVE.

Not often and not long do grovelling men
    The face of love behold.
One instant seen, his look divine again
    In Life's coarse screens is rolled.

He floats on high, an urn within his hands;
    And where its brimmings fall,
One moment's breath of heaven's own altar brands
    Thrills and bespirits all.

And sometimes in the gleams of mutual eyes,
    And sometimes in a bosom-rose's dew,
The half-too-late-seen glance of love defies
    The hungered after view.

Upon the parched up meadow of the heart
    He lights one second long;
Through fresh green grasses dazzling flowerets start
    Of instantaneous song.

NOTES OF A LECTURE BY GEORGE MACDONALD.

WE love to pry into the kitchens of great men. Genius hallows whatever it touches, investing the trifles of life with fictitious importance. Johnson's twenty-four cups of tea, Lamb's stutter, Thackeray's spectacles—these things have for most of us a strange interest. We delight in learning the minutest trifle regarding the private life and habits of—I shall not merely say great, but celebrated—men. A famous author or infamous criminal is equally an object of intense curiosity. An autograph note by Dryden sold not long since for a fabulous sum. Some years ago the doorsteps of a vile poisoner were literally chipped away by foolish people eager to obtain some memorial of his sin. In the latter case, curiosity springs from a certain inexplicable pleasure or fascination which most men find in the horrible; in the former, the knowledge of the foibles and manners of the great delights us by appealing to our vanity. We love to be assured that kings and peasants, Tennysons and John Smiths, are after all not so very different from each other. Greater it may be is Crœsus or Bacon, richer or wiser, but yet subject to like temptations and errors, interested by like objects, and in their friendships and enmities, their pleasures and sorrows, their habits and conversation, very much like ordinary mortals. It is hard at times to realize this fact. Newton and hot rolls, Bacon and cowardice, Poe's poems and Poe's life—these things are not to be associated in our minds without an effort. In reading a poem or work of fiction we unconsciously imagine to ourselves the likeness of its author. To us who have never seen him his face is familiar as that of a friend. From his own pages have we built his image, and instinctively, unconsciously, fashioned and coloured it according to the character of his work. Sometimes we hit the mark, most often we are wrong. Poe, whose works are pure and perfect as a marble statue by Praxiteles, had yet—if his photograph is to be trusted—the face of a fallen angel. Smedley, whose novels are the delight of schoolboys from their glowing descriptions of boating, racing and wrestling, was himself a cripple and confined to his couch. The poet whose works have charmed us by the sublimity of their sentiment and the subtle sweetness of their rhythm, is not in reality the man we imagine him to be. He is as often as not quite a common-looking man, not very amiable in character nor choice in language, addicted to much brandy and old clothes, and very different indeed from the pure and radiant ideal which his poetry had prepared us for. Wordsworth, on his first visit to Scotland, refused, when in the neighbourhood, to visit Yarrow, fearing with poetic sensitiveness that the actual should fall short of the ideal and the charm be broken. It was with feelings of a similar nature that I went one night two years ago to hear George Macdonald lecture. I had read his works, and admired their artistic beauty, their rhythmical sweetness of style and the subtle delicacy and Christian tenderness running through them, and I had formed my own opinion of the author's *personnel*. As to the character of these anticipations it were presumption in me to say a word. What impressions I received from the lecture is another thing; and I trust that the following sketch, though hasty and imperfect, will not be awanting in interest to such of my readers as are familiar—and who is not?—with the writings of our greatest Scotch novelist after Scott.

My first impressions of the author of "David Elginbrod" were not altogether favourable. I was seated too far back to see his features distinctly, but his general appearance struck me as odd. Tall and slenderly built, of uncouth appearance, with a massive head round which the long unbrushed raven locks hung thickly, a strongly marked face, small eyes, large mouth, and great black beard and moustaches—I asked myself "Can that be George Macdonald?" Afterwards, indeed, when I became familiar with the tender expression of his face, his quaint earnest manner, his simple humour, and his pleasant little appreciative laugh, I became reconciled, and wondered how I could have imagined him to be other than he was. The tone in which the opening words were uttered proclaimed his nationality—there was no mistaking it. "I have understood Tennyson," he said, "but Wordsworth understood me." The words were pronounced slowly, with a slight drawl, and the true North-east country accent. In this way he began his lecture, or rather chat. The subject was Wordsworth; but those who had expected to hear a succinct account of the poet's life, or a philosophical criticism of his writings, must have been disappointed. The only fact, if I remember aright, which Mr. Macdonald mentioned regarding Wordsworth's life, was, that he was born in a particular year, and even in making so simple a statement he stammered and gave the wrong date. It may have been intentional—to raise a laugh—but I hardly think so. His own goodnatured explanation wàs, that "he had made a blunder once regarding the precise date, and had ever since stuck to it."

Gradually, as he warmed with his subject, his manner lost its air of strangeness, his Highland accent seemed less marked, until at length every unfavourable impression vanished, and the audience sat delighted. The lecturer began by showing the immense influence which the French Revolution had exercised on Wordsworth and his contemporaries; and referred to Atheism in these terms— " Don't say that a man is bad because he does not believe in God. I believe in God, and I believe that God cares for those men and loves them, *if* they don't merely *pretend* to believe or disbelieve in Him when they don't." " Wordsworth, however," he continued, " was indebted to other influences. I don't know"—here he looked up with a sort of mystified expression as he slowly drew his hand across his forehead and eyes—he has a trick of this—" I don't know *what* Wordsworth would have done without his sister. Hamlet failed in being a hero because he had no one to help him. His mother was not good, and—and" (this in a hesitating manner) "Ophelia—withdrew. But perhaps the greatest influence of all on the poet's mind was nature. The feeling used to be so strong in these northern parts, that if you talked about nature with anything like enthusiasm, you were worshipping a heathen goddess. Friends, *it is rank paganism—* worse than paganism. The devil did not make the moonlight, nor did God place us here to strive against the lovely influences of sea and land and sky, amid which he has set us. The man who loves nature aright is a good man—a man of tender heart. . . . Man has had too much to do with the town, and God too little. The influence which nature exercised on Wordsworth was very strong. Like his own "Wanderer," he was 'overpowered' by it. In his "Prelude," especially, he tells us how nature worked to bring him back to peace. And in some such way does nature work on every one of us. What, for instance, would our notions of God and infinity be, if for the sapphire skies overhead we had this ceiling?" Here the lecturer stopped short in affected perplexity. "Now," he went on, looking up and around, "for a ceiling this is well, and so are the walls, *but*"—— Here he broke off with a laugh—a sort of quiet chuckle at his own humour, which set the audience in a titter. Not that the joke was a good one, or that there was any joke at all. Indeed, much of Mr. Macdonald's humour struck me as forced and awkward. What carried away his hearers was not the wit, but the speaker's own simple satisfaction with his own sallies, as shown in the short, hearty little laugh which invariably accompanied them. "The world," he continued, "is but another body around our bodies, and capable of expressing all the changes and shadows of life. From this, nature fell down on Wordsworth. If any one here doubts the influence of nature, let him out to some wild, waste, tenantless moor, *alone*, with nothing within sight to remind him of man. Only the sad wind soughing through the dying ferns, and leagues of barren moorland around him, with nothing to catch the eye or break the dull monotony. There silent and alone in the sacred hush of the closing day, when the shadows deepen on the hill, let him gaze upon the silent face of God. . . . To show you how strong a hold nature had on the poet, allow me to read you these lines." Here he read the well known passage, beginning, "One summer evening, led by her, &c.," and went on to say,—" That's the kind of thing he got out of nature. Wordsworth's calling was a high one— to mediate between nature and human nature. But more than this, Wordsworth got amusement out of nature. Now, amusement *is* a good thing: and though of good things nothing is really low, still is amusement relatively the lowest. There are some people who have no right to be amused, and there are those who can't be amused. You find them continually staring at things, and they think it a fine thing not to laugh or show surprise at anything. But to return, Wordsworth, as I have said, *did* get amusement out of nature, and I'll prove it to you from his poem of the 'Daisy.' On this subject of the daisy, by the way, I confess that I don't find the depth in Wordsworth that I find in Chaucer, *but only on this subject.* Well, then, I want to read this for amusement— not *your* amusement, for I don't think"—mark the quiet irony, intensely Scotch in its pauky slyness—"*you* will find it amusing, but it was so to Wordsworth :"—

"'With little here to do or see
Of things that in the great world be,
Sweet Daisy! oft I talk to thee,
  For thou art worthy.
Thou unassuming common-place
Of nature with that homely face,
And yet with something of a grace,
  Which love makes for thee.

Oft do I sit by thee at ease,
And weave a web of similes,
Loose types of things through all degrees
  Thoughts of thy raising;
And many a fond and idle name
I give to thee, for praise or blame,
As in the humour of the game,
  While I am gazing.

A nun demure, of lowly port;
Or sprightly maiden, of love's court,
In thy simplicity the sport
  Of all temptations;
A queen in crown of rubies dres't;
A starveling in a scanty vest;
Are all, as seem to suit thee best,
  Thy appellations.

A little cyclops, with one eye
Staring to threaten and defy,
That thought comes next—and instantly
  The freak is over,
The shape will vanish, and, behold!
A silver shield with bars of gold,
That spreads itself, some fairy bold
  In fight to cover.

> I see thee glittering from afar ;—
> And then thou art a pretty star ;
> Not quite so fair as many are
>   In heaven above thee !
> Yet like a star, with glittering crest,
> Self-poised in air thou seem'st to rest ;—
> May peace come never to his nest,
>   Who shall reprove thee !
>
> Sweet flower ! for by that name at last,
> When all my reveries are past,
> I call thee, and to that cleave fast.
>   *Sweet silent creature!*
> That *breath'st with me* in sun and air,
> Do thou, as thou art wont, *repair*
> *My heart with gladness, and a share*
>   *Of thy meek nature!*'

"Here we have poetry in one of her playful moods —fancy run wild. Imagination and fancy are related to each other as humour is to wit. The latter is in a measure untrue, building itself on chance appearances; imagination deals with truth. Wordsworth also found amusement in the lower animals. We have no notion of the intense humanity of brutes. But he found more than amusement in nature—he found gladness, which can make a man weep; amusement can only make him laugh. Take for example these beautiful lines,—

> "'I wandered lonely as a cloud
> That floats on high o'er vales and hills,
> When all at once I saw a crowd,
> A host of golden daffodils,
> Beside the lake, beneath the trees,
> Fluttering and dancing in the breeze.

Continuous as the stars that shine
And twinkle on the milky way,
They stretched in never-ending line
Along the margin of a bay :
Ten thousand saw I at a glance,
Tossing their heads in sprightly dance.

The waves beside them danced, but they
Out-did the sparkling waves in glee :
A poet could not but be gay
In such a jocund company :
I gazed—and gazed—but little thought
What wealth the show to me had brought :

For oft when on my couch I lie
In vacant or in pensive mood,
*They flash upon that inward eye
Which is the bliss of solitude,
And then my heart with pleasure fills,
And dances with the daffodils.*'

"Wordsworth as a poet has two faults; first, he sneers at all worldlings. Now we have no business to sneer, even at the butterflies of society. They are pretty—*very* pretty"—this in a tone of humorous pity,—"do nothing—but I suppose they must have *some* good in them, or God wouldn't have made them. We should be very cautious in attacking our brothers. There are good people who make their goodness questionable by their violent attacks on their neighbours, who, in their opinion at least, have not discovered the truth."

As an instance of true teaching from nature Mr. Macdonald read the well known sonnet, beginning "One who was suffering tumult in his soul." "Wordsworth," he said, "was troubled and in despair. Instead of doing the most sensible thing—praying, he did the next best, and went out into the midnight and the storm, a sort of homœopathic treatment of the soul which is often very effective. There the sudden sight of the blue lift of sky peeping through the drifting storm-clouds taught the poet the soothing lesson, that the troubles and passions of life reach but a little way up, and that all beyond is peace and rest.

"Wordsworth set about thinking how he could best teach mankind, and bring nature and human nature into sympathy with each other; and he came to the conclusion that this could be done best through the medium of poetry. Now, before we go farther, what is poetry?—a question more pertinently put in Wordsworth's age than now. There was then much quantity but a great dearth of quality—no end of rubbish accepted as the genuine material, and even what good poetry there did exist might have been better. * Of all the many definitions of poetry which I have seen I like Wordsworth's best.— "Poetry is the impassioned look of science upon the face of nature." I shall endeavour to make this plain to you by a homely illustration. Two friends, one of whom is an eminent scientific man and great in botany, go out in March in search of primroses. The man of science comes on the flower first. He explains to his friend the

---

* In this I cannot help thinking Mr. Macdonald is wrong. The beginning of the present century will ever rank in English history as the most illustrious in poetical development, not excepting the Elizabethan era.

first principles of botany—very kind and instructive, no doubt—and in his scientific zeal pulls the primrose to pieces to explain its formation. 'But,' cries his friend, unsatisfied by the learned disquisition, 'where is the primrose? The something which the leaves held—the meaning—the human look on the primrose's face—that for which all science (which if it be unconscious of its end is slavish) exists?—for 'poetry is the impassioned look of science upon the face of nature.' The next question which Wordsworth had to decide was, 'what form of poetry he should use,' and after much thought he adopted the language of simple-hearted, unsophisticated country people. For this he was immensely laughed at and ridiculed by a host of people, headed by the *Edinburgh Review;* but the great-hearted Sir Walter Scott backed him up, and after-years confirmed the brilliant Scotchman's judgment. One of the instances selected by the *Edinburgh* on which to discharge its bitterest ridicule was the following, which I shall read to you and allow you to decide between the poet and the Reviewer,—

"'She dwelt among the untrodden ways,
  Beside the springs of Dove,
A maid whom there were none to praise,
  And very few to love.

A violet by a mossy stone
  Half-hidden from the eye!
Fair as a star, when only one
  Is shining in the sky.

> She lived unknown, and few could know
> When Lucy ceased to be;
> But she is in her grave, *and oh,*
> *The difference to me!*'"

Having read the poem with great pathos and feeling,—" Words could say no more, and so, in the last line, the poet throws the reader back on his own individual experience—'And, oh, the difference to *me*.'

"Another thing besides *fine* language to which Wordsworth objected, was the undue prominence which poets gave to circumstance. The fault of sensational writing is that it interests you in people of no value but such as their position at the time may happen to give them. Once read, the book has lost its interest—*the characters have no secrets.* Is Macbeth sensational? No. Does one read it for the murder? *That* is only introduced to evolve and elucidate the history of two minds. Take, by way of example, the following verses as a sort of protest against this fashion. They are entitled "The Reverie of Poor Susan"—

"'At the corner of Wood Street'—

Now, observe, that's not very poetical; the poetry lies in the elucidation of the human heart,"

> "'At the corner of Wood Street, when day-light appears,
> There's a thrush that sings loud, it has sung for three years:
> Poor Susan has passed by the spot, and has heard
> In the silence of morning the song of the bird.
>
> 'Tis a note of enchantment; what ails her? She sees
> A mountain ascending, a vision of trees;

Bright volumes of vapour through Lothbury glide,
And a river flows on through the vale of Cheapside.

Green pastures she views in the midst of the dale,
Down which she has often tripped with her pail ;
And a single small cottage, a nest like a dove's,
The one only dwelling on earth that she loves.

She looks, and her heart is in heaven : but they fade,
The mist and the river, the hill and the shade ;
The stream will not flow, and the hill will not rise,
And the colours have all passed away from her eyes.'

" 'A very remarkable instance of association of ideas !' " says the man of science. Yes, certainly, very remarkable, and something more—it teaches us what the human heart of a poor sister feels.

"If you would learn what the animal creation taught Wordsworth, read those gems of poetry,—"The Nightingale" and "Ode to a Skylark;" though, by the way, I can't help thinking it a pity that in the second edition of his works Wordsworth omitted the second stanza of the latter poem as it originally stood.

"I have already specified one of Wordsworth's faults, another was his blindness to suggestions of the ludicrous. There are often two ways of reading his lines, and he didn't see the second way. For a perfect study of human nature read "Simon Lee." Watch that your heart has points of sympathy with every fellow creature—in this poem he has shown that he had.

"There are only three masters of blank verse, and three writers of first-rate sonnets in the English language.

Tennyson has only one sonnet.* Milton was a master of sonnet, so was Shakespeare, though not in the same way. The sonnets of the latter are very polished, exquisitely musical, but not *quite* crystallized." Here the lecturer hesitated for a moment, and characteristically added, "I'm ashamed of having said that of Shakespeare, but *it won't hurt him*. . . . Wordsworth was another master, though his ecclesiastical sonnets are not much worth. Some of Mrs. Browning's, too, are worthy of being mentioned along with those of these authors." After an apology for speaking so long—nearly two hours—the lecturer concluded by reading the sonnet beginning " Methought I saw the footsteps of a throne," —which, he remarked, was not so artistic as some— and that one entitled "London," composed on Westminster Bridge, just before sunrise.

Such is a rude, and necessarily very imperfect sketch of Mr. Macdonald's lecture. The words I have given are not the *ipsissima verba*, but they express the speaker's spirit and meaning. Scanty though these notes be, and far as they are from doing Mr. Macdonald justice, they may yet serve to give such as have not heard him some faint idea of his strange, rambling style, quaint delivery, quiet humour, and large-heartedness, and above all the Carlylean earnestness which animates whatever he writes or says. "Some people," I once heard him remark, "accuse me of being too prone to turn my stories into sermons. They forget that I have another master

* In this Mr. Macdonald is wrong. Tennyson has at least three sonnets to a " Flirt."

than the public, and I must serve Him first!" Well would it be for all of us, author and reader, if these words were oftener remembered. Mr. Macdonald's errors as a critic lean to virtue's side. He is, if anything, too tender. The same fault gives a tone to his writings. Amid much keen perception of human nature, and poetic genius of a high order, there runs a vein of weakness. If it were not that the term has been so much misused of late, I should have said the sentimental part of his nature is unduly developed. He has never outgrown, it is doubtful if he ever will outgrow—the first fresh enthusiasm of youth. He admires great men so much as to shrink from comparing them. "However much I love Tennyson," he once remarked, "I love Wordsworth more,"—then, after a moment's hesitation, added—"or would have, were it not for 'In Memoriam.'" His voice is rich and mellow, though I question if it has body enough to fill a large hall. His style of reading is strange but effective. I shall not soon forget the manner in which he recited the Laureate's "Brook," and "Northern Farmer." The latter poem he pronounced, "Clever—*very* clever, but not much more;" and he confessed that greatly as he admired Mr. Tennyson he did not think that even he could have written it. Mr. Macdonald has the knack of saying striking things, that stick burr-like to one's memory. Talking of Judas once, he remarked, "Judas was not such a bad sort of fellow after all. It was certainly unfortunate that he carried the bag; but I doubt not poor Judas looked upon an odd copper now and then as his right, or, as we should call them now-a-days, 'perquisites.'"

His lectures are no lectures in the usual acceptation of the word. He takes his audience by the button-hole, and, without as much as a scrap of paper, chats away to them pleasantly, often on every conceivable topic but the one on which he ought to speak; and after keeping them in delight and wonder for a couple of hours or so, suddenly and abruptly breaks off without any attempt at a peroration, as if he had stopped in the middle of his lecture, and could have gone on for any length of time longer. I have made no attempt to estimate Mr. Macdonald's place as a novelist, poet and thinker. I have merely endeavoured in these rude and hurried notes to record my impressions of one whom I deeply admire and respect, —one whose works amid the heat and passion of modern life and literature stand out remarkable for their pure and classic beauty, and show in every line how nobly the writer has acted up to his profession never to forget "that he has two masters to serve, of whom God is first."

PROOEMION.

In name of Him, that did himself create,
Incessant-active his eternal state;
In name of Him, from whom all these proceed,
Faith, Love, and Confidence, and Power, and Deed;
In His great name, who, titled o'er and o'er,
Remains unknown in essence as before:

As far as ear, as far as eye can go,
Only familiar things His image show;
And to thy spirit's lofty-soaring aim
Figure is wearied out, and likeness tame;
Thy steps are drawn, are torn in joy away,
And where thou journeyest, path and place grow gay:
Number is lost, and Time no more for thee,
And every step is all infinity.
                              Goethe—"*Gott und Welt.*"

PANTHEISM.

It may seem presumptuous to attempt, within the compass of a few pages, to offer anything like an adequate view of the multitudinous phases of Pantheism, more especially as it is proposed to examine these in their generating philosophical principles. To obviate this difficulty, at least in part, it will be necessary to confine our attention to one well defined type. All forms of Pantheism, which rest on anything like a speculative basis, are identified with, and spring from, one or other of the philosophies of Identity or Fatalism. The first represents the Deity as the universal substance, the second as the sole agent. The philosophy of Identity, again, resolves itself into two antagonistic forms, according as matter or mind is taken as the generating principle of all existence. Hence the various forms of Pantheism may be reduced to three well defined types, namely, the Dynamic, the Material, and the Idealistic. It is not pretended, however, that this is a perfect division, for Pantheism, it would seem, has other than mere speculative roots. For example, the Pantheistic faith of India appears to be not so much the outcome of any special philosophy, as a chronic distemper of the religious principle. True, it is associated with a philosophy, but that philosophy seems to be rather a development from a Pantheistic religiosity, than its producing cause. For a like reason, this form of religious belief has obtained a wide currency as a mere faith among a class who can have no adequate comprehension of its fundamental principles, and who must therefore be drawn towards such a faith for what it is in itself, and not on account of its speculative relations. The explanation lies in the fact that it has æsthetic as well as philosophical recommendations. Grand and imposing at a distance, its charms are overpowering for those dreamy, contemplative, mystical souls, who love to dwell in a hazy atmosphere, where nothing takes a definite outline, and all is in keeping with their own amorphous conceptions. We can even understand how it would be difficult to repress this faith in the contemplative minds of Eastern dreamers. Weak in moral purpose, more devoted to speculation than action, and continually witnessing the grandest processes of material nature, their personality is crushed and rendered unfit to present an effective barrier to the invading stream of infinite being. At present, however, we do not propose to deal with Pantheism as a beautiful thought, a pretty conceit, or a miserable affectation, but as the inevitable conclusion of a philosophy which puts forth an exclusive title to the name, and which claims for itself *absolute* certainty. Could it be shown that what aspires to this lofty pre-eminence is baseless and absurd, then those sickly sentimentalists, who know no criteria of truth but novelty and "pain-born beauty," might well be left to the enjoyment of their darling faith.

As before observed, it will be expedient to pass over, without notice, that form of Pantheism which rests on a materialistic basis, and confine our attention exclusively to the idealistic type. At the very outset we are startled by the assertion that Pantheism is the legitimate offspring of true science, of an absolute *gnosis*, which at once does away with the necessity of faith and the possibility of scepticism. If so, then it is no longer a mere sentiment soliciting acceptance, but a logical necessity exacting belief. No matter how we may exclaim against it, and urge our most intimate convictions—as, for example, our personality, which appears to hedge us off from all other being, or our feeling of responsibility, which seems to be inconsistent with the flow of a divine fate,—we must acquiesce, if these pretensions can be made good. In the determination of this point, one of two possible methods may be adopted. Proceeding implicitly on the veracity of our native and necessary convictions, and the perfect congruity of our legitimate knowledges, we may at once set about comparing Pantheism as a speculative result, with other convictions which are for us as certain as any others can possibly be. If it should prove that Pantheism harmonises these, or at least does not clash with them, then it may be true. But if, on the other hand, Pantheism be inconsistent with our intuitive perceptions or belief,—the supposition on which we are proceeding being legitimate—it must be unconditionally rejected. Indeed, its very definition makes such comparison impossible. If God be the all, then all existences are but parts or manifestations of the same fundamental essence, and our persistent belief in our separate individual existence an illusion. Even out of respect to the advocates of this faith, we must accept this as a true representation of their position; for, if the Deity is not all in the sense that there can be nothing else, he has no essential unity, and is conceived of as an arithmetical sum—a rude conglomerate of heterogeneous existences. But if the Deity is a true unity, our convictions as to personality must be explained away, seeing that they are in flagrant contradiction to the very conception of Pantheism. Such a method of criticising Pantheism, though not unfair, and perhaps practically sufficient, is, however, unsatisfactory from a philosophical point of view, because it rests on an assumption, and may be abused in the interests of scepticism. For what if Pantheism should prove to be a logical deduction from undoubted premises, as certain, at least, as any of those with which they are immediately brought into collision? Possibly it may be satisfactorily established that both sides of the antinomy are for us true. But what then? No conclusion can be drawn: knowledge is impossible, and absolute scepticism—the greatest of all absurdities, because the cessation of mental activity—is the inevitable result, since we cannot arbitrate between conflicting convictions equally rooted in our nature, it being impossible to lay hold of any criterion of truth outside of, or above, consciousness. At best, therefore, the ordinary mode of meeting the Pantheist, logically pursued, issues in an alternative—orthodox theism, or absolute scepticism. But even to this issue it will be difficult to bring matters, especially in the case of the Trinitarian. "Why," the Pantheist may demand of such an one, "do you urge your own personal existence as an argument against the existence of only one infinite substance or essence, seeing you maintain that there are three persons in one divine substance or essence? Your own religious belief is a sufficient answer to the only objection you can advance, for all your arguments resolve themselves into the one argument from consciousness or personality."

But by far the most satisfactory and most philosophical method is to examine Pantheism in its speculative ground principles, and if it can be shown that these are baseless, the common faith of humanity, and the possibility and congruity of knowledge are vindicated.

What then is the basis on which Idealistic Pantheism rests? We are told, and that in the most confident tone, that it is a legitimate conclusion of the higher philosophy, —not indeed of that miserable empiricism which under the name of Psychology feebly and painfully creeps along the ground, contenting itself with husks and probabilities, and feeding its votaries with blind faith,—but of absolute science, which, aspiring to lift itself above all experience, seeks to grasp and penetrate infinite being, or being in itself, and from this sublime attitude to develop and reproduce by the method of strict logical deduction the whole movements of the universe. Truly this is a grand ideal·! To be delivered from all seeming, all probabilities, to know not only what is but what must be, to penetrate into the innermost kernel of existence, so that all shall become perfectly fluid and ˙transparent, is surely for the finite mind a genuine apotheosis. And it is here that this form of Pantheism has its root—in the persistent struggles of speculative spirits to construct absolute science, *i.e.* a science which, starting from a principle absolutely apprehended, comprehends and explains by the method of rigid deduction the whole phenomenal universe, and in so doing furnishes a life of the absolute. To sober thinkers this will no doubt appear an insane and almost impious attempt to overleap the conditions and limitations of finite thought, and yet it is the principle, avowed or implicit, according to which the metaphysical potentates of Germany have constructed their systems. Such being their ideal, it will be evident to the student of philosophy that to realise it, even in appearance, two gigantic assumptions must be made at the outset, first, that thought and being are identical in essence, or thought is the all; second, that we can have a full and perfect comprehension of the infinite or absolute. Let us examine these propositions in their order.

Kant is generally allowed by modern metaphysicians to have shown conclusively that on the dualistic theory a scientific or demonstrated ontology is impossible. The reason is evident. Assuming that knowledge springs out of a relation subsisting between the ego and the non-ego, knowledge cannot be of the thing in itself, as it exists out of relation to our cognitive powers. Possibly, therefore, thought may be no adequate reflection of pure being, but rather of the nature of a chemical compound, which neither in appearance nor in sensible qualities resembles any of its components. True, thought *may* be a perfect representation of its object, and is, in fact, generally accepted as such, but this is nothing to the purpose of absolute gnosis, which excludes all faith. Scepticism on this point must therefore be ever possible, and consequently it must ever be impossible scientifically or demonstratively to bridge over the gulf between knowing and being. Besides, according to the ordinary theory of consciousness, knowledge only embraces the phenomenal. The knowable consequently reposes on a dark unknown and unknowable nucleus—on a hard persistent essence impervious to thought. This also is inconsistent with the character of absolute gnosis, which must thoroughly permeate its object on all sides. Such conclusions, it might have been thought, would have put a stop to the vagaries of absolute science and demonstrated ontologies. But no, "absolute science," say Fichte and others, "is possible:" and if, on the dualistic theory, it be impossible, then that theory is false, and some other must be adopted according to which it shall be made to appear that we have a knowledge of being in itself. No preliminary criticism, it will be observed, is instituted, as to the character and value of human thought. It is simply assumed that a cognition of pure being is possible to the human mind. This may be made to appear in two ways. Either, with Fichte, it may be maintained that thought is the all, or, with Schelling and Hegel, that thought and being are identical. Both suppositions virtually amount to the same thing, and both solve the grand philosophical problem by annihilating it. The passage from epistemology to ontology no longer requires to be made, for the two are identified. Science or philosophy is now possible, inasmuch as it has only one generating principle, viz., an infinite thought or activity which can thoroughly comprehend itself. It is evident that this principle logically involves Pantheism. If thought is the all, or if all existence is absolutely identical with our thought, there can be but one essence in the universe, whether that one being be the absolute activity of Fichte, the infinite subject-object of Schelling, or the logical process of Hegel. But must we sacrifice our necessary convictions and our individual existence for the sake of tiding over this preliminary difficulty, and be satisfied with a solution which is as much a hypothesis, as the solution which seems to be presented by the constitution of our minds? Is knowledge to be robbed of its distinctive character, and converted into an aimless regulated activity which exists by itself and for itself, simply in order to do away with the necessity of answering that puzzle which is ever presenting itself to the victim of absolute science as to the scientific proof of the conformity of thought with being? On what grounds, then, are we to assume, with Fichte, that the out-world is but the reflex of our own activity, or, with Schelling and Hegel, that thought and being are identical? No doubt the true reason is to be found in the exigencies of the ideal they had formed to themselves of the character and aims of philosophy. Still some ostensible reason must be produced in justification of their postulate, which must either be direct proof founded on what are supposed to be facts of consciousness, or an indirect presumption arising from the hypothetical solution which the principle in question may afford of the facts and phenomena of experience. If such direct proof can be furnished, the philosophy of identity is placed on an immovable basis, and Pantheism is proved to be the only rational theology. The cause at first sight does seem hopeless, for we cannot think of knowledge otherwise than as representing something not itself. If any fact of consciousness is clear and undoubted, this certainly seems to be that fact. What can appear more unnatural than Fichte's representation of thought as a mere activity without contents and with no object beyond itself? Schelling's theory is only in appearance more rational, for though he grants that there is such a thing as objective existence, thought can take no direct cognisance of its object, but only reaches it indirectly through the philosophy of the absolute, by which, it is contended, we have a scientific perception of the fact that thought in apprehending itself apprehends objective existence, seeing both are identical in essence and rhythmical movement.

But after all, ordinary thinking may be at fault upon this point, and philosophy may succeed in rectifying it, as science has rectified popular superstitions with regard to the operations of nature. So far as we know, only two distinct arguments, which pretend to rest on facts, have been advanced, the one to prove that thought is the all, the other to prove the identity of thought and being. The first of these is put forward by Fichte. Accepting the Kantian doctrine of the Categories, and the representative theory of perception, he argues, that since we posit or infer an out-world in virtue of the laws of our mental being, it cannot be real, rigid, persistent being, but only a projection of ourselves. To think otherwise, he contends, would be to hypostatise a mere law: or, in other words, the ego affirms an objective reality in order to release itself and account for a fact otherwise inexplicable, therefore the ego in affirming the non-ego creates it. Perhaps the most satisfactory method of testing this style of argument will be to apply it to his own philosophy. To account for the antithetical rhythm which obtains in consciousness, he is obliged to postulate an absolute ego, or unconscious infinite activity, susceptible potentially of all possible modes though actually undetermined. But how can this undetermined, unconscious activity be known, or rather how can it know itself as such, seeing that the condition of consciousness is limitation? Plainly, it can only be reached by inference, and if so then it is affirmed, and therefore created, by the conscious ego. But it is the unconscious ground, and therefore producing cause, of the conscious activity, consequently the absolute ego creates, and is created by the conscious ego, or, in other words, in order to account for its own existence, the conscious ego, constrained by an innate mental necessity, affirms and therefore creates the absolute ego. Therefore the ego creates itself. A plainer demonstration of the absurdity of the principle could hardly be desired.

The proof offered by Schelling may be very briefly stated. The subject and object always co-exist and presuppose each other: therefore they must be manifestations merely of the same essence. Add to this, that there is a beautiful correlation between mind and matter, the two running, as it were, in parallel streams, a fact which appears also to point in the same direction. But surely co-existence does not prove identity, at least it cannot prove an absolute identity, in the things themselves, otherwise they could not *be distinguished.* Even should the difference be but quantitative, as Schelling contends, this does not necessarily imply that they have their root in the same identical essence. There is, however, a fatal objection to the principle of making co-existence the test of identity of essence. It is a law of thought that contradictories always co-exist and imply each other, hence it would follow, if the above principle were adopted, that the possible and the impossible, good and evil, light and darkness, are identical. We are aware that Hegel accepts these conclusions, nay, he explicitly adopts the principle that underlies them, to wit, the identity of contradictories, to prove the identity of the ego and non-ego, and make it appear that zero is the productive germ of all being. Be it so, then truth and falsity are identical, so he cannot object if we hold by the falsity of his system. As to the harmony which obtains between mind and matter, a much more satisfactory explanation is to be found in the unity of a supreme creative intelligence.

This at once saves the facts of consciousness, and accounts for the correlation. The philosophy of identity therefore, so far as its advocates have been able to show, has no basis in the facts of consciousness. No one pretends to believe that we have an immediate conviction, that mind and matter are identical in essence, or that mind is the all, while on the other hand, the conviction which all must entertain, at least in their ordinary moods, as to their essential diversity, can be shown to bear all the marks and stand all the tests of intuitive truth. Even then should metaphysicians be able to furnish something better than inconsequential and absurd deductions from admitted facts, they could not possibly establish their indispensable postulate, but only develope a startling antinomy, and furnish a fresh irresistible argument for scepticism.

The only other question which remains for consideration is the presumption arising from the hypothetical solution which it may afford of the facts and phenomena of experience. Perhaps this is the most favourable view that can be taken of German Metaphysics. At best they are but logical romances, arbitrary in everything but their internal coherence, and not unfrequently even in this attempt hypothetically to construct, rethink or create *a priori* the whole universe of being. We do not at present pronounce on the possibility of the method, for that would involve another question hereafter to be discussed; neither indeed does it concern our present purpose. Admitting therefore the possibility of such hypothetic constructions of the universe, they must conform to one condition, they must take up and explain either as facts or appearances all known phenomena, otherwise they are useless, and if logical conclusions, the premises on which they rest must be false. A beautiful example of the fulfilment of this condition is furnished in Physics by the undulatory theory of light. But it ought to be observed that though the hypothesis that light is propagated by a species of undulatory movement serves to account for all the facts, yet this by no means converts the assumption into an absolute certainty, for there may be other suppositions which would serve equally well. For the same reason, even could it be shown that the principle of identity affords a perfect explanation of all known facts, this could not entitle it to stand in competition with intuitive truth or to rank as an absolute certainty. But does it give a solution of all the known facts of thought and being? We do not ask, does it fall in with every popular notion, but does it, when it deviates from or contradicts them, at the same time account for them as illusions? Physical science has explained away not a few popular superstitions, and why should not philosophy? This, however, is essentially a weak point in these philosophies. Unlike physical theories in general, they contradict the most deeply rooted convictions of humanity in their fundamental postulate, while in their development they neither explain nor account for the facts which they ought to elucidate. They are imposing no doubt as word-theories—mighty monuments of the power of perverse genius, but as sciences of existence they are caricatures throughout. It would be most tedious and uninstructive to compare their results with the facts of experience, for this, by general confession, is not their strong point. Indeed, by the great majority of sensible thinkers their conclusions would be accepted as *reductiones ad absurdam* of the principles from which they are deduced. What genuine student of nature, for example, could be led to believe that all the glories and mysteries of the external world either are, or are identical with, the workings of his own mind, so that all he had to do, or indeed could do, in deciphering its secrets, was simply to register the movements of his own little soul? Verily if mind and matter are identical,—if the movements of mind are those of matter,—the material universe must be a strangely chaotic and contradictory thing. Are we not therefore amply justified in rejecting a principle which has neither direct evidence nor hypothetical probability in its favour, and which has absolutely no foundation save in the exigencies of a baseless ideal? In so far, then, as Pantheism is identified with the principle of identity it is irrational and absurd.

There is yet another assumption essential to the philosophy of the absolute, which logically involves Pantheism. Let us revert to the scientific ideal which the philosophers of this school place before themselves. "Science," say they, "starts from a principle absolutely apprehended; and from it demonstratively deduces all the movements of infinite being." Plainly to realise this conception, not only must they start with a single principle, but that principle must be a knowledge of infinite being in itself, for, if the infinite be not in the premises, it cannot be in the conclusion. And here, it is to be observed, that not only a knowledge of the fact that the infinite exists is claimed, but a full and adequate comprehension of it—such a knowledge of it as shall warrant them in making it the major premises of an argument which shall embrace the infinite modifications of infinite being. Let it be granted that it is competent for us logically to manipulate this idea, and the Pantheist is prepared to demonstrate that there is, and can be, but one existence. Many arguments may be produced to show this necessary connection, of which we need only give the following as a specimen :—The infinite is that than which there can be no greater. But if the individual ego which posits the infinite affirms at the same time (as it seems to do) its own separate individual existence, then the infinite, plus the ego, is greater than the infinite by itself—that is, the infinite can and cannot be augmented, which is absurd. The reasoning is perfectly valid, the definition being granted, and the definition must be allowed, if it be held that our knowledge of the infinite, such as it is, is adequate and complete. This at once brings matters to a crisis. Either we must surrender our belief in our personal existence, or, holding by that, deny that we have an adequate conception of the infinite. The only remaining alternative is scepticism. But it is impossible to give up our belief in our personal existence, for it is in virtue of this fact alone that we can posit anything. The infinite, therefore, as conceived and defined by the ego, cannot be the infinite of reality, for it is impossible to believe that the mind, in affirming the infinite in the same breath, affirms and denies its own existence. Nor is it to the purpose to urge, that because all necessarily think the infinite, whereas they regard their own being as contingent, therefore contingent ought to give place to infinite being. True, all necessarily think the infinite as the correlative of the finite, not, however, with an absolute, but a relative necessity, that is, a necessity consequent on their own contingent being. The necessity is therefore merely that of consequence, for the finite is, in our thinking, logically prior to the infinite. An illustration may perhaps help to make our meaning more clear. Time and space are the necessary conditions of our thinking; are they, therefore, apart from our thought, necessarily existent in any sense? Surely not, for they are consequent on the contingent existence of finite minds.

But the startling contradictions which spring out of the logical development of our conception of the infinite, are not the only proofs which go to show that we have no positive conception of the infinite *as such*. From the time of Kant, downwards, it has been abundantly shown that our pretended conception of the infinite is a mere bundle of contradictions. A faithful analysis of the conditions and limitations of thought leads also to the same conclusion. Consciousness implies relation, and relation limitation, hence the infinite *as such* cannot be known. Again, we only know as we distinguish, and distinction implies comparison, relation, and limitation. The force and validity of these arguments have been felt by all who have seriously studied them. Fichte even held that the infinite could not know itself till it limited itself. Hence, in his philosophy, the infinite is a mere inference in itself, unknown and unknowable. Thus, absolute science in his hands broke down at the very threshold. Schelling, too, had a perfectly clear perception of the fact that the infinite cannot be apprehended in consciousness, and so was obliged to invent a special faculty for its cognition—a faculty outside of consciousness, and which, unfortunately for its inventor, ever persisted in keeping both itself and its contents aloof from consciousness. The same may be said of Hegel, who, to avoid the difficulty which had hitherto proved insuperable, made zero, as manipulated by the aid of his fundamental principle, to wit, "the ideality of contradictories," the generating principle of his philosophy. Or, to put the matter more correctly, he rears the whole superstructure of infinite being on the relation of contradiction which obtains between zero and being. In passing, it may be observed that zero and being, apart from the relation of contradiction in which they stand to each other, are nonentities, and that consequently Hegel makes the relation between two nonentities the productive germ of all being. From what has been said, it will be evident enough that Hegel, in place of taking the infinite as the terminus·*a quo*, makes it the terminus *ad quem* of his system, thereby reversing the necessary laws of deductive reasoning.

Spinoza, however, the father of modern Pantheism, claims for himself a clear logical conception of the infinite. It would seem, notwithstanding, that he never seriously contemplated the question. At least, he has not attempted to justify his claim, except in so far as he insists that the infinite is clear as a term and necessary as a thought. To all this it may be replied, that it is not the case that we have a clear, full, and adequate conception of the infinite, and that its necessity in thought, so far from proving its necessary existence, may only imply a necessary law of thought.

So far, then, as Pantheism is a necessary deduction from the philosophy of the infinite, it rests on a sandy foundation. We have, and can have, no such conception of the infinite as shall warrant us in making it the major premises of a deductive argument which shall embrace and explain scientifically the whole sphere of the knowable. No matter whether it be held that our conception of the infinite is purely negative, or positive so far as it goes, the conclusion is quite the same, so far as Pantheism is concerned. The question is, have we, or have we not, an adequate logical conception of the infinite, as such? The controversy, therefore, as between Mansel and Mill respecting our conception of the infinite is superfluous, so far as our present argument is concerned, since both alike hold that our conception of the infinite is inadequate. Taking for granted, then, that our conception of the infinite is inadequate, we can vindicate our claim to a separate individual existence without at the same time denying the existence of the infinite. The antinomy arising out of the conception of our own finite individuality, and the conception of the infinite, is due to our necessary ignorance. Still, it must be conceded that there are real difficulties connected with the philosophy of the infinite. All, however, that is contended for here, and all that is pertinent to our purpose, is that the infinite, *as such*, cannot be known, or only inadequately. That the infinite is, we must believe; what it is, we can only know in part through its finite manifestations. But despite these facts and their own liberal concessions, such men as Schelling proceed under cover of the real difficulties attaching to a philosophy of the infinite to develop their inadequate and practically false notions of the infinite into a philosophy essentially Pantheistic. One can understand how Spinoza should proceed with remorseless tread to solve the awful mystery which hangs over the relation between the infinite and the finite, by virtually annihilating all finite beings; but that Schelling and his disciples should follow in the same track, is both strange and inconsistent on their part. True, it may be asserted that intellectual intuition is competent to a knowledge of the infinite. But what of that? The idea must be developed under the conditions of ordinary consciousness, and to be developed must be conceived, which is impossible, according to his own representation.

There is yet another objection which cleaves, like an avenging Nemesis, to all philosophies of the absolute. What, we ask, develop the life of the absolutely infinite? Is not the absolutely infinite at the same time the perfect, for imperfection is a limitation; and does not the perfect exclude all virtuality, all potentiality, and therefore all progressive life or movement? Assuredly, if our conception of the infinite is perfectly adequate, all such developments in the life of the absolutely perfect are absurd; for not to be what it is possible to become, is surely a limitation. The existence of the absolute must therefore be the stillness and repose of an eternal death. But if this be so, then the so-called infinite which lies at the basis of these philosophies either is not the infinite, or, if it is so, it ceases to be so in the process of development. If finite or imperfect prior to development, it never can become infinite, for this were to make the finite beget the infinite. If, again, we start with the absolutely infinite or perfect, every future development must be a falling away from perfection, otherwise two absolutely perfect beings may be conceived which are not identical, which is absurd. Such are the conclusions into which we are forced if our conception of the absolutely infinite and perfect be regarded as adequate. Let it not, however, be imagined that we hold that anything like a progressive life is impossible for the Deity. We only say such a development or movement is absurd on the supposition that our notion of the Deity is perfectly adequate. Nay, we believe in the doctrine of the Trinity, though unable to form a rational conception of *the how* of that mystery, while our necessary ignorance shelters our belief from the charge of absurdity.

Such are but a few of the absurdities necessarily involved in that vaunted Autonomic Philosophy with which Pantheism is identified. If, as is contended, these are the only principles on which Idealistic Pantheism rests, in place of being, as is often claimed for it, the only rational theology, it is encumbered with *absurdities* and pregnant with contradictions. In point of fact, this type of Pantheism has no basis whatever but the exigencies of the chimera of absolute science, and no recommendation but such as belongs to a grand philosophical romance.

J. D.

FROM THE BELLEROPHON OF EURIPIDES.

Frag. 288.

Why call me vilest, so you call me rich.
"If he be rich," we *all* would know: not one,
"If he be good:" we ask not "whence?" or "how?"
We ask "how much!" and all the world around
A man is worth so much as he is worth.
Can we be rich, and yet be vile? no, no.
Let me live rich: poor, I would rather die.
'Tis worth to die so: for you gain by dying.
O Gold, thou sweetest palmful to mankind,
How far inferior is mother's love,
Or children's, or a father's tender care,
To their delight within whose homes *thou* dwellest!
And if the looks of Venus be of gold,
No wonder that she has ten thousand loves!

DRAMATIC REPRESENTATIONS IN THE UNIVERSITY.

IF executed with the requisite learning and critical ability, a study of the poetic literature connected with our College would be curious and instructive. We might point to the "Pleasures of Hope," the "Course of Time," and "Festus," besides a great amount of miscellaneous poetry—religious, romantic, and humorous—both by functionaries high in the government of the University and by students. Then there are fugitive College poems, prize poems, translations, occasional verses; verses which had perhaps a brief existence in the poet's corner of some daily paper, or which ere yet they had rightly opened their eyes on the light of day, were sepulchred at birth in the pages of a University Album. A still more unique collection might be made of those brilliant efforts which the triennial contest of a rectorial election scatters lavishly in the courts in the short space of one week. These, if gathered together, would convince the most sceptical, that though the College in past time has not been absolutely shunned by the muses, their stay has seldom been long and never continuous.

The muse of Tragedy in particular has avoided the old halls. Two centuries ago, indeed, she received anything but a cordial reception, and in later days this positive dislike has been modified into an equally repellent indifference. Why stage representation was so long objected to we need not discuss. Whatever the reasons may have been, it is certain that plays were deemed heathenish and regarded with aversion. Like many bad things, however, they were found to offer a certain amount of attraction, and it became the aim of the church even at a very early period to turn them to the best possible account, partly in the way of amusing and instructing the people, partly in increasing her own influence and maintaining her monopoly of learning. For the clergy alone knew what tales or legends could be represented with profit to themselves and the people; they alone had the literary ability required to adapt, to compose and allot each actor his part, and they were, moreover, the only class who could allow the necessary amount of freedom in the treatment of the story, or could overlook an occasion when the freedom degenerated into license. From all this it followed, that for a long time during the middle ages, the clergy were themselves the principal actors of their mysteries and miracle plays, and in some parts of Europe even to the present day they have reserved to themselves the power of presenting these plays, or at any rate of superintending and conducting their performance.

Both as being under the management of churchmen, and as imparting training to those who intended subsequently to enter the church, the Universities would afford and encourage only such relaxation as could be shared in by such persons—and if interludes or plays were performed at all they would be of the kind in which ecclesiastics could join. From the records of the University it appears that such shows were given, by an account of the preparations made for certain solemnities in which the members were to take part, and the expense of which was to be defrayed by subscription raised in the College.

"On the 2nd of May 1462—about twelve years after the University was founded,—there assembled a congregation of the Faculty of Arts, at which the Masters agreed that in all future times, on the Feast of the Translation of St. Nicholas (the 9th of May), there should be held, on the intimation of the Dean at the doors of the cathedral, a general congregation for electing two discreet masters, who should provide the necessaries and utensils for a banquet in the College of the Faculty of Arts, on the Sabbath day, or feast following the said day of the Translation of St. Nicholas as should seem most suitable to the Faculty and as the weather should permit. For which every beneficed master in congregation, or present in the City of Glasgow, should give to the providers three shillings, and every non-beneficed master as well as licentiates, bachelors and students eighteen pence."

Moreover, it was ordained that on the day fixed by the Faculty, all the Masters, Licentiates, Bachelors and Students, should, under a penalty of two shillings, assemble at eight o'clock a. m. in the Chapel of St. Thomas the Martyr, and there hear mass, after which, each should in a becoming and solemn manner receive flowers and branches of trees, which the said providers should cause to be brought there at the common expense, and all should proceed on horseback in a grave and stately procession through the public street from the higher part of the city to the cross, and return the same way to the

College of Arts, where, amid the joy of the feast, the Masters should take counsel concerning what might promote the interests of the Faculty and its members, and give their diligence to remove all discords and quarrels.
. . . The banquet being finished the members and students in a body, should repair to a place more fitted for amusement, where some of the Masters and alumni should perform an interlude in a becoming manner for the delight of the people. And because it was just that those who devoted their labour and money for the honour of the Faculty should not want a reward, the Faculty further ordained that the Masters and Students, who made such shows for the honour of the Faculty, should have special favour and prerogatives in their promotions and petitions.

We can well imagine, that encouragement of this sort would foster the production of stage plays, and the festivals on which they were accustomed to be given would be looked forward to with considerable expectation and curiosity.

But the Reformation which intervened surely though gradually made its influence felt even in the matter of amusements. Miracle plays, portions of scripture dramatized, interludes, all stage exhibitions, whether of a sacred or secular character, were discouraged or forbidden, and in the histories of the sixteenth and seventeenth centuries will be found instances of the difficulties which actors had to encounter. The whole system thus fell away in those countries which dispensed with the guidance of the church, and in no country ultimately more so than in Scotland. The freer play of thought allowed by the Reformation gave dramatic authors, indeed, a greater choice of subjects. A wider current of facts and ideas, of character and passion, was opened for them in which to move, and the increased independence and nobility of man invested his actions and his course of life, with that uncertainty—the mystery of fate—which the old miracle plays could not reproduce, founded as they were upon stories familiar to the audience,—stories in which evil ended evilly and goodness was joy. But though the drama thus gained artistically in eminence—the old feeling against acting and actors not only survived, but with such life and force that it was with the utmost difficulty sometimes that permission could be obtained from the authorities to act a play.

A hundred and fifty years had barely gone when a general reform seemed called for in the country. The people had relaxed in their national and domestic morality, and had lost much reverence for what was dignified, grand and sacred. Some few were left, however, who, impressed with the belief that life is too serious to be made the subject of a jest, that the crudities of human existence are matters for tears rather than for ridicule, animadverted sharply upon all those who encouraged stage plays and such amusements for playing into the hands of the spiritual enemy of mankind. This idea, though derived in part, no doubt, from the early Fathers, seems certainly native to the strict discipline of the Puritan system, and it may therefore be expected to recur whenever there is a corresponding reaction against the ways of a luxurious age, wasteful, as it always is, of time in its intellectual or æsthetic relaxations.

The view of the old writer who said that "the dance is the devil's procession, and paint and ornaments the whetting of the devil's sword, the ballet is the pomp and mass of the devil, and whosoever entereth therein entereth into his pomp and mass," was adopted in all its entirety by those who believed implicitly in an embodied principle of evil, with which all at the present time do not sympathise, and which some seem to find difficulty even in understanding. Being at that time in power, these purists succeeded in closing theatres and other places where plays and shows could be exhibited, and also in convincing a large part of the people that such amusements were not only inexpedient but morally wrong. The governing bodies, both of the towns and universities, sooner or later exercised their power with austerity, and steadfastly opposed the doubtful amusements. So that it happened about the beginning of last century, in the year 1721, that the University of Glasgow saw fit to withdraw that encouragement which, as we have seen, it had formerly given to theatrical shows.

There was at that time a considerable number of English and Irish students at Glasgow, who had been less restrained at home in the matter of stage plays than the Scotch students, and who accordingly saw no harm in acting Tamerlane and Cato. "The actors went one night very inadvertantly into the Common Hall to rehearse. Upon this a Faculty was immediately called, where they were rebuked for their insolence in putting that place to such a profane use, and gravely advised to desist from acting the play. This was what they said, they could not do, having invited their friends and been at considerable charges in getting things ready for it. This issued in appointing them to appear before another Faculty, and in the meantime the Principal and Mr. Carmichael endeavoured to persuade them to lay aside their design. They told them it was very indecent for men to put on women's clothes as those gentlemen must do who were to act the part of the ladies in the play. To this purpose some passages in the Leviticus were urged with much gravity; and when one of the young gentlemen had the pertness to tell the Principal in the systematical style, that he looked upon that place in Leviticus to be only a part of the Ceremonial Law and consequently abolished under the Christian Œconomy, he was very readily answered that though it was indeed but a Ceremonial Law yet it was founded on a moral precept. To avoid, therefore, this great inconvenience it was proposed by Mr. Carmichael that the women's part should be left out, and then they might act the remainder with decency. 'But this,' say they, 'is what cannot be done without breaking the action and making no play at all of it.' 'Why then,' replyes that learned gentleman, 'you must e'en see and get some skilful hand to change those love parts into a scene of friendship, as I remember was very judiciously done by my schoolmaster with one of Terence's comedies when acted by his boys.' But whatever was done by that great man his schoolmaster, it was to be feared there could no such skilful hand be found about the University of Glasgow, and therefore the gentlemen persisted in their resolution to act the play without transforming it.

"The Faculty which met in a few days upon the affair was pretty full; for several of the masters, being resolved not to deny themselves the pleasure of being present at such an agreeable entertainment, went thither purposely to prevent the young gentlemen's being hindered to perform. The Principal introduced the debate with a very learned speech, wherein, after the repeating the several arguments already mentioned, he concluded with telling them that really he was an enemy to all comedies, and so could not allow of the students acting Tamerlane. He was seconded by his echo the professor of Divinity, and then by several others of the party, some of whom did at great length and with much elegance both of style and sentiments, show that in all polite nations it was reckoned a very illiberal thing for persons of any character to act on the stage. It was in vain to urge the example of Roscius and the intimacy of Scipio and Lælius with the comedians of their time, in answer to this. For those gentlemen, being well read in antiquity, could easily have refuted such arguments by showing that among the ancient Romans, the Players, as well as the Grammarians and Philosophers, were generally slaves; and, therefore, when any persons of distinction admitted them into their intimacy it was only a mere condescension and could not be drawn into precedent.

"It would be too tedious to report all the fine speeches made on this occasion. The majority of the Masters would not be so unjust, as to let the gentlemen lose all their expenses for nothing, and so allowed them to act the play, but not within the territories of the University. *And to prevent these great enormities for the future an act was made, debarring the students from doing such things in all time coming.*

"These difficulties over, the gentlemen acted their play with very much applause, several of the Masters being present. A Prologue and Epilogue proper for the occasion were repeated, written by two of the students."

The Prologue was the work of an Irishman, by name James Arbuckle, M.A., Glasgow, student of divinity at the time when Tamerlane was acted. He was author of two or three poems, and some prose works, among which is a pamphlet containing "A short account of the late treatment of the students of the University of Glasgow," which appeared at Dublin, 1722, and from which the preceding extracts have been taken. Thomas Griffith was the author of the Epilogue.

"It happened, very unluckily, that there were some passages in both, which the Principal and his friends would needs understand to be meant of themselves. Mr. Griffith in the Epilogue had handsomely rallied those gloomy mortals, who looked upon theatrical representations to be the devices of Satan and remnants of Popery. This was reckoned to be plain satire upon the Principal, and a wounding of religion through his sides. In the Prologue Mr. Arbuckle was so unfortunate as to mention the tragedy of Tamerlane having been opposed by a tyrannizing faction on a neighbouring stage; the neighbouring stage could signify nothing but the common hall, and the tyrannizing faction, the facultie, who had censured the students for rehearsing in that place. The criticism, indeed, would not have been very unjust, had not the Prologue been written before the rehearsal, and had not a Jacobite faction in the late reign laid that performance under a kind of prohibition, and persecuted a set of honest gentlemen for a riot who had encouraged the acting of it in the Royal Theatre in Ireland. But these were circumstances the Principal's passion made him overlook; and therefore he proposed to some of his friends that the two gentlemen should be punished, and thought that expulsion was the least sentence could be inflicted upon them. This was agreed to, but the question was, how could it be done seeing if it come before a full Faculty, it was apprehended, the matter would not carry. For an expedient, therefore, it was thought the Principal, Professor of Divinity, and two or three other Masters might have a private meeting, and do it themselves. But Mr. Carmichael, to whom the business was proposed, not agreeing to such a clandestine way of proceeding, it was found convenient to drop the whole affair, tho' not without first giving Mr. Griffith such a severe reprimand as obliged him, already disgusted with their former management, to leave the University and prosecute his studies elsewhere."

Such a dispute as this would probably prevent for some time any attempt at acting by members of the University. At any rate the next mention of a performance, or at least of rehearsals, of which we know, is by

Dr. Carlyle. It was in 1744, more than twenty years after the Arbuckle and Griffith disturbance, that a number of ladies and gentlemen prepared to act Cato— the same tragedy as in the former case—to a select party in the College. The controversy had probably been forgotten, and the opponents of the play, if they survived, may have been mellowed by time and by the knowledge that the drama had meanwhile been domiciled in Edinburgh. Glasgow could not boast of a theatre till some years later. Though the actual performance in the present case never really took place, the cast was made, the play thoroughly rehearsed, and one of the chief purposes of the actors attained, " which was to become more intimate with the ladies. Lord Selkirk would not join them, though he took much pleasure in instructing Miss Campbell, who was to impersonate Marcia."

Times have changed, and we must have changed with them, when in the middle of the nineteenth century, without a qualm as to whether a statute of the University were infringed or not, Glasgow students could act, and the whole College could countenance and encourage, the performance in a regular theatre of a tragedy which was asserted without any hesitation to be the work of a Glasgow Professor.

The play chosen for representation on this occasion was the tragedy of "Wallace," which had been published anonymously in 1856, at the time when the movement for the now nearly completed Wallace Monument began. It was to have been brought out in the Theatre Royal,

Glasgow, by the late Mr. Edmund Glover, and the requisite licence, one of the last officially signed by the lamented John Mitchell Kemble, had been obtained, when Mr. Glover was seized with the illness which terminated in his death, and the representation in consequence was never carried out. The Prologue which was to have been spoken on this occasion, and of which we have obtained a copy, thus pleads for the supposed imperfections of the play,—

"If, as the poet sings, '*the world's a stage*,'
A mighty actor in a bye-gone age,
An actor shrined in every Scottish heart,
To-night before you plays his mimic part.
 And well that part—no mimic part—he played,
Scotland! for thee, in that dark hour and dread,
When o'er thy realm of mountains and of flood
The heaths were reddened with heroic blood,
And but for *one*, and his devoted band,
Tyrants had slaved our never-conquered land!
 Scotsmen! who home where, to the Atlantic tide,
Rolls his rich argosies, majestic Clyde,
Cradle of poets crowned with world-applause,
O not to *their mark* strain the critic laws,
But gently judge the poet for the cause.
 Here where your *Campbell* lisped his earliest lays,
And wreathed his boyhood's glorious brow with bays,
Here where your *Baillie*, with Ithuriel Art,
Unmasked the innate traitors of the heart,
Syrens, that woo to sin, or lure from good,
To rack with misery, or drench with blood,
And sang in strains had Shakespeare's self approved,
'*How Montfort hated, and how Basil loved.*'
 Here where your *Knowles*, on fresh young pinions flew,

> A stripling Shakespeare—poet and actor too,
> And to the fair ideal of his brain,
> Gave breath and body *on this very scene*,
> Another son, another suitor, woos
> A kindly verdict, for a feebler muse.
> O gently scan *his* daring, would presume
> To hang his garland on so proud a tomb :
> And let the name of Wallace, that of yore
> A Nation's war-cry on to Vict'ry bore,
> A Nation's Watchword still, the poet shield,
> And bear him scathless through his maiden field,
> While generous England with a softened eye,
> Approves the scene where patriots dare and die."

There was no farther attempt made to produce the play until the two representations by the students on the 20th and 21st March, 1862, in the Prince's Theatre. Although it was acted without the author's sanction, there is little doubt that it was selected out of compliment to him and to the University, from which it had emanated, the anonymity being at the same time strictly observed. During the previous part of the Session it was made known that a dramatic performance was contemplated, and as the time approached, and the results of rehearsals oozed out, the ability of the actors and the likelihood of a successful performance formed the topic of lively discussion in the courts. The eventful night at length arrived, and those who were present will not soon forget the audience which assembled in the theatre, the discriminating manner in which praise was measured òut to the actors, and the really meritorious acting of the students to whom the more important parts had been entrusted. What helped, besides, to make the undertaking agreeable was the way in which the members of the University gave their support to the performance, instead of making an attempt to suppress it. The end was thus attained, and with the exception of a single concert given a few years ago, and a memorable torch-light procession, the students have not since appeared collectively in any capacity which by some straight-laced critics might be considered unacademical, and more likely to engender habits of dissipation than of strict discipline and study.

The tragedy, as originally published and as acted by the students, consisted in reality of two distinct tragedies, though one was printed as the first act of the other,—the principal one. This shorter tragedy, the scene of which is laid in and around Lanark, is occupied with the adventures of the outlawed Wallace, his visit to Ellen Bradfute, his escape from the English garrison in Lanark, the execution of Ellen, and the revenge which he executes upon the Governor, Heselrig, and vows against the whole of the English. In the second edition of the play* this portion was separated from the rest of the drama, and printed as a short tragedy in two acts independent of "Wallace," but still serving as an introduction to it, and entitled "Heselrig." In the latest edition of all†

* "Tragic Dramas from Scottish History. Heselrig. Wallace. James the First of Scotland." Thomas Constable & Co., Edinburgh. 1859.

† "Tragic Dramas from History, with Legendary and other Poems." By Robert Buchanan, M.A., Late Professor of Logic and Rhetoric in the University of Glasgow. 2 vols., 8vo. Edinburgh: Edmonston and Douglas. 1868.

"Heselrig" is entirely suppressed, and the play of "Wallace" now stands in what we may suppose is its final form.

As these two volumes contain several other dramas which have not been previously published, and are perhaps the only complete dramas, claiming at the same time to be poetical, which have ever issued from within the College walls, we trust we shall be pardoned for devoting a little of our space to them.

The five plays which these volumes contain have all of them a historical basis. Two of them, "Wallace" and "James the First," contain events in Scottish history dramatically treated; while, of the other three, one, "The British Brothers," is taken from a legend contained in the chronicle of Geoffrey of Monmouth; another, "Gaston Phœbus," is developed from a portion of Froissart, and the third, "Edburga," is based upon incidents recorded in the Anglo-Saxon histories. The author, however, knowing the difficulties which a too strict adherence to written history entails upon the dramatist, has judiciously refrained from marring the symmetry of his work by forcing his plans into useless conformity with it. His rejection of nothing, however anachronous, provided it increase the effect, is perfectly correct, and is justified by the practice of the greatest masters. Of all kinds of artistic composition, the historical drama, while apparently easy, is in reality one of the most difficult. At first sight it would seem to require nothing but to transform the indirect narrative of the historian into the direct language of the personal actor, but were such an attempt made it would be found that the result was merely a shadow of what may have been originally a very interesting history. It is necessary for the dramatist or poet to fill up from his own knowledge and experience all those minute details of person, place, and circumstance which a history never gives completely, and seldom, if ever, describes at all. Above all things, he must supply from his own study of his own heart, the clue to the motives which prompted those actions which he is pourtraying. The deeper he sees into human life, the more powerfully he holds, and the more sensitively he plays the reins of the soul, the better a dramatist will he be, provided only his personages speak clearly. He must know that after all there are but few types of motive, though in practice they are infinitely modified; he must be able in particular cases to see the type in the instance, the law of the fact, because he may be called upon to extend an incompleted portion of the character, and this harmoniously with the rest. He will then know, that however it may be required in art, to accommodate the limited range both of the creative and sympathetic faculties in the mind,. that there should be what is technically called a plot, actual life has no plot, that we cannot arbitrarily fix a limit to any action and determine that its influence shall stop as we choose. We are only active witnesses of a series of events, powerful and yet passive units in the evolution of history, conscious at the same time both of power and of passivity, but unable to explain their relations to each other in ourselves, much less to alter or avert them. Under such complicated conditions as these

—and in reality they are more burdensome than can be known—the dramatist has to work, even when he has the greater freedom of gathering his material from any source; but, in addition to these, the writer of historical dramas fixes for himself the magic circle out of which he must not step. He has to reconcile many opposing elements; the historical acts of his hero—these often inconsistent with each other, and giving discrepant views of the character,—with the ideal, which the acts, guided by his own knowledge of mankind, induce him to pourtray. He must select, condense, bring into the space of a few hours on the stage, or a few pages for the study, everything thought, spoken or done, which, spread over years, made the life interesting to the rest of the nation, or of the world. He must know the idea of the life and embody that, and if in so doing he find it necessary to leave the guidance of history, he must not be found fault with for arbitrarily making his facts suit a theory. Discrepancies indicate not that the theory is wrong, but point, as in theories of the material world, to higher, but yet unattained laws, which include and harmonize present generalizations and exceptions.

The poet when employed in his actual work very possibly does not indulge in such a tone of mind as this, and will succeed all the better that he is free from it. The ideas, however, exist potentially in him, and are reflected according to circumstance more or less distinctly from his work. In the present case we have got certain plays which seem without any straining to embody some great ideas. All that we can do is to indicate these, and leave our readers to study for themselves the way in which they have been worked out.

The name inscribed over the first and best known of these plays, "Wallace," indicates at once the topic. It is the triumph of true patriotism; the success of the man in his great aim, whose thought is undivided devotion to his country, who, taunted by his doubting, and betrayed by his faithless friends,—opposed, vanquished, captured by his material enemies,—yet works to reassure the waverers, forgets that there is such a thing as treachery to guard against, and maintains an endless fight against the superiority of numbers. If he ever has a thought for himself in danger or out of danger, it is that he may live for the nation, that he may be present when there is need of counsel or of a sword, or if he must die that he shall lie below the soil he has always loved. Man, however, is by himself impotent against the forces moral and physical which he provokes, and thus sooner or later comes a harsher doom. Even here there is a personal victory, for in a knowledge of the justice of the cause he beholds its triumph: the torch which is dropping from his hand is caught up by one whom he has gained to his cause, and who, he sees, will complete what he began :—

"The lot of Heaven
Doth fall on thee, the younger and the worthier :
And thou, or I misread thy noble nature,
Wilt justify the call. Methinks from far,
I catch the cloud-break of thy coming day,
Bright for thyself, and for thy country, glorious,—
And, in the blessed foreview, die content.

This may or may not be the historical or most authentic Wallace, but it is the Wallace of the drama and the Wallace that is most familiar to Scotchmen, and whose memory might still stir them to not altogether unworthy deeds.

In the play of "James the First" there is represented what may take place in a remote transition age, the temporary check and discomfiture of law and order, by recurrence of the violence of unreasoning rights and privileges. We have therefore most striking contrasts presented between the party of the king, and those who had suffered by his stringent execution of the law. Considered in respect of the difficulty of portraiture, James I. is one of the author's most successful designs. To display the man of his time in Scotland perhaps the most gifted by nature, and the most accomplished by education and culture, who was not only an admirer of poetry but himself a poet, fond of the chase and of games, and with all this a calm and temperate but skilful and decisive ruler, appears to have been the author's intention. In this he was to some extent assisted by what we know of James from his own writings, and also by the contrast between his taste and refinement and the superstition and ignorance of many of the barons who were opposed to him. Of these the delineations of Græme and Sir Robert Stewart seem to us the most dramatic: Græme actuated solely by a desire to avenge the slaughter of his kinsmen on the king, suffers from a revulsion of feeling when he has gained his wish; Stewart actuated by mixed motives, accomplishes nothing, but makes himself even more detestable by his selfishness, by his treachery, by his inability to comprehend purity or self-devotion, by his savage passions, than if he had been guilty of great crimes.

"The British Brothers" depicts a situation, rather than an idea, and thus while it is sufficiently interesting from the exceptional story it presents, it is less satisfactory than the others as regards artistic development. It differs from them too in ending happily, so that while it contains enough of crime or of apparent or attempted crime to produce the tragic spirit, it may be more properly described as belonging to the higher comedy. The plot is brought forward more prominently in this than in the other plays, and the interest depends rather upon the denouement than upon the evolution of character. Perhaps Gunegil in the latter respect is best drawn. With what man is apt to think her sex's perverseness she loves the memory of the wicked brother her first lover, better than all the adoration and the royal rank of the living brother, her future husband. Nay, rather than do violence to her own passion she will not give him up even at his own request, and entreats to remain single for the sake of him. This conjoined obstinacy and love may be regarded as almost the main spring of the scenes which the dramatist has chosen. The conditions in which the actors find themselves prior to the drama are determined by other causes, but when the action is entered upon the evolution from the motives which Gunegil's love supplies to the man she supposes dead, naturally begins, and after a lapse of adverse circumstance Gunegil is rewarded by the first embrace of him she has brought back to human feeling. The external scenery has an air of woodland freshness, and, we imagine, would make it a pleasant piece if acted.

"Gaston Phœbus" and "Edburga," though much more disagreeable both in plot and in character are more dramatic and in some scenes intenser than the plays already referred to. Gaston Phœbus is in some respects the best of all the plays. In its construction it is more involved, and the interests of the dramatis personæ while more selfish are more interlaced, so that the attainment of his desire by one strikes athwart the projects of others. The characters all stand higher or lower than usual, and there is more of direct connexion between what they think and what they do. Charles is one of the most elaborated of these, and his wily, unscrupulous nature is quite in keeping with the surname of Bad which history has given him. In some respects he, as often happens, has usurped the place of hero, which belongs by right to Gaston, his brother-in-law. But the latter, fiery and jealous, destitute of that nobleness with which passionate men are often imbued, is less qualified to be the prime mover in a tragedy where poison is to be employed, than Charles. Though, then, he escapes the snare Charles hides for him, he is not less his victim or at least his tool, and the author has done right in allowing the events to determine who should be the character fullest of interest. We turn therefore again and again to Charles to examine his motives, to see the influence he can gain over weaker men, and how he can take advantage of a single slip to compel a man, who has every wish to do right, and, when opportunity offers, does it, to share in his crimes without daring to murmur. The picture of the mediæval philosopher and naturalist, Giovanni, is well drawn, and the reflections which he utters are appropriate. In his relations to him however Charles forgets that in his acquaintance with nature Giovanni wields a power which he himself is as weak to resist as any of his own too numerous victims. There is an amount of justice in making the tool inflict the death-wound upon its user, even though it be broken itself in the act. Unlike the others this drama ends with the accomplished desires of the bad entailing ruin upon good and bad alike.

> "I die accurst,—
> My light extinguished, and my labour lost,—
> Might have commanded for my living fame
> Empires for theatre, and at my death
> The tears of nations for mine Epitaph."

So concludes Giovanni, and with death, madness and despair, the curtain sets on universal gloom.

Edburga is one of those portraits, to draw which effectively requires great tact and even reserve on the part of the writer. The drama is intended to show the growth of sin in a sensuous character of a not uncommon type, and the real end of the crime of which she is guilty. Having made choice of his theme the author has not been afraid to develope its moral consequences. It falls into two main parts, the first of which is much the longer in the play. These are Edburga, queen, jealous, revengeful, debased, sowing the wind, and Edburga the outcast, unrepentant, unchanged in nature, reaping the whirlwind. The tragic tone of the play is maintained, not alone by the actions themselves, gloomy enough if their morality be considered, but much more by revelation of the minds and motives of the actors, and by a continuous suggestion of the grave doubts which the existence of an essentially and unchangeably bad person awakens. The author has succeeded in individualising Edburga better than any of the other characters. Kenred, her lover, is guilty of quite as great crimes, persons in the other plays are quite as wicked in their lives, but all these have some remnant of morality left them, while Edburga *is* sin. In any course of action she chooses what is wrong, not because it is her interest or inclination, but apparently because it *is* bad, and at the close of all she herself destroys the hope that she may feel regret for her past life, and locks in her grave the mystery of evil she embodied. This play, which, if it consisted mainly of the guilty love of Edburga for Kenred and the guilty deeds which their ambition, jealousy, and fear of discovery dictate to them, would be of rather a repulsive kind, is relieved by the characters of Ethelbert and Ethelburga, Edburga's sister, and her opposite in all respects. The scenes in which they appear and in which their affection for each other is traced, have a purity and grace with which the author has nowhere else favoured us, and which are peculiarly fragrant and grateful by contrast with the lurid meetings of Kenred and Edburga. A comparison of the two sisters runs through the whole play, and it is indeed upon the motives which the contrast supplies to each that the external events of the tragedy hinge. Up to a certain point Edburga seems to triumph over her unintentional rival, but the murder by Kenred of her sister's husband, which, by the way, is a highly wrought and, we should think, exceedingly effective scene on the stage, is the turning point in her life. She goes rapidly from bad to worst, until she dies a beggar, and delirious at the feet of her sister.

These are, briefly, the general results which the perusal of these dramas has left on our minds, but which we can hardly expect all our readers to confirm. For the details and the subtle poetical interest which no one person can make palpable to another we must refer to the works themselves. Had this been a fitting occasion it would have been easy to have referred to other general points, at length. In any case however it would be unfair to leave the impression that Edburga, the wanton, was the only female character who had been successfully depicted. On the contrary the female characters in the other plays, though generally speaking less prominent in the action, afford the author opportunity for some of his most genial descriptions. Gunegil and Ethelburga have already been referred to, and we might besides instance Isabel in Gaston Phœbus, merry, but gentle and loving to death; Elizabeth Douglas fond of a roguish jest at the love of her cousin Catherine for Walter Luvale, but withal tender and kind: Catherine Douglas herself, famous for ever by her broken arm, in the mouth of whose lover the poet has placed one of his most passionate eulogies for her heroic act; the Queen, riper in years than her two companions, with her mellowed love for her husband, which supplies the place of more robust qualities but which makes her almost superstitiously anxious for his safety, and afterwards rouses all her energies to avenge his murder. All these are genially depicted. Even Lady Comyn errs, not by sin but by misplaced love. In her rash affection for Wallace, she is led to wound him in his tenderest memories, to work his capture, to bribe him to love her by a promise of freedom, to assist in his death, but when he is no more she is the most passionate in her remorse and self-upbraiding, most undisguised in her hatred and contempt for his betrayer and executioners.

The female characters, however, having less prominent parts to fill, are less likely to impress those who may merely glance at these plays. But such will probably find but little to please them in these volumes at all. What is thoughtfully written must be thoughtfully read; what is artistically designed and elaborated requires an artist's knowledge and sympathy. Looking at these plays as a whole, we do not think we wrong the author by saying, that they seem to be the fruit of leisure hours always looked forward to, at times ardently longed for, and luxuriously enjoyed. They show that though the thoughts were gained in moments of inspiration, the setting is the work of time and careful study. Their continuous polish, their perhaps rather too uniformly grave and unbending diction, their felicitous idioms and scrupulous selection of words, hint to those who can feel this delicacy, the labour bestowed on them, and the manner in which the author has returned to them with wider experience and maturer taste.

If we might complain at all it would be that the author, while justly allowing himself license enough in the treatment of his materials, has shrunk from throwing much personality into his work. One feels that a little *abandon* would have contrasted with, and heightened, the more serious parts of the dramas. The language, which is well sustained in the more fervid scenes, is apt to become somewhat too full in phraseology when lighter events are to be pourtrayed. This careless ease, however, is one of those qualifications which may be cultivated but can hardly be acquired by study, and when it does exist is apt to be repressed or refused utterance, by some of the more pretentious powers of the mind, instead of being fostered and encouraged.

While we can see in the dramas themselves the care that has been given to them, and in their themes the nature of the mind which selected them, it is in the shorter poems at the end of the second volume that the poet has himself permitted insight into his own character. As being occupied too much with personal feelings, and as being thus irrelevant to our present topic, we should not have referred to these at all, had it not happened that some of these shorter pieces refer to a general feature of the dramas which deserves to be specified. By subtle allusions in the words of the actors themselves the author has contrived to saturate the plays with the natural scenery by which the actors are surrounded. The difference between the air of Wallace, the British

Brothers, and parts of James the First, and that of the others, is something which it is easy to feel but difficult to describe. This is, perhaps, the only personal feeling—if we except his patriotic love for his country—which the author habitually reveals—his love of natural scenery, and it is in the shorter pieces that we find this feeling in part explained. Scenes of outer nature he turns to, wearied with the study of impalpable thought. Travelling, he naturally expresses the feelings with which the scenery impresses him, and we must regard the admiration of King James at the rugged grandeur of Killiecrankie Pass as an expression of his own quiet pleasure. Nature in all her moods he loves, though it is the spring season to which he seems most attached; in all her displays he enjoys her, but while he feels the awe of her savage mountains and glens, he tries to reproduce the more touching scenes of moonlight and cultivated repose. We can do nothing more than refer to those poems in which he links more intimately the progress of nature and the changes in himself; these open up the personal feelings upon which we are not called to speak.

In conclusion, we would say of the dramas that one of their merits seems to be their adaptibility for performance. In treatment they are broad, there are no minute details, the conversations are rapid and to the point, the scenes are never overcrowded and follow each other with sufficient variety, and they always contain an incident well developed to further the plot and display the characters. If then, anything that has been said induce those of the students who may feel themselves possessed of histrionic powers to add another performance to those which have already originated in the University, we may point to these tragic dramas from history as well suited for their purpose, and as calculated to interest an audience derived both from past and future members of the Old College.

ANSWER.

THE rosebud which I had from thee,
Which thy dear fingers culled for me,
Is dead of grief, to leave thy side;
It scarcely reached to eventide.
And now, behold its spirit flee,
A little stanza, back to thee.

From Uhland.

THE TRADITION OF THE ELDERS.

ON a summer morning did our Schoolman, as he narrated to me himself, walk among the tombs. These were not such tombs as those of the great English Abbey which the man of the small countenance has told us how he did pass through. These tombs were not "erected by a grateful nation" nor yet "by sorrowing admirers of a genius dead," nor do they lie encanopied under Gothic arch and religious shade, with the voice of organ or of myriad feet of men at stated intervals pealing or pattering through them. Still less do they lie, like the tomb of a great Duke whom our nation delighteth to honour, in murky blackness lighted up for the stranger's profit by a tallow candle, and most voluble Cicerone of the Cockneyest breed, where the hearse fashioned from cannon spoiled from Indian Maharajah and French citizen still rises like a car of Juggernaut in the dark dead-smelling vault, not unaccompanied by six black horses, stuffed with horse hair and straw. For the tombs through which our Schoolman walked are quite simple tombs overgrown with moss and grass, only the music of the wind passes through them, and they are encanopied only by the blue lift. This old God's acre lies in a long meadow beside the sea, around the standing walls of an ancient Kirk, where men these many years are not wont to worship, save only by leaving their dead under the shadow of its walls. And about four stone throws from the crumbling Kirk, upon the same sea meadow, are the standing walls of an old castle; the gateways, the courtyard and the tower stand strong as of old; nor are there wanting the marks of window-stanchions and portcullis. But no man now dwelleth within the halls of Ivor: in the wall-crevices grow up the nettle, the bower tree, and the sea-fern, and the memory of them that held the great castle has died away from among the people of the place. For hard by the castle, along a white bay of shore, is a village of fisherfolk: and they have called their clachan Ardechat, from the long rocks at the end of their bight and from the ship wherewith they do traffic or gain sustenance. For they still speak that antique language, which clings yet to the remoter corners of our island, and in many of their doings and sayings do they recall the old savage time. Not within miles many told from Ardechat is heard the puff of that genie which cries begone, begone to all things old and quaint. Were that tush-calling genie to visit the place, or even the vicarage thereof, then would the hamlets of Ardechat, like Helice and Burris cities of Achaüs, sink into the sea, and men would say that the days of miracle and Moses-rod had appeared on earth again. Rarely from the chapel meadows is seen out at sea the smoke of the ship which uses no wind nor sail : but such galliots stop not at Ardechat nor even pass before it, so far does this clachan lie outside of what men are pleased to call the world. Nor yet, since the destroyal of the old chapel, has there been raised in Ardechat a new kirk. Only at this day is stone and mortar taken to raise a fabric named the Parish School, which, men of prudence and motherwit have been known to say, has before it in these our little days, a work greater than that of old chapel or new kirk.

Now our friend the Schoolman, living near by this village, did walk one morning through the tombs that lie around the old kirk. In his hand was a scroll, written by the ancient Sage, styled the master among them that know, and in his mouth besides the words of wisdom was a clay calumet, the gift methinks of a lady gay, and as he walked he pondered over an antique curious stone, in the centre whereof was imaged a man in the antique garb, with a peaked pile in his crown, having in his right hand as it were the lofty standard for an host, and in his left the sword to do the battles of the Lord. Above his head was graven the sign of holy cross, and a roundure, the symbol percase of Eternity: for which and through which this warrior priest or priest-warrior had his being. Below him was figured the strife of a lion and a unicorn, with fearful horn and open jaw, to signify, meseemed, that the beasts which mark this lower world he had laid for ever under his feet. And all round about these figures, which were as centrepieces, were carven intricacies, inextricable of line and curve, and these lines passed through the banner which he held in hand and grown into the topmost ends of the cross, and eke to the tails of the lion and of the unicorn: whereby was thrown out, perchance, as in a riddle, that this our mortal life is encompassed, yea, liveth in the midst of mysteries manifold, not to be scared away by sacredness either of banner or of cross;—and as our Schoolman saw these things he said thus and thus with himself: "This stone windbattered and salt bitten now was one day new, nay, is yet new to me while I meditate upon it, and the works of him who made it do in some sort follow him. For of a truth there is nothing old under the sun, and the man of wise proverbs was in error." So saying with himself, he heard a voice behind and close to him, tremulous, as of an old man: and turning he found by his side a man old indeed and bowed. His cheek was colourless, and over his haffits hung long lyart hair; his voice and limbs as in one for whom the palsy waits. In his right hand was an old sickle wherewith he had been shearing the grass that grows rank over the graves. Then, by his clouted clothes and the pouting of his lower jaw, our Schoolman knew him for one of the most ancient folk of Ardèchat, a poor man, and too weak to win a living. Still, for his visage and aged form, the sickle in his hand, and the place wherein he stood, he might not ill have resembled even the angel of Dede. Then, for that the old man was garrulous, he began to tell how "his father, who for a poor man was a good scholar, had told him that the stone whereon they were looking had come from Kullumkeel that was in Mull, and that a priest who had passed by that way had easily read to him the meaning of all the images in the stone, and the Schoolman himself being a gentleman knew them perhaps as easily, but that for himself he knew but little for he was a poor man: and though he said any thing amiss the gentleman should not lay it to his harm, for he meant no ill, but only could not say well his thought in the English."

Then he began to go about all the other stones which his father had told him had been brought from Kullumkeel, the kirk that is in Mull: but on these stones the pictures had not remained graven as on the first, save that on one was the work, as it seemed, of a drawn sword. Then the old Donald, laying his hand on one stone said "it was the first that had been laid outside the chapel walls though it seemed those were older lying beside it." And so he led to where at the chapel end was a window from which they could see the inside. Then Donald again began; "that when the Priest came by he had had long talk with him about the place, forbye what he had heard from his father, who though a poor man was a good scholar. And the Priest had told him that in that hole in the wall," to which he pointed as well as he could with his sickle, "used to be held the holy water, which they touched this way"—and he crossed his breast—"when they went into the chapel, and which the Priest gave them with the holy wafer for the assoilziement of their sins, and he had asked the Priest about the age-time of the church building, and the Priest said that it was built at the time the great kirk in Glasgow was built, but I told him that there was.. a kirk there afore our Lord came into the world, afore, or at any rate at, the time that Christ became flesh, though I canna say it right in the English,"—at this point our Schoolman began to suggest, in his learned way, that there might have been a heathen worship in that same ground before the time Christentie had come so far. But his pedantic interruption only broke the thread of the old man's thoughts, and he had grappled for his words before he went on again, "and the Priest seemed to take it ill though it wasna' ment so. Then I said to him, Priest, I wish to ask you but one question: you take some water from the sea say or from the burn and put it in a hole like a boine or a boat, and ye says here take this and this wafer and look on this picture of our Lord, and ye shall be soilzied of your sins: but I say to you what's that image but pipe clay, and that wafer but flour or siclike, and that holy water but sea water in a boine, and how'll that soilzie me from the sin that's in my heart? and then I said, and how can you set me free from the wickedness that is in me?" and as Donald said this he brandished his sickle with such force that it came straight in our Schoolmaster's face; "and mickle he didna say but that he wasna married," and "I'm no married mysel," I answered, "but will you tell me that ye are no as well as I, born of a woman, gotted of a man, and our souls are full of sin that winna flee away from flour, pipe clay, or Priest." And yet the Priest was an honest man, and though he could say nothing didna take it ill. "For it was the truth I tauld him," he said, "for you and for me, aye, it was and is the truth." And so saying, not without excitation, he returned to the shearing of the grass, and left our Schoolman to go on his way.

www.ingramcontent.com/pod-product-compliance
Lightning Source LLC
Chambersburg PA
CBHW020229240426
43672CB00006B/460